December 2021

To my fine friends, Jr and Ray—
my "Tuesdays person."

Best to you,
Mary Alice Dillman

MW01504452

THOUGHTS IN MOTION:
A COLLECTION OF ESSAYS

Thoughts in Motion

A Collection of Essays

MARY ALICE DILLMAN

WHITE POPPY PRESS
Amherst, MA 01002

THOUGHTS IN MOTION: A COLLECTION OF ESSAYS

Dustjacket design by Carol Bracewell.
Printed and bound in the United States for limited distribution only.

ISBN: 978-0-9997705-1-1

WHITE POPPY PRESS
495 West Street, Suite 1C
Amherst, MA 01002
(an imprint of Modern Memoirs, Inc.)

Dedicated to my dear son Brad,
who inspired me to write, committed hours editing this volume of essays, advised me in all matters of accuracy, style, context, logic, intention, and truth for the modern world, and has supported me throughout my life.

In memory of my beloved husband Tom (1931–2021) who inspired and supported me in my writing.

Books give us ways to see and know our world that are truly unique and help form educated minds. And the interaction between the author's words and the reader's mind has its own kind of magic. In publishing, we are the shepherds to this gift of The Book, doing everything we can to help bring the author's voice to the reader.

—*Carolyn Reidy*
"In Loving Memory"
The New York Times, *May 22, 2020*

CONTENTS

INTRODUCTION

The essays in this collection represent forty years of my writing career. Without question, these essays are a legacy of writing into my ninetieth year of life. Intertwined in these exemplars are a pattern of my thinking, my personal philosophy, my values, my search for truth, my goals, and my dreams. Ultimately, writing has been my search for inner truth within myself. Parul Sehgal describes a writing life as "a lifetime apprenticeship, a daily devotion, a process of constant gleaning, and a self-interrogation of inner thoughts."

Through the years, the capacity and desire to read has been the beginning of my writing. Reading other authors helps clarify what I believe. Writing projects my thinking to others who may then want to discuss, debate, or enter a conversation with me about the topic. Sources I mention in my writing may entice others to read further.

In 1990, at the age of sixty, I wrote a dissertation describing John Steinbeck's writing ability. This challenge set a pattern in my writing: reading other authors, researching the subject, organizing the material, and then writing a response. In this way, I best express my intellectual self. My talent lies more in analytical, speculative, philosophical, and interpretive terms of thinking rather than writing novels. Novels require a broad imagination that demands a visionary, inventive language with a multicolor syntax. Writing essays best fits my writing strengths.

In my writing, I constantly try to be creative. Creating clear, concise English with correct syntax is a challenge. Creating sentences with a musical lilt in their rhythmic contours is a test of skill. Incorporating words or phrases with alliteration, metaphors, similes, or imagery for literary purposes measures dexterity within the English language. Frankly, the art of writing is difficult, but it inspires creative thinking. As my writing matured, I began to notice a commonplace beauty at looking at my thoughts in the written word.

Through the years, I have had a keen interest in researching the lives of notable individuals such as Thomas Jefferson, Sojourner Truth, Edward Coles, Norman Mailer, Lorraine Hansberry, and John Steinbeck. This research interest requires a vast amount of reading from many authors.

Indeed, these authors inspire my thinking. I relish taking a plethora of ideas I have read and organizing them into an essay. This collection of essays is grounded in the works of other writers, but the essays reflect my own thoughts and ideas, formulated in creative prose. I make connections with other authors to create original ideas of my own. My essays often serve as a review of a book or article. The practice of reading, researching, and writing essays invites my creative talent into invigorating, compelling, and stimulating thinking.

In January 1996, the Delaware Unitarian Universalist Fellowship, a lay-led congregation, invited me to present commentaries periodically. Taking on this minor role in leading worship services became a creative way for me to expose my thoughts and my writing to others for their consideration. I presented commentaries on modern issues like climate change as well as historical, political, and religious topics. Delivering messages to a diverse audience in the format of an essay became a challenging application of my writing.

A note on style: In an effort to assert my core value of the worth and dignity of every human being through my writing, I have made deliberate word choices, particularly when describing racialized power dynamics and positions. For example, in keeping with practices adopted by the Associated Press, *The New York Times,* and others, I capitalize the word "Black" when referencing cultures and people of African origin in non-quoted material. I also use the term "enslaved person" rather than "slave" in order to separate identity from oppressive circumstances while also placing verbal responsibility for those circumstances on the enslaver. I am indebted to the community-sourced document "Writing about Slavery/Teaching About Slavery: This Might Help," created by P. Gabrielle Foreman, et al., for informing my thinking around these style choices and many others.

Arriving at the milestone of age ninety, I want to share this collection of essays with others. The essays reflect my thoughts and values. The usefulness, worth, and importance of these essays will dwell in the reader. My purpose in writing and publishing them will have been achieved if the reader finds pleasure in reading them, gains knowledge about a variety of subjects, ponders the ideas, and feels inspired to read more.

Mary Alice Dillman
Delaware, Ohio, 2021

PART 1

Reflections

Writing and Life

Anne Lamott's *Bird by Bird* (meaning step by step) is a one-of-a-kind composition handbook for advanced college students. Even though today's fast-paced, digital generation might find the book a bit outdated, it is witty, creative, and appealing to all writers. Lamott stresses that writing can complement everyone's life; it is not just an activity for professional writers.

Devotion, commitment, and dedication are rewards in life; writing gives these same rewards. Writing gives solace, direction in thought, wisdom, truth, and pride. "It is spiritually invigorating…, intellectually quickening…, a perfect focus for life."[1] Writers find experiences in life to "stimulate and nourish the spirit. These will be quiet and deep inside."[2] Recording life experiences in writing gives the soul "a sense of liberation."[3]

Throughout the book, Lamott gives writing advice to students:

- Pay attention and observe everyone and everything carefully. Then write down everything you remember about a subject.
- Don't worry if what you write is no good, because no one is going to see it.
- Don't worry if you spend the rest of the day rewriting or destroying what you have written.
- Sit down to write at approximately the same time every day.
- Just start. Don't worry about doing it well.
- Clean off your desk. All the "sensory overload" is distracting.
- Stay at the desk and stare if you must.
- Limit the topic.

- Begin with short assignments like a paragraph with one small memory, one exchange, or one small scene.
- Remember that perfectionism on the first draft ruins your writing because it blocks inventiveness and playfulness.
- Never fall in love with your first draft. Fix it in the second draft.
- Do research. If you're writing about canoeing, go canoeing.
- Let someone else read your paper.
- Relax, get rid of critics. Just practice by moving your hand across the page.

Lamott relates the benefits of writing in the context of life. "One of the gifts of being a writer is that it gives you an excuse to do things, to go places and explore.... Writing motivates you to look closely at life."[4] Lamott quotes C.S. Lewis in *Surprised by Joy* that writing opens "a zoo of lusts, a bedlam of ambitions, a nursery of fears, a harem of fondled hatreds."[5] On the other hand, "writing has so much to give, so much to teach, so many surprises."[6]

"If you give freely, there will always be more [to give]."[7] "You are going to have to give and give and give."[8] Getting something published is not the important issue, "but there is in learning to be a giver."[9] Writing gives you a voice to love someone and have their legacy live forever in words. For example, when Anne Lamott's father was dying of a brain cancer, she started writing two books as presents for him. "I composed funny stories and tender moments about my days with my father and brothers."[10] Indeed, these stories helped her father as she read them to him in the months before his death. "I showed [these stories] to my father, who thought it was great that all this pain and fear and loss were being transformed into a story of love and survival.... I was giving him a love letter that was a living legacy for life."[11]

In the movie *Chariots of Fire*, Eric Liddell wants to run because he is fast. Likewise, writes Lamott, "God made some of us fast in this area of working with words."[12] However, writers "have days of frantic boredom, of angry hopelessness, of wanting to quit forever."[13] Then, "the sun comes up again" and you start with an idea that works.[14]

According to Lamott, writing is a social activity, an effort to say something to someone for some purpose. If the writing is read, at least it is a record of your thinking and feeling, and you give something to someone. In writing, you take yourself outside to an audience, and you go inside yourself. Lamott recalls that "Flannery O'Connor said that anyone who survived childhood has enough material to write for the rest of his or her life."[15]

Lamott says that "writing a first draft is very much like watching a Polaroid develop."[16] The picture is a murky, grayish green at first, but it slowly comes into focus. For example, take the Special Olympics. Sitting in a stadium one day, Lamott saw far in the distance a picture of sheer beauty of effort. A teenage girl running on crutches, way in the distance, came into focus behind all the other runners. But her sheer happiness that she made it shone in her eyes and through her sweat. Lamott wrote about it because "it was tragedy transformed over the years into joy."[17]

Lamott recalls writing about all the people at a convalescent home she used to visit regularly. She believes that she would have characterized these people wrongly if she had written about them right after the first visit; she would have focused on surface observations, on their "bleak existence."[18] "Though these people are no longer useful in the traditional meaning of the word, they are there to be loved unconditionally, like trees in the winter... stripped of leaves, color, and growth."[19] Good writing allows us to notice this in detail. "Writing is about learning to pay attention and to communicate what is going on."[20] Lamott believes that you sometimes have to use a pair of binoculars to observe the truth closely—to see the parts of a whole universe. According to Lamott, "I honestly think in order to be a writer, you have to learn to be reverent."[21] Reverence is "awe," a "presence in and an openness to the world."[22]

Lamott relates how one can see the beauty of a sick person in an AIDS clinic. "You could see the amazing fortitude of people going through horror with grace.... Each ravaged body or wounded psyche can and should still be cared for as softly and tenderly as possible."[23]

Lamott reveals that "the purpose of most great writing seems to be to reveal in an ethical light who we are.... As we live, we begin to discover what helps in life and what hurts" through characters we conceive in writing.[24] "If your deepest beliefs drive your writing, you can internalize some decency in the world and make...characters take a risk or make a sacrifice for someone else.... Characters let us see that there is in fact some sort of moral compass still at work here, and that we, too, could travel by this compass if we so choose."[25] When we create characters in writing, we see courage and goodness, "we get to see something true that we long for."[26]

"A writer always tries...to be a part of the solution, to understand a little about life and to pass this on."[27] "We no longer need Chicken Little to tell us the sky is falling, because it already has. The issue now is how to take care of one another."[28]

In his novel *The Things They Carried,* Tim O'Brien tells us that the stories and novels and writing we do save our lives. His novels are all written about the Vietnam War. In Vietnam he committed murders, and he witnessed tragedies, violence, and misery among Vietnamese peasants and American soldiers, so his stories eased his guilt and kept him sane. Stories, O'Brien says, make the lifeless or dead live again.

So why does our writing matter? Lamott proposes the following answer:

"Because of the spirit, I say. Because of the heart. Writing and reading decrease our sense of isolation. They deepen and widen and expand our sense of life; they feed the soul. When writers make us shake our heads with the exactness of their prose and their truths, and even make us laugh about ourselves or life, our buoyancy is restored. We are given a shot at dancing with, or at least clapping along with, the absurdity of life, instead of being squashed by it over and over again. It's like singing on a boat during a terrible storm at sea. You can't stop the raging storm, but singing can change the hearts and spirits of the people who are together on that ship."[29]

Writing gives us the chance "to see in everything the essence of holiness, a sign that God is implicit in all of creation."[30] The natural world is full of beauty and pain, and the human world is full of the mind and heart, so try to capture those in words. Writing offers hope to others and truth to ourselves.

Notes to Writing and Life

1. Anne Lamott, *Bird by Bird: Some Instructions on Writing and Life* (New York: Anchor Books, 1994), 232.
2. Lamott, *Bird by Bird,* 233.
3. Lamott, 233.
4. Lamott, xii.
5. C.S. Lewis, *Surprised by Joy,* quoted in Lamott, xxi.
6. Lamott, xxvi.
7. Lamott, 202.

8. Lamott, 202.
9. Lamott, 203.
10. Lamott, 185.
11. Lamott, 186.
12. Lamott, xxviii.
13. Lamott, xxix.
14. Lamott, 9.
15. Lamott, 4.
16. Lamott, 39.
17. Lamott, 42.
18. Lamott, 82.
19. Lamott, 82.
20. Lamott, 97.
21. Lamott, 99.
22. Lamott, 99.
23. Lamott, 129.
24. Lamott, 104.
25. Lamott, 105.
26. Lamott, 106.
27. Lamott, 107.
28. Lamott, 108.
29. Lamott, 237.
30. Lamott, 100-101.

Outliers

V. S. Naipaul starts his novel *A Bend in the River* with the line, "The world is what it is; men [and women] who are nothing, who allow themselves to become nothing, have no place in it."[1] In an interview late in his presidency, Barack Obama said that he often thought about this line, particularly when considering foreign policy questions, but that he fought against "that very cynical, more realistic view of the world" in which human beings seemed to have no place.[2] Even when human beings seem to have nothing and cannot rise above nothingness in their lives, they still have an important place in the world.

Malcolm Gladwell states in his 2008 book *Outliers: A Story of Success*, "People don't rise from nothing."[3] Success always requires the contributions of many people. Successful people benefit from hidden advantages, extraordinary opportunities, and cultural legacies that allow them to learn and thrive in ways many of us cannot. The culture, legacies, and history of a country, as well as our individual abilities, opportunities, parentage, and wealth, "shape the pattern of our achievements in a way we cannot begin to imagine."[4] Gladwell defines Outliers as "men and women who do things that are out of the ordinary."[5] They are the remarkable ones in the world. Fortunately, success is not necessarily determined by wealth. For Outliers, success comes with "a combination of ability, opportunity, achievement, and utterly arbitrary advantage."[6]

Let's look at some examples. First, when you are born matters. In Canada, nine-year-old and ten-year-old hockey players born in January, February, and March have an arbitrary advantage. When the eligibility cut-off date for hockey programs based on age is January 1, these players can join early in the year and play with more experienced players until the end of the year; they experience more coaching, they play more games, and they have more practice. This spells success, for these youth are more likely to be selected for all-star teams than those with birthdays in later months of the year.

A second example relates to musical ability. According to the Berlin Academy of Music, a professional performer needs to have had ten thousand hours of practice by age twenty.[7] At age twenty-one, Mozart had been playing and composing for more than ten years. Putting in the hours of practice certainly contributed to his success, but he was also fortunate to have had a father who was a music teacher and to have grown up in a household immersed in music.

Finally, Bill Gates is a brilliant math whiz, and as a teenager he put in his "ten thousand hours" of practice with computer software, but wealth and opportunity also contributed to his success. His father was a wealthy lawyer in Seattle, Washington; his mother was the daughter of a well-to-do banker. He was fortunate to attend a private high school that was affluent enough to install an ASR-33 Teletype Terminal with time-sharing access in 1968. Gates was able to use this terminal freely. He was a programmer by the age of thirteen.[8] Gates happened to find work writing payroll software for a company called ISI. He happened to live within walking distance of the University of Washington, which had free computer use in the medical center and the physics department, so he worked nights there from 3:00 to 6:00 a.m. He dropped out of Harvard in his sophomore year and started his own company, using financial help from his parents. "But what truly distinguishes [Gates' history] is not [his] extraordinary talent but [his] extraordinary opportunities."[9] On top of his talent, where he grew up and when he grew up created advantages that contributed to his success.

In addition, Bill Gates and Apple founder Steve Jobs were privileged to be born in 1955, because by the time they were twenty, the personal computer revolution had just begun. Their success was "a product of the world in which they grew up."[10] Many wealthy people like them—and politicians, too—incorrectly claim that their success has little to do with family connections or unique historical influences. Jeb Bush, for example, claimed in 1993 that he was "a self-made man" whose success "was the result of his own pluck and work ethic."[11]

"Geniuses are the ultimate outliers."[12] But being smart, with an IQ score of 115 to 130, isn't enough to make one successful. Indeed, "success in a popular sense must incorporate certain traits of personality and character."[13] "Being a successful lawyer is about a lot more than IQ."[14] Practical intelligence and creative intelligence are different from analytical intelligence. "Common sense is an effective tool" in making decisions.[15]

According to Gladwell, successful Outliers come out of particular environments. "Cultural legacies [of the South and of the North in the United States] are powerful forces.... They persist generation after generation... and play a role in directing attitudes and behavior."[16] For example, in the 1600s, Quakers from England settled in the North Midlands of the Delaware Valley while Puritans from the Netherlands settled in Massachusetts; their cultural legacies still influence people in those U.S. regions today.

Of course, maturity, hard work, opportunities, and parentage matter. So do inherited genes, family attitudes, and individual skills. All in all, Outliers find success based on when and where they are born, what influence parents and culture have on them, and what circumstances and advantages they have in a particular place and in a particular time in history.

Gladwell's understanding of Outliers can be applied to Justice Sandra Day O'Connor and Justice Ruth Bader Ginsburg. In her 2015 book *Sisters in Law,* Linda Hirshman describes the two justices as "sisters in law" who did "the work of transforming the legal status of American women."[17] How do we measure O'Connor and Ginsburg as Outliers? First, the influences of the particular place where each was born matter. O'Connor was born in 1930 near El Paso, Arizona; Ginsburg was born in 1933 in Brooklyn, New York. Their families had relatively modest homes. O'Connor lived most of her formative years on a working cattle ranch. She adopted a conservative belief in individualism. Ginsburg's parents were Russian and Polish immigrants who sewed garments for the garment industry. Growing up as a "country girl" in conservative Southwest Arizona was culturally quite different from growing up as a "city girl" in New York. Where you are born and when in history you mature matter for success.

O'Connor and Ginsburg also had personal abilities that propelled them toward achievement and opportunities. They were both intelligent and socially inclined, so they made many contacts with important people. O'Connor was sent to live with her grandmother in El Paso to attend a private school for most of her education. At age sixteen, she entered Stanford University. She was particularly influenced by a professor named Harry Rathbun whose seminars led O'Connor to ask herself: Who am I? What potential do I have? Where am I bound? In 1950 she entered Stanford Law School where she was one of only four women in her class. William Rehnquist was her classmate. O'Connor married John O'Connor in 1952, and in 1957 they settled in Phoenix, Arizona. John became an attorney in a distinguished law firm.

Ginsburg began her education with weekly trips to the public library with her mother. Her school in Brooklyn, New York educated students K through eighth grade and was populated with one thousand students. Diversity was its hallmark. Ginsburg attended James Madison High School where she was a cheerleader, an honor student, and a member of the orchestra and the school newspaper. Her mother died of cancer when Ginsburg was seventeen. Ginsburg graduated sixth in her high school class in 1950 and entered Cornell University, a coed institution where men outnumbered women four to one. She received scholarships earmarked for female children of immigrants and the working class. At Cornell, Ginsburg absorbed liberal ideas about protection of freedom of speech, freedom of the press, and the right to assemble.[18] She became "committed to liberal politics."[19] She developed a strong belief that every person has a right to think, write, and speak freely.[20] Right after graduating from Cornell, she married Michael Ginsburg, whom she had dated since her freshman year. After two years at Harvard Law School, she transferred to Columbia Law School and received her law degree in 1959 with the highest grades in her class.

Both O'Connor and Ginsburg achieved a superior education, which helped catapult them to highly successful careers. But like other Outliers, they also seized opportunities and turned obstacles into opportunities. Persistence and good luck also helped them. O'Connor began her career with disappointment. As a rancher's daughter growing up in an isolated part of the country and receiving an education in the post-war West, O'Connor did not suspect that being a woman was a problem. She believed she could do anything as long as she worked hard. However, she was shocked when none of the forty law firms to which she had sent job applications offered her a position as a lawyer. One firm in Phoenix—Gibson, Dunn, and Crutcher—told her, "This firm has never hired woman lawyers.... Our clients wouldn't stand for it."[21] However, they did offer to hire her as a legal secretary.

In the early 1960s, O'Connor took a break from her law profession to focus on raising her children. She became active in the Republican Party as a precinct committeewoman, then as the county vice chairman, and finally, as the president of the Junior League of Phoenix, "a powerful volunteer organization."[22] With help from local Republican Party leaders who had connections with the attorney general of Arizona, she became the first woman to be appointed an assistant attorney general in Arizona.[23] Moving forward to 1973, O'Connor became the first woman in America to become the majority leader of a state senate. Arizona was a hostile landscape for women; abortion was a criminal act. In the Arizona Senate, she supported laws that denied state funding to the poor for abortions and prevented any workers from participating in an abortion.[24] At this time, O'Connor had a feminist awakening. When the Equal Rights Amendment (ERA) was proposed, she was caught between her ambitions in the Republican Party and her support for women. She supported passage of the ERA, but it was never approved by the Arizona legislature. She supposed she was supporting women with a career by cooking dinner every night for her husband and her sons. She saw a future in supporting Barry Goldwater, the Republican candidate for president.

O'Connor's experiences as a child on an isolated ranch made her impervious to social pressure,[25] although she had keen social skills for entertaining large groups of people in which she made contacts.[26] Her political philosophy moved her in the 1970s to support the promotion of William Rehnquist to chief justice of the Supreme Court; he was no friend of the women's movement and repeatedly failed to strike down laws that discriminated against women.[27] She worked hard to reelect Richard Nixon in 1972.[28] As Arizona Senate leader, she played a role in redistricting Arizona to favor Republicans. She took the Republican line on gun control, the death penalty, and school busing. During the 1970s, O'Connor was influenced by the place in which she lived, her race, and her socio-economic status; she was white, middle-class, and married. In 1981, Reagan appointed Sandra Day O'Connor as the first woman justice on the Supreme Court.

As a member of the Supreme Court, "O'Connor was not a robust voice of social change."[29] She was not a strong advocate for gender equality. She defended "women's proper role in society," but she was not "a committed strategist for women's rights."[30] But several major positions she took on the Supreme Court made an enormous difference. In the 1992 case of *Planned Parenthood v. Casey*, she joined the majority opinion which stated that in abortion decisions, "the destiny of the woman must be shaped to a large extent on her own conception of her spiritual imperatives and her place in society."[31] O'Connor also cast the fifth vote to end the Florida count in the presidential contest of *Bush v. Gore*.[32] After this vote, for the following five years, she often voted more liberally on cases involving civil rights and equality for men and women.[33]

Ginsburg's education propelled her into varied opportunities. She clerked for Supreme Court Justice Felix Frankfurter. In 1959 she received a clerkship with New York Federal Judge Edmund Palmieri, who was one of the few federal judges at the time willing to hire women. An opportunity to study court procedures during Sweden's feminist revolution was given to her in 1961. That year strengthened her belief in equality for men and women. She carried this philosophy into her teaching at Rutgers Law School and at Columbia University Law School. By 1970, she was giving speeches everywhere in the country to support the ERA, but American society was more conservative at that time and the amendment was never ratified. She believed that the court should treat sex discrimination like racial discrimination.[34] She was a major force in founding the Women's Rights Project within the ACLU in 1972. In the decade from 1971 to 1981, she argued six gender discrimination cases before the Supreme Court. Chief Justice William Rehnquist continued to oppose Ginsburg's arguments for legal equality for women.

Other opportunities opened for Ginsburg. In 1977, the Rockefeller Foundation presented her a residency in Italy; the following year she was a delegate to China for the American Bar Association; by 1979, she was picked for the United States Court of Appeals in Washington, D.C. President Bill Clinton nominated her to the Supreme Court in 1992, and in 1993 the Senate approved her by a vote of 96 to 3. Ginsburg was sixty years old, a "brilliant, beautifully educated, experienced" woman who would lead the court in fighting against all forms of discrimination.[35] With the appearance of a second woman on the court, a women's bathroom was added in the Judges' robing room.[36]

After twelve years together on the Supreme Court, O'Connor and Ginsburg respected each other highly, despite their differences. They clearly broke some gender barriers. As remarkable women in American society, they became Outliers. They were similar in some ways. While on the court together they heard twenty cases about women's issues. Similarly, they were born in the same decade. Humble parents launched them into wealthy futures, too; both had lawyer husbands, providing well for them. Both women traveled extensively, giving speeches and classes around the United States.

But they had differences as Outliers. They came to the court during different political eras. Reagan nominated O'Connor to the court during the conservative resurgence of the 1980s, while Clinton nominated Ginsburg during the liberal, pro-globalization era of the 1990s. One incidental difference in philosophy was that, while the O'Connors were long-time members of a Phoenix country club that historically excluded Black people, the Ginsburgs in 1983 resigned from the Woodmont Country Club in Maryland because its personnel waived the $25,000 initiation fee for "high-ranking Washington people" but declined to do the same for a talented African American golfer, Harry Edwards.[37]

Individual merit toward success is important, but Outliers must "unravel the logic" of "beneficiaries of hidden advantages and extraordinary opportunists and cultural legacies that allow them to [succeed]."[38] Like a towering oak tree that grew from the hardiest acorn, "people come from hardy seed."[39] But, like a tree, they must have sunlight to warm them, deep, rich soil in which to put down roots. Outliers learn, work hard, and make sense of who they are in the world. However, one Outlier cannot reach the top of the ladder of success without other people assisting him or her on the ladder. Success for Outliers is grounded in advantages, inheritance, opportunities, and where and when one is born. Some Outliers are the remarkable among us—the skilled, the talented, and the driven—who successfully do things that are out of the ordinary.

Notes to Outliers

1. V. S. Naipaul, *A Bend in the River* (New York: Alfred A. Knopf, 1979), 1.
2. Michiko Kakutani, "How Reading Nourished Obama in Office," *New York Times*, January 16, 2017.
3. Malcolm Gladwell, *Outliers: The Story of Success* (New York: Little, Brown & Co., 2008), 19.
4. Gladwell, *Outliers*, 19.
5. Gladwell, 17.
6. Gladwell, 37.
7. Gladwell, 39.
8. Gladwell, 51.
9. Gladwell, 55.
10. Gladwell, 67.
11. S. V. Dáte, *Jeb: America's Next Bush* (New York: Tarcher, 2007), 80-81.
12. Gladwell, *Outliers*, 76.
13. Gladwell, 79.
14. Gladwell, 89.
15. Linda Hirshman, *Sisters in Law: How Sandra Day O'Connor and Ruth Bader Ginsburg Went to the Supreme Court and Changed the World* (New York: Harper Perennial, 2015), 195.
16. Gladwell, *Outliers*, 175.
17. Hirshman, *Sisters in Law*, xv.
18. Hirshman, 10.
19. Hirshman, 11.
20. Hirshman, 11.
21. Hirshman, 13.
22. Hirshman, 20.
23. Hirshman, 23.
24. Hirshman, 60.
25. Hirshman, 139.
26. Hirshman, 138.
27. Hirshman,118.
28. Hirshman, 122.
29. Hirshman, 172.
30. Hirshman, 230.
31. Anna Quindlen, "Public & Private; One Vote," *New York Times*, July 1, 1992.
32. Hirshman, *Sisters in Law*, 255-256.

33. Hirshman, 259.
34. Hirshman, 40.
35. Hirshman, 200.
36. Hirshman, 231.
37. Hirshman, 138.
38. Gladwell, *Outliers*, 19.
39. Gladwell, 20.

Respect for the Dignity of Each Individual

The contents of a small card slipped under the mat at my front door immediately caused pandemonium in my thinking. The card—from a conservative, Protestant church in Delaware, Ohio—invited me to "one of many exciting services" based on "The Bible Way to Heaven." My response to the card is not a criticism of any particular religious belief, but rather a direct expression of my view concerning the dignity of each human being.

The card stated that the four ways to heaven are found in Romans 3:10. First, you must RECOGNIZE YOUR CONDITION: All have sinned, so no matter how much good a person does, it will not be good enough to go to heaven. Second, you must REALIZE THE PENALTY FOR SIN: The punishment for our sins is death in hell. Third, you must BELIEVE CHRIST DIED FOR YOU: While we were sinners, Christ died for us through God's love. Fourth, you must TRUST CHRIST ALONE AS YOUR SAVIOUR: Life is a gift of the blood of Jesus and offered to everyone through faith in him. Finally, the card offered a prayer to Jesus: "I know I'm a sinner. Please forgive my sins...save my soul from Hell...take me to Heaven when I die. Thank you for saving me, Jesus."

The provocative statements in the card do not respect the dignity of an individual. They claim that sin is so deeply rooted in an individual's personality that he or she has no worth or dignity. They require a person to bow in supplication to a God who has already condemned him or her without a trial. The overall aura of the card devastates an individual's self-esteem, self-respect, pride, and self-assurance that he or she can survive. It suggests that a person will constantly require a savior instead of a conscience. Hell is always near; only Jesus—not good deeds—can save a person from it.

To define sin as a transgression against divine law, a wickedness, a willful violation of some religious or moral principle, or a reprehensible or regrettable action is problematic. Whose divine law or principle is violated? Islamic, Buddhist, Protestant, Jewish? Is it a sin to waste time? Is it a sin not to attend church? The Unitarian Universalist literature very sparingly uses the word "sin"; instead, each individual is accountable to himself or herself to respect his or her own dignity and self-worth and the dignity and worth of every other human being. Dignity comes from a personal name, from self-assessment, and from how others view us. One needs self-respect to respect others.

A name identifies and gives dignity to a person. In the movie *The Valley of Decision,* the rich, humble son of the family asks the house maid he loves to please call him by his first name to be more intimate. Instead of "Hey," "Looka here," "Well now," or "Mr. Paul," how about just Paul? Thomas Jefferson recorded the names, births, rations, and work assignments of the people he enslaved, but, as Nicholas Kristof points out, he excluded them from those deserving human freedom.[1] When we label the Tutsis in Africa as "sub-human" and the Vietnamese as "godless gooks," we remove the dignity of *all* persons in those categories. Today, millions of people around the world are stuck in refugee camps or subjected to forced labor, human trafficking, or nonconsensual marriage. We don't know their names, but surely they have talent, faithfulness, enduring strength, and gratefulness that make them worthy of dignity.

Individuals with self-respect discover that their own self-affirmation results from the ability to affirm the worth and dignity of others. Thereupon, one can have compassion and empathy for others and from others, for dignity comes from the way an individual relates to others. Take the case of four janitors in the Physics Department at Ohio Wesleyan University, where my husband taught for nearly fifty years. They took pride in their work: highly polished floors, sanitary drinking fountains and restrooms, and meticulously cleaned offices. These friendly janitors earned the respect of everyone in the department.

Finding the dignity and worthiness of an individual depends on the perspective one observes. Some people will earn praise based on their rank, office, station, popularity, or nobility. Some will find loftiness in service to others through the military, the Peace Corps, or Doctors without Borders. Some of us admire those who work with dedication, no matter what their circumstances are, or those who pursue their dreams. In an op-ed in *The New York Times* on October 22, 2013, Joe Nocera profiled Michael J. Fox, a popular TV star. Fox was diagnosed with Parkinson's disease at age thirty, but he kept the fact to himself. Finally, when he could not work on episodes of the sitcom "Spin City" because symptoms of Parkinson's were becoming too noticeable, he retired and became a spokesman for those suffering with Parkinson's. He did interviews with commentators such as Barbara Walters and reporters of *People,* and he testified before Congress. This helped him in an important way to maintain his sense of dignity and purpose. In addition, Fox established the Michael J. Fox Foundation to support scientists and industry in the search for a cure for Parkinson's. In conjunction with this, after a Phase III drug failed for Fox, the doctors tweaked his medication, and his body movements stabilized enough to allow him to do a new TV show, "The Michael J. Fox Show." Fox joked, "I can play anybody so long as he has Parkinson's."[2] The tenacity of his character is commendable, as is his commitment to dignity.

Another example of dignity of character is found in Abraham Nemeth, creator of the Braille Code for Advanced Mathematics. Although blind from birth, he loved playing piano using Braille books, and he loved mathematics. In 1940, while working at the American Foundation for the Blind and playing piano in Brooklyn bars, he customized the Braille code for complex mathematics and made a Braille slide rule. He earned a master's degree in psychology and a doctorate in mathematics. The Nemeth Code that he developed "enable[s] blind people to learn, work, and excel in science, technology, engineering, and mathematics," said the Chairman of the National Federation of the Blind.[3] His deeds lifted the dignity of so many other individuals.

Whereas Unitarian Universalists are dedicated to respecting the worth and dignity of each individual, we acknowledge that human beings are woefully flawed. Sometimes we treat others with prejudice or even consider them to be enemies. Naturally, we can't love and respect everyone in the world, so each one of us blocks the unworthy individuals by his or her own means. Consider our attitudes regarding the dignity of Palestinians. Most of their ancestral land has been occupied by Israel, and many of their homes have been demolished since 1948. In the 2006 novel *The Lemon Tree* by Sandy Tolan, Dalia, a sympathetic Israeli, is speaking to Bashir, a Palestinian who has just spent fifteen years in an Israeli prison. She says, "We need to make sacrifices if both of us are to live here.... And I know it is not fair for me to say that.... But I think we need to strengthen those people who are willing to make some compromise.... By not accepting the state of Israel or by not accepting the state of Palestine, I think none of us has a real life here."[4] For Dalia, the key to co-existence is to acknowledge mistakes, apologize, and make amends.

Bashir replies that for thirty-seven years since they had met, "there have been more settlements, land confiscations, and now this wall—how can there be a solution? How can there be any Palestinian state? How can I open my heart, as you say?... [A solution is] having one state, and all the people who live in this one state are equal, without consideration of religion, nationality, culture, or language. Everyone is equal, has equal rights, has the right to vote and choose his own leadership."[5] Bashir was among those considered unrealistic and fixated on returning to his former home.

Earlier in the novel, Dalia had told Bashir that after the Holocaust, "Israel was the only safe place for us." Bashir reminded Dalia that the whole world did not persecute Jews: "The Nazis killed the Jews. And we hate them. But why should [Palestinians] pay for what they did?"[6] In this dialogue, the eternal question is, is there any compromise that will provide dignity and worth to both parties?

We also should not forget that animals have worth and dignity. The lumbering elephant, the swaggering ape, and the graceful giraffe are precious creatures. But the lion should not be a coat, elephant tusks are not for decoration, and the bone of the hippopotamus is not a medicine. Wildlife and domestic animals have been abused by hunters, slaughtered by poachers, stolen by criminals, and demeaned as unworthy forms of life. Brad Goldburg of New York writes, "Farm animals end up on our plates with no hint as to their inherent intelligence or the suffering inflicted on them in the process. We have a moral obligation to educate ourselves and our children so these wonderful, nonhuman beings get their due consideration and respect."[7] As for birds, Eliot Brenowitz, professor of psychology and biology at the

University of Washington, "marvels at the capacity of birds to migrate thousands of miles using landmarks and star constellations, to use clever tools to capture their prey, to construct astonishing complex nests, and to practice bird songs from their parents."[8] Birds do all this with brains that may be no larger than a marble. So next time someone calls you a birdbrain, thank him or her for the compliment.

In the end, the invitation I received on my doorstep from the conservative Protestant church is demeaning to someone who believes in the dignity of every human being. Dignity and worthiness begin by assuming that the Creator has given each individual the gift of a conscience. Such an individual assumes responsibility for his or her actions. Human beings are not all wallowing in "sin" from the very beginning of life. To save all human life and restore human dignity to all life, individuals need to act first in accordance with environmental controls and climate change. Further, Unitarian Universalists believe that we should have respect for the interdependent web of all existence of which we are a part.

Notes to Respect for the Dignity of Each Individual

1. Nicholas Kristof, "Slavery Isn't a Thing of the Past," *New York Times*, November 7, 2013.
2. Joe Nocera, "The 3 Roles of Michael J. Fox," *New York Times*, October, 22, 2013.
3. William Yardley, "Abraham Nemeth, Creator of a Braille Code for Math, Is Dead at 94," *New York Times*, October 7, 2013.
4. Sandy Tolan, *The Lemon Tree: An Arab, a Jew, and the Heart of the Middle East* (New York: Bloomsbury, 2006), 258.
5. Tolan, *Lemon Tree*, 259.
6. Tolan, 160.
7. Brad Goldburg, letter to the editor, *New York Times*, October 23, 2013.
8. Eliot Brenowitz, letter to the editor, *New York Times*, October 23, 2013.

Spirited Resilience

I have always been amazed how some people bounce back after disheartening, daunting pandemonium has crushed their spirit. A mental revival must take hold and transform them. Perhaps some intellectual or emotional force saves them. Such force is a mystery, but I believe it might be a resilience of spirit that sustains them. Dr. Elizabeth Kubler-Ross puts it this way: "The most beautiful people we have known are those who have known defeat, known suffering, known struggle, known loss, and have found their way out of the depths. Beautiful people do not just happen."[1]

Resilience is the ability to return to the original form or position after being bent, compressed, or stretched. Resilience allows a human being to recover from an illness, instability, sadness, depression, or adversity. Buoyancy is a type of resilience, a corralling of courage and strength to lift one's spirit and rebound from adversity with a relative lightness and cheerfulness. We see resilience (and sometimes buoyancy) in migrants crossing the Mediterranean Sea, in Palestinians stuck in Gaza, in refugees from Syria, Iraq, Yemen, and South Sudan, and in families knowing injustice.

Let me tell you about a few incidences of resilience that I have discovered in some newspaper articles and books. In *The End of Your Life Book Club*, author Will Schwalbe tells an amazing story of courage. A friend Judy Mayotte had polio in college, but she taught herself to walk all over again. She became a nun for a decade and then a world expert on refugees as the chair of the Women's Commission for Refugee Women and Children (now called the Women's Refugee Commission), a global advocacy organization. In 1993, Judy was in southern Sudan, helping a community that desperately needed food. Airplanes were scheduled to come in from one direction to make airdrops, but they unexpectedly came in from a different direction. A two-hundred-pound sack of food that was dropped from the sky missed its target and landed on Judy's leg, crushing it in ten places. Miraculously, a doctor doing relief work was right there. First, Judy's lower leg was amputated in Africa. Then, at the Mayo Clinic most of her upper leg had to be amputated, too. But Judy survived and continued to work with refugees. She remarked to a *Chicago Tribune* reporter on a return trip from Africa, "Fortunately, I'm lucky. The leg knocked off was my polio leg."[2] Resilience often requires adapting one's attitude in the face of setbacks.

Stuart Scott, a former sports commentator for ESPN, used to enliven his sportscasts with a blend of pop culture references, slang, and exuberant phrases like "As cool as the other side of the pillow." Scott ushered in a new style of sports commentary and entertained us and inspired us with his courage and love. During the years he was battling cancer, Scott received the Jimmy V Perseverance Award at the ESPY Awards. After four operations in the previous week before he died, he accepted the award with these words: "When you die, that doesn't mean you lose to cancer. You beat cancer by how you live, why you live, and the manner in which you live. So live. Fight like hell, and when you get too tired to fight, [lie] down and rest and let someone else fight for you."[3] Although Scott died of cancer in 2015 at age forty-nine, he was resilient in spirit.

Nirmal Joshi, Chief Medical Officer for Pinnacle Health System in Pennsylvania, wrote an op-ed in *The New York Times* about how addressing communication failures between doctors and patients can lead to better treatment outcomes. She recounts the story of a diabetes specialist who sat down with a patient to understand why he was not taking his diabetes medication regularly. The patient told the specialist, "I can't continue to do this anymore. I've given up." The specialist placed a hand on his shoulder and sat with him before saying, "You still have a heart that still beats and legs you can still walk on—many of my patients don't have that privilege."[4] Five years later, the patient told the specialist that this brief discussion was the reason why he started to take better care of his health. Taking a few minutes to express concern for someone inspired him to be resilient for many years thereafter.

Another resilient person was Peggy Cooper Cafritz, a patron of Black artists who died in 2018. The artist Hank Willis Thomas described her as "one tough cookie." "She's seen a lot coming from the South, and she also realizes how fortunate she is to have had the family she had. Maybe that's why she's so resilient and so voracious."[5] Cafritz's father tried to send his children to Catholic schools in Mobile, Alabama, but was thwarted by a bishop in the diocese. During law school, Cafritz's father died. After law school, she became the youngest scholar at the Woodrow Wilson International Center. During a trip to Paris, she was attacked and kidnapped.

Later in life, a fire destroyed Cafritz's house which was full of artwork that she had collected. Heartbroken by the fire, she sued her utility company for failing to maintain the fire hydrants in her neighborhood. On top of that stress, she suffered health problems that required a gall bladder operation in Croatia that put her in a coma and two back surgeries. Amid all the turmoil in her life, with voraciousness she vowed "to look at everything anew." She rebuilt her art collection with new works, "collecting work that she loves, championing young artists and embracing the pioneering work being made by diverse artists from around the world."[6]

During the depths of the Ebola crisis in Sierra Leone, Bureh Beach Surf Club members found resilience in surfing at this beach in a "quiet, palm-fringed cove."[7] By January 2015, three thousand Sierra Leoneans had died from Ebola, and hundreds were still infected. But nobody at Bureh Beach was "talking about viral loads or death rates, treatment centers or protection suits."[8] Life went on. Surfers found peace in "the rhythm of the waves, the pull of the ocean, the sets coming in."[9] On the beach they could temporarily return to the ordinary order of life. They enjoyed their passion for surfing as a way to cope. All around the cove, survivors were "struggling to put their lives back together."[10]

In a review of the documentary *On the Way to School* in *The New York Times* on February 6, 2015, Ben Kenigsberg summarizes the film's main message: "Too often we forget how lucky we are to go to school."[11] Children from three continents are depicted on their daily journeys "toward knowledge." In India, a handicapped boy in a wheelchair is pushed by his brothers for two miles to attend school. In Kenya, a boy and his sister have to watch out for elephants on their nine-mile walk. A girl in Morocco has to walk for four hours in the Atlas Mountains. In Argentina, a boy and his sister ride a horse for an hour and a half. These grueling commutes to school by children attest to their hunger to learn and their resilience.

One of the most captivating stories of spirited resilience is Tommy Caldwell's and Kevin Jorgeson's seemingly impossible 19-day free climb of the 3,000-foot Dawn Wall of El Capitan in Yosemite National Park. Caldwell and Jorgeson were the first to ascend the Dawn Wall in a single expedition, using only their hands and feet to pull themselves up. Just how these two quiet men could imagine accomplishing such a quest is a mystery. Luckily, the "uncharacteristic stretch of dry weather" was a blessing. Their resilience was magical.

At the top of El Capitan, Jorgeson said, "I hope it inspires people to find their own Dawn Wall, if you will. We've been working on this thing a long time, slowly and surely. I think everyone has their own secret Dawn Wall to complete one day."[12] Questioned about the climb, Jorgeson explained, "You try not to linger too long on doubts.... I wanted to see what I was capable of and this was the biggest canvas and the most audacious project I could join and see to the finish." Caldwell chimed in, "I love to dream big.... This just lights a fire under me, and that's a really exciting way to live."[13]

Nature is resilient, too. Humans have cut down or damaged at least three-quarters of the world's forests, but there is a growing environmental movement toward preservation of forests in countries such as Brazil and Indonesia that are home to tropical forests. In Costa Rica, reforestation has played a big role in limiting the damage done to the environment there. Costa Rica is considered a forest success: Forests have regrown to cover more than half the country. Large, dense, natural forests are not being used for timber production. The spirited efforts of many scientists, governments, and conservationists have restored nature.

In *When Elephants Weep,* Jeffrey Moussaieff Masson and Susan McCarthy describe animal behavior. One story illustrates the resilience of a mother elephant:

> One evening in the 1930s, Ma Shwe, a work elephant and her three-month-old calf were trapped in rising floodwaters in the Upper Taungdwin River in Burma. Elephant handlers rushed to the river when they heard the calf screaming, but could do nothing to help, for the steep banks were twelve to fifteen feet high. Ma Shwe's feet were still on the river bottom, but her calf was floating. Ma Shwe held the

> baby against her body; whenever [the calf] began to drift away, she used her trunk to pull the calf back against the current. The fast-rising water soon washed the calf away and Ma Shwe plunged downstream for fifty yards and retrieved it. She pinned her calf against the bank with her head, then lifted the calf in her trunk, reared up on her hind legs, and placed the calf on a rocky ledge five feet above the water. Ma Shwe then fell back into the torrent and disappeared downstream.
>
> The elephant handlers turned their attention to the calf, which could barely fit on the narrow ledge where it stood shivering, eight feet below. Half an hour later, a British manager of the elephant camp wondered how to rescue this calf when he heard "the grandest sounds of a mother's love." Ma Shwe had crossed the river and got up the bank and was making her way back as fast as she could, calling the whole time—a defiant roar, but to her calf it was music. The two little ears, like the maps of India, were cocked forward listening to the only sounds that mattered, the call of her mother. When Ma Shwe saw her calf, safe on the other side of the river, her call changed to the rumble that elephants typically make when pleased. The two elephants were left where they were. By morning Ma Shwe had crossed the river, no longer in flood, and the calf was off the ledge.[14]

Scientists of animal behavior would like to say that Ma Shwe committed an act of love. But animals supposedly cannot love like people can because animal bonds are not spiritual. This evolutionary perspective stresses that survival is valued above love; animals act based on the dictates of their genes. They are survival machines wanting to spread their own genes in the gene pool. But if we stretch our interpretation of survival-based care, this act of resilience by a mother elephant may be evidence of feeling love.[15]

Finally, all these examples of resilience in individuals, animals, and nature bring me to the incredible, true story of Louie Zamperini, as recounted by Laura Hillenbrand in a biography she wrote about him titled *Unbroken: A World War II Story of Survival, Resilience, and Redemption.* Louie was a free-spirited child. One of Montaigne's maxims applies to Louie: "A spirited mind never stops within itself; it is always aspiring and going beyond its strength." He reacted to every limitation as a "challenge to his wits, his resourcefulness, and his determination to rebel."[16] At age nineteen, he was the youngest teenager to qualify as a 5,000-meter runner at the 1936 Berlin Olympics. His athletic training in track and boxing gave him self-discipline and confidence throughout his life. After graduating from the University of Southern California in 1940, he enlisted in the United States Army Air Forces in 1941. During a rescue mission on May 27, 1943, the B-24 bomber he was in malfunctioned and fell into the Pacific Ocean. (Note: In World War II, 70 percent of Air Force service men in the Pacific arena died in plane malfunctioning accidents, not enemy action. New, untested technology, storms, fuel leaks, and human error were responsible for many plane accidents.)

Louie drifted forty-seven days in a raft with his co-pilot Phil and the tail gunner (who died after thirty-three days). They ate fish and drank rainwater while braving the elements. After they had drifted 2,000 miles, the Japanese captured Louie and Phil (after shooting at their raft) and took them to a prison on Wotje Island, then to a prison on Kwajalein Island in the Marshall Islands. By this time, Louie weighed only 75 pounds. The two friends learned the dark truth as prisoners that "dignity is as essential to human life as water, food, and oxygen."[17] Self-respect and self-worth were the "innermost ornament of the soul…, the humanness."[18]

Marched through POW prison camps, Louie and Phil had no guarantee for their lives. To kill POWs was easy for the Japanese during war. On the Pacific island of Kwajalein, they were taken to a tiny wooden cell that had a thatched roof, a hole in the floor as a latrine, and a 1-inch-square window in the door. The floor was gravel with maggots, flies, and mosquitoes hovering in the hot weather. After a month they were moved to the Yokohama Ofuna interrogation camp on the eastern coast of Japan. POWs were forced to perform calisthenics until they collapsed. They sat outside in all kinds of weather.

When Louie was moved to a POW camp near Tokyo in September 1944, his endurance was tested to its limit. Japanese guards beat the POWs for folding their arms, cleaning their teeth, talking in their sleep, misunderstanding Japanese orders, and shielding their face during beatings. In a guard's presence, a POW was not to speak, sing, read, or look out the window. To be captured in war was "intolerably shameful" for a Japanese, so with their absolute power over POWs, guards were brutal and dehumanizing. POWs had very little food and often fell victim to beriberi.

The Japanese officer who assumed command of the camp, Corporal Mutsuhiro Watanabe, was a psychopath. First Lieutenant Zamperini, who outranked a Corporal, had his temple and ear pounded with a belt whip, leaving him deaf in his left ear for several weeks. POWs were encouraged to write letters home, but all their letters were burned. The U.S. Army sent a death notice to Louie's family in June 1943, but in November 1944, Radio Tokyo broadcast a list of POW survivors with Louie's name included. He was twenty-seven years old. On November 27, 1944, American aircraft bombed Tokyo. Louie was transferred to Naoetsu Prison northwest of Tokyo in the midst of winter...for his safety. Watanabe was still in command. Japan held 132,000 POWs from the United States, Britain, Canada, New Zealand, Holland, and Australia. One in four (36,000) died. According to Louie, "I could take the beatings and the physical punishment, but it was the attempt to destroy your dignity, to make you a nonentity that was the hardest to bear."[19] POWs became "torn-down men." Their memories were filled with torture, humiliation, shame, and unworthiness. They were dehumanized, lonely, and isolated human beings.

On February 15, 1945, 1,000 American planes bombed Tokyo. Then, on February 24, 1945, 1,600 more planes bombed Tokyo. After the war ended, Louie was liberated in October 1945, sick and wasted.

The ravages of war did not end when Louie was liberated. At home in California, he fell into alcoholism. Alcohol was to Louie what acorns are to squirrels.[20] He would often wake up in the middle of the night screaming and sweating. Although he spoke harshly to his wife Cynthia and they nearly divorced, their marriage ultimately lasted fifty-four years until her death. During the post-war mental and physical turmoil, Louie experienced an epiphany while attending a large religious meeting led by the evangelist Billy Graham. He began to believe that he was a good man.[21]

In this conversion, Louie turned his attention to his wife Cynthia, his daughter Cissy, and his son Luke. He became a real estate agent. He made ninety-five speeches for the War Department. In 1950, he returned to Japan to confront Watanabe, who was being tried with more than one thousand other Japanese for war crimes. He opened the Victory Boys Camp in 1954 for troubled boys. He lectured in schools and at the First Presbyterian Church. At age sixty, he was climbing mountains; at age seventy, he continued skateboarding; at age eighty-five, he returned to Kwajalein Prison to recover the bodies of nine marines. In 1998, he triumphantly ran the Olympic torch past Naoetsu Prison in Japan. He remained incorrigibly cheerful until his death at ninety-three.

Louis Zamperini epitomizes an unbroken, resilient spirit. Considering the mayhem of war, Pacific POW veterans died four times as fast as other men their age. Thirty percent of Pacific POW veterans succumbed to suicide, and many became alcoholics. When Louie was liberated after World War II, most postwar Pacific POWs were emaciated; the majority had neurological damage and diseases such as beriberi, TB, malaria, and dysentery.[22] The effects of these diseases and other ailments often persisted for decades after the war ended. Louie overcame these maladies. According to Hillenbrand, he believed that "everything happened for a reason and would come to good."[23]

The final words on the cover of the book *Unbroken* are the following: "Zamperini would answer desperation with ingenuity; suffering with hope, resolve, and humor; brutality with rebellion. His fate, whether triumph or tragedy, would be suspended on the fraying wire of his will." The mystery of his life was his resilient spirit.

Amazing people, animals, and nature have corralled courage and strength to rebound from adversity with a spirit of lightness and cheerfulness. Buoyancy of spirit develops surprisingly from inner sources of the mind and physical stamina. Resilience channels survival of human life.

Note to Spirited Resilience

1. Elisabeth Kubler-Ross, *Death: The Final Stage of Growth* (Englewood Cliffs, NJ: Prentice-Hall, 1975), 96.
2. Will Schwalbe, *The End of Your Life Book Club* (New York: Vintage Books, 2013), 166.
3. Richard Sandomir, "Stuart Scott, ESPN's Voice of Exuberance, Dies at 49," *New York Times*, January 5, 2015.
4. Nirmal Joshi, "Doctor, Shut Up and Listen," *New York Times*, January 5, 2015.
5. Penelope Green, "Peggy Cooper Cafritz: Everything in a Big Way," *New York Times*, January 15, 2015.
6. Green, "Peggy Cooper Cafritz."
7. Jeffrey Gettleman, "No Moon Suits, Just Trunks and the Healing Surf," *New York Times*, January 11, 2015.
8. Gettleman, "No Moon Suits."
9. Gettleman, "No Moon Suits."

10. Gettleman, "No Moon Suits."
11. Ben Kenigsberg, "On the Way to School," movie review, *New York Times*, February 6, 2015.
12. John Branch, "Pursuing the Impossible, and Coming Out on Top," *New York Times*, January 15, 2015.
13. Branch, "Pursuing the Impossible."
14. Jeffrey Moussaieff Masson and Susan McCarthy, *When Elephants Weep: The Emotional Lives of Animals* (New York: Delacorte Press, 1995), 64-65.
15. Masson and McCarthy, *When Elephants Weep*, 65-66.
16. Laura Hillenbrand, *Unbroken: A World War II Story of Survival, Resilience, and Redemption* (New York: Random House, 2010), 148.
17. Hillenbrand, *Unbroken*, 183.
18. Hillenbrand, *Unbroken*, 182.
19. Ira Berkow, "Louis Zamperini, Olympian and 'Unbroken' World War II Survivor, Dies at 97," *New York Times*, July 4, 2014.
20. Hillenbrand, *Unbroken*, 90.
21. Hillenbrand, *Unbroken*, 338.
22. Hillenbrand, *Unbroken*, 346.
23. Hillenbrand, *Unbroken*, 384.

Stories Can Save Us

"Telling stories seemed a natural, inevitable process like clearing the throat...It was a way of grabbing people by the shirt and explaining exactly what had happened.... By telling stories you objectify your own experience. You separate it from yourself. You pin down certain truths."[1] Stories can save us. A story is about people, about human beings, richly rendered in communication. "In a story, which is a kind of dreaming, the dead sometimes smile and sit up and return to the world."[2]

In 2001, former Senator Bob Kerry revealed through the media that he regretted his murderous deeds during the Vietnam War. Likewise, in 1990, Tim O'Brien, a Vietnam veteran, wrote a penetrating novel, *The Things They Carried,* in which he tells personal stories of killings by Alpha Company, a platoon of men in the Vietnam War. By writing these stories in *The Things They Carried* and five other novels, O'Brien relieved his guilty conscience and restored his sanity for the rest of his life. In *The Things They Carried,* he writes, "After seven months in the bush, I realized that those high, civilized trappings had somehow been crushed.... I'd turned mean inside. Even a little cruel at times. For all my education, all my fine liberal values, I now felt a deep coldness inside me, something dark and beyond reason.... I was capable of evil."[3] Such a horrifying realization that the gore and terror of Vietnam jungle warfare could turn a person into a killer filled O'Brien and many other Vietnam veterans with deep guilt. O'Brien carries this burden in his stories with a lovely, stirring grace that is about the redemptive power of stories as much as it is about Vietnam.

Courage, O'Brien says in *The Things They Carried*, accumulates from childhood to adulthood. It is like an inheritance; we earn interest in daily acts of courage as we steadily increase our moral capital in preparation for a day when we will need immense courage. Thus, in stories, we are saved by tales of courage and revived by the store of courage we have accumulated. By telling and writing stories, O'Brien claims that you pin down certain truths, such as, you can choose to love, not hate. You can clarify incidents to others and to yourself. You can relieve guilt and pain. You dream as you tell a story so "others might dream along with you."[4] You find it natural to communicate with others and objectively see your own experiences. "You take your material where you find it, which is in your life, at the intersection of past and present."[5] And in stories the dead come alive; for example, grandparents who are no longer here can talk, move, cry, act out funny stories, and save our memories.

To illustrate some of these points, O'Brien relates the story of Henry Dobbins, a soldier who wore pantyhose around his neck as a good-luck charm. The pantyhose kept him safe throughout the entire war; he was never wounded. Dobbins thought that they gave him "access to a spiritual world, where things were soft and intimate."[6] They were like "body armor," so he carefully tied the nylons around his neck before he went off with the platoon.[7]

O'Brien tells stories justifying why he killed a young Vietnamese man. It was self-defense, one comrade reminded him. For O'Brien, "I wanted to tell exactly what happened, or what I remember happening.... I did not see [the man] as the enemy; I did not ponder morality or politics or military duty.... I was terrified. There were no thoughts about killing. I wish I could have warned him.... I did ask myself what the dead man would have done if things were reversed."[8] This pondering is why O'Brien keeps writing stories.

In *The Things They Carry*, O'Brien relates a story of returning to Vietnam with his imaginary ten-year-old daughter, Kathleen, twenty years after his tour in this country. He was looking for "signs of forgiveness or personal grace or whatever else the land might offer.... The place was at peace. There were yellow butterflies. There was a breeze and a wide blue sky.... Things were quiet."[9] Though O'Brien was sentimental in this place, he felt forgiven when he saw a farmer who stared across the field at him and then went back to work. Vietnamese life had been renewed, thought O'Brien.

O'Brien believes that stories can save us because the dead come alive in them. At age forty-three, he still kept dreaming about Linda, his elementary school sweetheart who died of cancer. In a story about Linda, he claims that sometimes a smile returns to the face of the one who is gone. "The thing about a story is that you dream it as you tell it, hoping that others might then dream along with you, and in this way memory and imagination and language combine to make spirits in the head. There is the illusion of aliveness."[10] "That's what a story does. The bodies are animated. You make the dead talk. They sometimes say things like, 'Timmy, stop crying.'"[11] In a story, O'Brien could save Linda's life. He could "steal her soul…, revive, at least briefly, that which is absolute and unchanging…. Linda can smile and sit up. She can reach out [to me]."[12] Imagination, saved in a story, revived life.

O'Brien stresses that telling a true war story is different. A true war story is never moral. If the story seems moral or if you feel uplifted at the end, you are the victim of a terrible lie. A war story does not encourage virtue or restrain men and women from what they do. There is no rectitude; the story is uncompromising allegiance to obscenity and evil. Furthermore, in most cases, it is difficult to separate the facts from fiction in a true war story. The listener must be skeptical. Also, a true war story never seems to end. You cannot forget it. You cannot extract the meaning without unraveling the deeper meaning to all persons. Nothing in true war stories is analyzed carefully, only generalized. How is it generalized? War is hell! But war is mystery, terror, adventure, courage, discovery, pity, despair, longing, and love. War is thrilling, war is drudgery. Undoubtedly, war makes one mature; but war can also make one dead. All these things about war are contradictory. The truth is that each of us wants to be our truest self—a good, decent human being. Each of us wants to be courteous and just. In a true war story, nothing is ever absolutely true. You cannot completely describe what happened. Besides, often in a true war story there is not even a point, or else the point hits you long after the war has ended.[13]

Some stories save us when they give us hope. In the chapter "The Power of Stories" in his book *The Force of Spirit,* Scott Russell Sanders outlines reasons for telling and hearing stories. Stories speak to our condition. They help us see through the eyes of other people and sense what it is like to be old or young, female or male, or beholden to a race, creed, geography, or class. They reveal the consequences of our actions. They help us deal with suffering, loss, and death, and they give us hope.[14] Furthermore, Sanders believes powerful stories shape our desires and behavior. They can push us away from greed and lead us toward generosity. They can inspire us to seek nature's bounty instead of material possessions. They can help us find meaning and purpose and joy in life. "Stories resist our habit of dividing the world into us and them, friend and foe, and that is certainly cause for hope."[15]

What we tell in a story always seems to have a story behind it that excites the imagination and reveals human possibilities. What we tell in stories—just like in ordinary conversation—reflects our values, priorities, joys, prejudices, and disappointments. Therefore, others come to know us more honestly. Through stories we put our own awareness into the world of others. Stories save us from complacency because we react to the stories we hear about injustice, genocide, or a tragedy in a family. Stories save our humanity when we realize the sacrifices, hardships, and pain others have had. They keep reminding us of our foundation, our heritage, and our identity. Jokes in a story save us because laughter improves health. A mother's stories save us from sleeplessness. But more than that, stories comfort us, they caress us with love, and they assure us of an imaginative world.

Stories are the oldest and most pleasurable way of organizing experience. Telling and writing stories enhances human intimacy. Stories save our humanity for eternity.

Notes to Stories Can Save Us

1. Tim O'Brien, *The Things They Carried* (New York: Penguin Books, 1990), 179.
2. O'Brien, *The Things They Carried*, 255.
3. O'Brien, 227.
4. O'Brien, 259.
5. O'Brien, 38.
6. O'Brien, 129.
7. O'Brien, 130.
8. O'Brien, 147-149.
9. O'Brien, 209.
10. O'Brien, 259-260.

11. O'Brien, 261.
12. O'Brien, 265.
13. O'Brien, 86-89.
14. Scott Russell Sanders, *The Force of Spirit* (Boston: Beacon Press, 2000), 85.
15. Sanders, *The Force of Spirit*, 89.

Transitions

"I've never felt this way before," the man said at the end of the evening, "but I feel as though my whole life was built on a frozen lake. [I] go on with [my activities], work on the house and play golf, and entertain and have our fights. I put in long hours at work and think I'm doing well. Then every once in a while I think, 'This is ice I'm standing on, and it's melting.... I try to forget, but I keep thinking 'that ice looks thin!'"[1]

Life runs thin sometimes. When one's past patterns of behavior stand in the way of transitions to new beginnings, it is as if the past is melting the future. Life stagnates when one cannot make changes for a brighter future. Instead of life's beginnings leading to endings, many endings lead to beginnings through transitions. William Bridges describes this process in his book *Transitions,* which proposes strategies for coping with the difficult, painful, and confusing times in one's life and trying to make sense of life's changes.

Life is not all wrapped up in sad endings; there are happy ones, too. For example, in the movie *Pride and Prejudice,* the Bennets' daughter Jane, after a year wondering about Mr. Bingley's affections, finds that he loves her and wants to marry her for a new beginning in life. Jane says to her sister Elizabeth, "To know I will be giving such pleasure to all my family. How shall I bear such happiness?" There are other examples of happy transitions from endings to beginnings: when a daughter, son, or grandchild completes a good lacrosse season and looks forward to next year's season; when a teenager's rebellion against his or her parents ends with an agreement to disagree; when one completes a book that took a year to write and begins writing a new one; when one ends an urban life-style by moving to the country; when one ends one's affiliation with a church and finds a new spiritual faith; or even when one cracks open an egg and starts to make a cake.

Other endings require struggles to cope with a new beginning. These events include a separation or divorce from someone, illness, the "empty nest syndrome," moving away from friends or family, getting demoted or fired, retiring after a long career, losing trust in someone, or losing one's innocence. What one must realize is that many endings bring a happy, unanticipated chance for a new beginning.

In a mechanistic culture, people expect to just turn on a switch and transition from one phase to another. But personal transitions contain risk. Such changes are either entered into willingly or unwillingly. If a person has been steeped in the rituals of an old life, endings are challenging, but they can be beneficial if, in the meantime, that individual doesn't disintegrate, malfunction, or need major repairs. If a person admits that new beginnings are inevitable, normal, and not a mistake, he or she can cope more easily. In other words, like cars, Bridges states, "[humans] have times of production and function and falling apart."[2] Human development is comparable to the life of a car; it begins when the item is in production and ends when the item is ready to drive. When the car "malfunctions," a mechanic tries to fix it. Like a car, life involves finding some faulty part, repairing it, and starting up again. To end transition and begin again is inevitable and normal in life.

Transitions are a bridge between endings and beginnings or between beginnings and endings. Moving from one shore to the other shore may cause disorienting emotions. The transition process realigns and renews one's energy despite the emotional and mental chaos a person is immersed in. Taking risks temporarily deprives a person of security. Letting go of the past is difficult. One may have built a comfortable role and identity as a spouse, political ally, provider, or parent. Deep bonds with a place and time have been developed. To say goodbye to neighbors, friends, and loved ones can be crushing. The uncertainties of transition can haunt the imagination. But new beginnings can bring self-renewal, a new self-image, new relationships, new goals, new projects, and new opportunities. Imagine the possibilities: a job promotion, returning to college, remarrying, having a baby, or reconciling with parents, siblings, or friends. Gradually but resolutely, "our most important beginnings take place in the darkness outside our awareness."[3]

No one escapes transitions; we have to accept a lifetime of them. They are often difficult to maneuver, like traveling through a dark tunnel to the small light that pulls us to opportunity. Life crises occur at any age. There is a rhythm in one's life just as there is in nature: the falling of leaves, the thawing in winter, the blossoming in spring. Letting go of old dreams and past seasons, one discovers new rhythms, new patterns, new self-knowledge, new achievements, new service, and more of what one is meant to be. One takes these beginning leaps of faith and risk at different times in one's life and in different forms. Certainly, "each of us is on a unique journey with a ticket marked, 'Good for this trip only—no transfers.'"[4]

Honor goes to people who have made transitions adeptly:

- At fifty-seven, Handel wrote *The Messiah* while transitioning through deep debt and a stroke.
- At fifty-one, Joshua Slocum sailed around the world alone.
- At seventy-eight, Grandma Moses discovered her artistic talent.
- At thirty-eight, Meb Keflezighi became the first American to win the Boston Marathon since 1985.
- At thirty-five, Eleanor Roosevelt discovered that her husband was having an affair with her most trusted friend. She transitioned through her shyness and "shattered dream of domestic safety" and began a career serving the world. She advised her audience, "Somewhere along the line of development we discover what we really are and then we make our real decision for which we are responsible. Make that decision primarily for yourself because you can never really live anyone else's life...."[5]

When an ending happens, when a neutral zone makes a transition plausible, a genuine beginning dangles as a possibility. According to William Bridges, individuals accept opportunities "to do what they seem to have been destined to do."[6] "The beginnings...of all human undertakings are untidy," states the English novelist John Galsworthy.[7] Beginnings begin as a "faint intimation that something is different."[8] Money and time are the obstacles that most people cite as the reasons why they cannot manage new beginnings. Bridges believes we are accustomed to expecting careers with linear trajectories and no interruptions. Radical shifts complicate adulthood. But beginnings are accessible to everyone. They are similar to "moving up in the air," to breathing more freely. Beginnings emerge within us when we awaken to possibilities instead of building "a spider's web of precautions" against change.[9]

How we handle transitions may determine the decision to begin anew. For example, a mother at forty years old, divorced, with three children, one handicapped, completed an advanced university degree and became a teacher of disturbed children. Also, a U.S. veteran of four tours in Iraq who lost both legs ran the Boston Marathon. If we avoid shifts in life, we may be less likely to adjust to inner reorientations. When we make commitments and take responsibility for them, stability follows. For example, a percussionist in an orchestra rebuilt his life economically by investing carefully, living in a smaller house, and setting up a trust fund for his children. Transitions may make us more understanding. The actor Michael J. Fox began a new television series despite having Parkinson's disease.

There are many examples in literature of transitions to new beginnings:

- In the novel *The Things They Carried,* Tim O'Brien relates that his college career ended when he received a letter from the War Department stating that he had been drafted for military service in Vietnam. He transitioned through the nightmare of the war and returned wounded. But he began to write novels and short stories about the war, and that beginning saved his sanity and eased his guilt and pain.
- In Henrik Ibsen's drama *The Doll's House,* Nora ends up being a "doll" in the house of her father and her husband. She makes a transition to end her marriage to a rich bank executive and leave her three children. She shuts the door behind her and begins a new life, wanting an education so she could be self-sufficient.
- In the drama *A Raisin in the Sun* by Lorraine Hansberry, a family of five lives in a crowded apartment in Chicago. Mama takes the insurance money of her deceased husband and buys a house in an all-white neighborhood in Clybourne Park. Her son says, "We come from people who had a lot of pride.... And that's my sister over there and she's going to be a doctor—and we are very proud."
- In contrast, in the drama *Death of a Salesman* by Arthur Miller, not a single character makes an ending, a transition, or a

beginning—even after Willy dies. The ending of the drama is depressing because no member of the family can make a change.

Americans have always been in transition, Bridges claims. Alexis de Tocqueville noted in his diary in 1831: "Born often under another sky, placed in the middle of an always moving scene, ...the American has no time to tie himself to anything, he grows accustomed only to change, and ends by regarding it as the natural state of man. He feels the need of it, more, he loves it; for the instability, instead of meaning disaster to him, seems to give birth only to miracles all about him."[10]

In Washington Irving's nineteenth-century tales of Rip van Winkle, Rip wakes from a deep spell after an eighteen-year transition that was puzzling and dramatic. In the era of the Vietnam War, Alvin Toffler wrote in *Future Shock,* "Change is avalanching upon our heads and most people are grotesquely unprepared to cope with it."[11] Those who cope through transitions surprisingly find within themselves a power to do what they wanted to do in what they thought they could not do. The rewards are pride, discipline, and self-confidence.

Notes to Transitions

1. William Bridges, *Transitions: Making Sense of Life's Changes* (Reading, MA: Addison-Wesley Publishing Co., 1980), 21.
2. Bridges, *Transitions,* 30.
3. Bridges, 18.
4. Bridges, 55.
5. Quoted in Bridges, *Transitions,* 141.
6. Bridges, *Transitions,* 140.
7. Quoted in Bridges, *Transitions,* 135.
8. Bridges, *Transitions,* 136.
9. Bridges, 142.
10. Quoted in Bridges, *Transitions,* 2.
11. Quoted in Bridges, *Transitions,* 4.

PART 2

Biographies

Edward Coles: Making a Difference

"Edward Coles was a common man who made uncommon history," according to historian Kurt Leichtle and scholar Bruce Carveth.[1] His family, his Virginia friends, and many citizens of the United States in the early nineteenth century considered him "crazy" for freeing the people he had enslaved. Perhaps his magnanimous gesture was less significant than the actions of Rosa Parks, who refused to give up her seat on a bus, or Nelson Mandela, who fought apartheid in South Africa, or Martin Luther King, Jr., who preached equality and freedom; nevertheless, Coles staked a claim for justice against the ingrained social structure of slavery. The twentieth century produced other "common" individuals who, like Coles, made a difference in the world. For example, Richard Rockefeller founded Doctors without Borders in the United States, researched cures for sleeping sickness in Africa, and became an advocate for ocean conservation. At the age of seventy-five, feminist writer Germaine Greer bought 150 acres of despoiled land in Queensland, Australia to restore it to native rainforest. Nadine Gordimer, a novelist and 1991 Nobel Prize winner, fought apartheid in South Africa. And during the London 1948 Olympic Games, high jumper Alice Coachman became the first Black woman to win an Olympic Gold Medal.

Born in 1786 into a wealthy, aristocratic family of Virginia, Edward Coles grew up on a plantation with seventy-one enslaved individuals, and which produced lumber, brandy, tobacco, and hemp. In fact, cherry tree lumber from the estate was sold to Thomas Jefferson for use as parquet flooring in the music room at Monticello.[2] Coles stood six feet tall with fine features and chestnut hair. He was educated at the College of William and Mary until 1807, but when his father died, he was required to tend the plantation.

At the College of William and Mary, Coles was swayed by the philosophy of Rev. James Madison, the First Bishop of the Episcopal Church of Virginia and the second cousin of the future president, James Madison. Bishop Madison was committed to the eighteenth-century Republican ideology that the authority and power of natural laws are laid down by a superior being.[3] God is the final judge of all actions. Coles fell into discussions with Bishop Madison and forced him "to admit that slavery could not be justified on principle and could only be tolerated" if God's natural laws included human rights.[4] Coles noted that citizens in the colonies were taking advantage of a "lawful privilege" to enslave Black people. However, he was "bound to obey what he considered the will of God where it concerns a right of [a human being]."[5] Some higher law controls the universe! This law forced Coles to "renounce slavery as immoral."[6] The institution of slavery had corrupted the natural law expressed by the Founding Fathers that "all men are created equal." "Holding slaves constituted a dangerous breach of virtue—dangerous to the republic and dangerous to the individual."[7]

According to historian Suzanne Guasco, Coles abided by the law to "do as he would be done by."[8] He was schooled in the belief that one must "act according to the maxims of his [or her] understanding and not...behave inconsistent with...his or her conscience."[9] Before making a decision, humans should not follow blindly the advice and direction of others but should inquire diligently, favor skepticism, and voice intellectual curiosity.[10]

In the early nineteenth century, Coles believed that collective action would be more effective than individual action in the struggle against slavery. It would be nearly impossible for individuals alone to break "the profound hold that slavery had on Virginia society and its entwined notions of white virtue and honor, the legal barriers to emancipation."[11] The enslaved were Virginia's "single-largest tangible asset."[12] For tax purposes in Albemarle County, where Jefferson's plantation Monticello was built, 4,409 enslaved persons were counted: 54 percent of all households had at least one enslaved person; 42 percent had three or less; and 1 percent enslaved fifty or more people.[13] In 1800, when Thomas Jefferson became president, many

Virginians fully supported slavery because of a labor shortage. "Benevolent treatment of an inferior race" was viewed as emblematic of honor and white liberty.[14] Coles could not understand how the supposedly virtuous leaders of virtuous citizens could encourage a class of people to deprive another class of people their liberty for economic gain.

Coles never discussed his thoughts about slavery with his father because his family depended upon the labor of enslaved people, and he feared that his father would likely change his will and not allow Edward to have an inheritance in the plantation if he knew that Edward planned to emancipate those held in bondage. But when John Coles died in 1808, Edward and his six siblings inherited the "holy trinity" of enslaved laborers, tobacco, and land that constituted their father's commercial empire. Edward accepted 782 acres of land on the Rockfish River in Amherst County, Virginia, as well as the rest of this inheritance.[15]

At the reading of his father's will, Edward shared his views about slavery with his family, and the family was shocked. A painful discussion erupted. The family asked, "Don't you appreciate the work of your parents? Freeing slaves is a 'senseless and destructive fit of foolish, unproductive, dangerous generosity' because other slaves on other farms might make demands on other slaveholders."[16] His family wondered why he hadn't honestly declared his opposition to slavery to his father. They warned that if he followed through with emancipation, he would be separated from his family, cast out, and ostracized from Virginia planters. The family's attacks weighed on Edward's conscience. Although at the age of nineteen he had pledged to himself that he "would not and could not hold a fellowman as a Slave,"[17] it would be more than a decade after his father's death before he freed those he held in bondage.

During Jefferson's second term as president of the United States, the Virginia legislature enacted a law requiring formerly enslaved people who were freed to leave the state within a year of their emancipation; enslavers were required to pay for their transportation. Lawmakers feared that the presence of freed Black people might incite hope of freedom among all enslaved people; but if they left the state, they would not intermingle with the white and Black races in Virginia.

Coles realized that his intention to free the enslaved people he inherited from his father put him out of step with the social order in Virginia.[18]

Therefore, in 1809 at the age of twenty-three, Coles moved to Washington, D.C. and became the secretary to James Madison, the newly elected president. Coles fared well in the Washington social milieu where he planned balls, private dances, and dinner parties for the elite. But three years later at the age of twenty-six, he became disenchanted with the social whirl of Washington and unsympathetic to farming on his marginally successful plantation. "Coles was faced with choices, but lacked a clear way to sort them out. The mental turmoil may even have affected his health."[19] He was ill during one-third of his tenure in Washington, but in the process of healing, he had time to think. By 1809, 22 percent of the population in Washington City were enslaved (5,395).[20] Witnessing the horrors of Black people in chains, ready for markets in the South, Coles felt that the "wretchedness and human degradation" of slavery was "disgraceful to our character as citizens of a free government."[21]

Coles was loyal to President Madison and supported his policies. By the time the War of 1812 ended in the winter of 1815, "Coles had faith in the virtues of his fellow citizens, but he was worried about the virtues of its leaders.... Congress is an unspeakable mess."[22] Coles observed enslaved people being brought to Washington by legislators. Many enslavement auctions occurred in Washington; many individual enslaved people in the city had been separated from their families. According to Leichtle and Carveth in *Crusade against Slavery*, Coles knew that he was associating with many officials who perpetuated "the worst sins of slavery."[23] "Slave ownership was, in the view of many, a white man's burden that produced honor when carried with compassion and a sense of responsibility."[24] True to his conscience, Coles never took a servant with him to Washington. He found ways to be candid about slavery. He never bought or sold any enslaved people, but he did arrange transportation and contracts for them. When he did so, he betrayed his beliefs, no matter how much he tried to treat enslaved people with kindness. By playing the South's "game," he expressed loyalty to his immediate family in Virginia rather than to his own conscience, and he denied the humanity of those held in bondage.

Seven months before the end of the War of 1812, Coles wrote to Thomas Jefferson, "the father of freedom" and a revered patriot, about slavery and the future of the republic. "Coles was growing hungry for the bread of freedom" for the enslaved.[25] He believed that because Jefferson was loyal to the republic, a longstanding enslaver, and a powerful persuader, he would serve the cause of emancipation. However, Jefferson was very cool in his response to Coles. In retirement, Jefferson would not "invest as much as a [reply] to the cause—the end of slavery."[26]

Coles wrote a second letter to Jefferson, strongly believing that "if [one of] the writers of the Declaration of Independence made an appeal against slavery, the nation would surely listen."[27] Coles also thought that if Jefferson spoke out, posterity would always remember him for leading the cause of the emancipation and securing the human rights of Black people. Coles reiterated that no man has the right to enslave his brother. He pointed out that Jefferson had based the liberty and independence of his country upon not remaining "a slave" to Britain. Likewise, Coles implored Jefferson to free all those he enslaved. Furthermore, Coles stated, "I [am] capable of reflecting on the nature of political society, and of the rights appertaining to [human beings]. I have not only been principled against slavery, but I have had feelings so repugnant to it to decide me not to hold them; which decision has forced me to leave my native State and with it my relatives and friends."[28]

In his reply, Jefferson claimed that he was too old to be active in this cause of emancipation; he ventured that, in time, the young would solve the problem of slavery. In fact, Jefferson argued, Coles could best serve the antislavery cause in Virginia by being a kind of model so-called master and by being active in politics. "[Jefferson] would not participate directly in efforts to abolish slavery in Virginia."[29] He did, however, offer Coles his prayers.

Not more than two weeks after refusing to accommodate Coles in his worthy cause to abolish slavery, Jefferson wrote a letter to Dr. Thomas Cooper, a British Unitarian, who was asked to join the faculty of the University of Virginia. Claiming that the enslaved were better cared for in America than laborers were in England, Jefferson added, "I am not advocating slavery. I am not justifying this wrong we have committed on a foreign people, by the example of another nation committing equal wrongs on their own subjects. On the contrary there is nothing I would not sacrifice to a practicable plan of abolishing every vestige of this moral and political depravity."[30] While Jefferson met Coles' challenge with "prayers," withdrawal, and abdication, he hypocritically portrayed himself to Cooper as a forthright abolitionist.[31]

In a rebuttal letter to Jefferson, Coles disagreed that the young should lead the task of "cleansing" Virginia of the "foul stain of slavery."[32] Why should the young carry the burdens of the nation when the aged had the wisdom and influence necessary to tackle the problem? The "aged worthies"—respected representatives in society like Jefferson—had an obligation to awaken fellow citizens "to a proper sense of Justice and to the true interest of their country."[33] The great emancipation of the enslaved should be a rallying point for Jefferson's influential friends. Jefferson's sanction of emancipation might have a "propitious and happy result." Coles also pointed out that Benjamin Franklin proved instrumental in ridding Pennsylvania of the evils of slavery when he was older than Jefferson.

The disappointing correspondence with Jefferson increased Coles' resolve to leave Virginia, as did the fact that the issue of slavery began to own his existence and his thoughts. Edward Coles "is often used as an example of the second generation leaving Virginia, fleeing slavery to end his own involvement in the institution."[34] In February 1815, he submitted his resignation to President Madison. He journeyed west to the free state of Illinois and bought 3,000 acres of farmland in Illinois, 5,890 acres in Missouri, and several plots in St. Louis.[35] But his plan to move to Illinois was interrupted by his recall to Washington to accept a diplomatic post in St. Petersburg, Russia in September 1816. When he returned to Virginia from Russia in 1817, he sold his Rockfish Plantation to his brother Walter. Coles went to Illinois alone in March 1818 to obtain a job as register of lands in Edwardsville, Illinois, so he would have an income. In the following spring, he carried his plan for emancipation to fruition. Now thirty-three years old, he assembled all of the enslaved people from the plantation, "perhaps around the tobacco shed behind the main house," and explained to them his plans to accompany them to the free state of Illinois.[36] Anyone who wanted to go with him was eligible to be transported freely. Each family would be given 160 acres of farmland with which they could start a new life. Coles assured them that they did not have to go against their will.[37] The following people consented to the arduous displacement: Ralph Crawford (age 47–48), wife Kate (43–44), and their children Betsy (16–17), Thomas (13), Mary (11–12), William (9); Robert Crawford (brother of Ralph, 25); Polly (sister to Ralph and Robert, 16–17); Thomas Cobb (38 or 40); Nancy Gaines (16–17); Sukey, husband Manuel, and their five children.

According to Leichtle and Carveth, Coles went to Staunton, Virginia for supplies. He purchased two horses for $250 and a two-horse wagon for

$175. On April 1, 1819, he hired two flatboats for $70 to ferry the rivers. One flatboat was twenty-three feet long and held the horses; the other was thirty-seven feet long with two cabins for people. With Zadok Cramer's book *The Navigator* in hand, Coles directed the passage down the Monongahela, Allegheny, Ohio, and Mississippi Rivers. At Pittsburgh he purchased a third horse ($50), gear for two horses ($15.50), six weeding hoes ($5.32), and four axes ($6.66). At Brunot's Island on the Ohio River, Coles paused for a solemn ceremonial service. The people were stunned. Coles recorded in his journal that "they stared at me and at each other, as if doubting the accuracy or reality of what they heard. In breathless silence they stood before me, unable to utter a word, but with countenances beaming with expression which no words could convey, and which no language can now describe as they began to see the truth of what they had heard, and to realize their situation, there came on a kind of hysterical, giggling laugh. After a pause of intense and unutterable emotion, bathed in tears, and with tremulous voices, they gave vent to their gratitude, and implored the blessings of God on me.... Ralph [thought that Coles] ought not to [emancipate the enslaved] till they had repaid me the expense I had been in removing them from Virginia, and had improved my farm and gotten me well fixed in the new country."[38]

Coles wanted the people he freed to have immediate and unconditional freedom, so he prepared "a general certificate of freedom for the now-freed Black pioneers proving proof of their new legal status."[39] He longed for them to prove their success in their new lives. If these freed people demonstrated that they were willing and able to succeed with "the blessings of liberty,"[40] perhaps their example would encourage a universal emancipation in the nation.

While at Brunot's Island, the freed people unloaded the horses and wagon from the flatboat to land and traveled through Indiana for three weeks while Coles rode ahead to Illinois on horseback. When they were united in Illinois, the caravan settled in Ridge Prairie Township east of Edwardsville. Coles' Prairieland Farms of 474 acres was comprised half of timber and half of prairie. Coles advocated corn for the prairie crop. Using two oxen instead of four horses, the farmland was plowed once with a "knife coulter," second by a "small bar shear," and last by an "iron-tooth drag."[41] Hard labor on the farms was freely assumed by the formerly enslaved people, who built homes on each family's 160-acre plot which Coles had given them. They carefully attended to their land.

In Edwardsville, Illinois, Coles found that the state was hostile to free Black settlers. White citizens of Illinois who couldn't purchase land during the Panic of 1819 resented Coles for giving land to those he emancipated.[42] Southern-born, white settlers wanted land at a reasonable price. They brought their prejudices with them when they moved west, promoting sectional divisions even in the state of Illinois. Many white Southern farmers moved to Illinois to escape the disproportionate political power of enslavers.[43] Independent white people in states where slavery was legal often suffered biased treatment; if they didn't own human "property," they were considered on the level of an enslaved person.[44]

Coles settled his prairieland with optimism that the people he had formerly enslaved would be welcomed under his supervision and not be a burden on the county. He gave books to all the children in his group, promised to pay for teaching them, and offered premiums to those individuals who learned to read and write.[45] He wanted to prove that free Black people were energetic, cooperative, and productive. Fortunately, his neighbors were congenial in his community and they shared labor, materials, produce, and other resources.

In their brief history of slavery in Illinois, Leichtle and Carveth note that slavery entered the area in 1719 when laborers were needed in the salt mines. By 1750, enslaved Black people were 32 percent of the population. The Northwest Ordinance of 1787 forbade slavery north of the Ohio River and east of the Mississippi River. However, residents in Illinois who already legally enslaved people could continue doing so. By 1790, Article II of the state constitution prohibited the entrance of any additional enslaved people into the state. In 1807, Illinois passed an "indenture law" that, in essence, initiated a form of slavery. Enslaved people as young as fifteen could be imported and registered under "voluntary indenture agreements."[46] Starting in 1814, slaves could enter the state as "indentured persons." However, usually "people [came] to Illinois expressly to escape from slavery."[47] By 1818, Madison County in Illinois increased its white population by 250 percent. By 1820, free Black people lived in Madison County, and others continued to settle there. Congregations of Baptists and Methodists fought any introduction of "slavery" into Illinois. Peter Cartwright, a Methodist, "bitterly opposed slavery."[48] The Missouri Compromise, nevertheless, kept the slavery issue alive in Illinois.

Coles established himself as an agricultural advocate; he joined the Agricultural Society of Illinois for six years and became its vice president. Also, he was employed by the federal government as the register of lands, "administering the orderly sale of land."[49] He was considered "fair and honest."[50] Within these associations, Coles met many people in his "public service and scientific agriculture."[51] Thereupon, on October 20, 1821, the *Edwardsville Spectator*, "the state's only antislavery newspaper," announced the candidacy of Edward Coles for governor of Illinois.[52] He was fifty-five years old. Coles campaigned in the first governor's race since Illinois achieved statehood and won the election in 1822 by fifty votes. In his inaugural address on December 5, 1822, he pledged to improve farming, guarantee education, make internal improvements (roads, canals), and maintain a stable currency. In conclusion, Coles crusaded against slavery, an issue that was gaining momentum in Illinois. He advocated for abolishing all slavery in Illinois, revising Black laws, and strengthening laws against kidnapping (essentially of free Black people). He maintained that slavery was "immoral by natural law and illegal under the Northwest Ordinance."[53] With this stance, he faced conflict during his governorship.

An avalanche of criticism descended upon Coles, according to Leichtle and Carveth. First, critics claimed that his "short residency in Illinois" was not long enough to qualify him to be its governor. Second, the newspaper editor Hooper Warren attacked Coles in his editorials because Coles was "too Virginia bred," he was a "name dropper," he "chattered" too much with his storytelling, and he was too political to control Illinois. Third, Coles was summoned to the sheriff's office to pay a $20,000 fee for bringing "slaves" into the state of Illinois. However, Coles did not bring "slaves" into Illinois; he had already freed those he had enslaved in Ohio before he arrived in Illinois. The Black Code of 1819 stipulated that enslavers had to post $1,000 bond for each enslaved person who entered into Illinois. Since the Northwest Ordinance of 1787 barred slavery in Illinois, the state legislature declared that a constitutional convention should be convened to change the state constitution and legalize slavery. A resolution to convene such a convention lost by one vote in 1822, but in February 1823 it passed the legislature by one vote. Finally, this contentious issue to permit slavery in Illinois flared into a "feud that swallowed the state."[54]

Of course, Coles worked to defeat such a convention to legalize slavery. He was convinced that stopping slavery at the Ohio River—as the Northwest Ordinance stipulated—would prevent the spread of slavery throughout the western frontier. Coles was a "skilled writer and researcher and a well-connected and energetic organizer."[55] He printed pamphlets and articles with antislavery information when two suits were brought against him in 1824; he loaned money to a bankrupt newspaper, *The Illinois Intelligencer*, and gained control of the editorial section wherein he fought the convention issue with the persuasion of words. Churches helped to spread the antislavery movement by making it a moral crusade. Unfortunately, the slavery issue caused political unrest in the state. Families became divided. Murder cases increased. When the statehouse was burned, Coles refused to rebuild it immediately. Two weeks after the burning of the statehouse, fire destroyed Coles' Prairie Farm: Two-thirds of the buildings and enclosures were burned, and two hundred peach trees planted by Kate and Robert Crawford, people he had emancipated, were burned.[56] Also, the fencing Coles had made to keep out wildlife was demolished.[57] Finally, the convening of the Constitutional Convention was defeated on August 2, 1824 by 11,688 votes. This victory in 1824 "demonstrated a democratic affirmation of federal authority to restrict slavery" based on the 1787 Northwest Ordinance.[58] However, states' rights established the power to permit or undo slavery. Southern states were seceding by the 1860s, compromising the ability of the government to hold the nation together.

Being governor was a painful experience for Coles; he believed that public service was an honorable undertaking.[59] He was attacked personally, and his principles were questioned. "The list of miseries that opposition to slavery had visited on Edward Coles was by now extensive."[60] He left the governorship, however, as a popular man because he was deemed an honest, consistent politician. But he didn't even want to be a professional politician; he wanted to be a gentleman politician. When the new governor of Illinois was elected in 1826, Coles faded from public service; when he attempted a comeback as governor in 1831, he ran a dismal third among candidates in the election. "For Coles, the defeat was traumatic and masked his political decline."[61] In October 1831, single and fifty-five years old, he left Illinois and returned to Philadelphia, where Quakers welcomed him as an abolitionist.

Edward Coles married Sally Logan Roberts, a member of the upper class of Philadelphia, on November 28, 1833 at the age of fifty-six. Coles cultivated business and cultural interests, but "his family remained the center of life."[62] "His opposition to slavery had done nothing to weaken his ties to the rest of his slaveholding family."[63] In addition, he was proud that the people he emancipated had made successful lives for themselves, especially Robert Crawford, who "epitomized the hope Edward Coles had in developing his experiment in freedom."[64] Crawford became a property owner, a leader of Black churches, and finally, an influential preacher in the prairielands of Illinois.[65]

Abraham Lincoln was elected president in 1860 when Coles was seventy-three years old. In 1862, Coles' son Robert, a Confederate soldier, died in action. Coles was sequestered in his home most of the time during the Civil War.[66] He was too ill to greet the crowds of Republicans and the speaker Lincoln for whom he voted. He died on July 7, 1868, at the age of eighty-two. With the ratification of the Emancipation Proclamation, signed on September 23, 1863, "[Coles] would live to see the end of slavery."[67]

Edward Coles "has made cameo appearances in many books on the antebellum South to illustrate the high road not taken [on slavery] or to explore the paradoxes of Jefferson's character."[68] He is not a "celebrated American," but he is "historically significant" because he believed his actions opposing slavery had to speak as loudly as his words. History books which dwell on the emancipation of enslaved people would do well to illuminate the brave people on "a sure road to obscurity" who performed admirable deeds in their private life. Wealthy Virginian Robert Carter III, whom many historians had overlooked until the last few decades, issued a "Deed of Gift" in 1791 that eventually led to the freeing of nearly 450 people he enslaved. Despite criticism from many compatriots, Virginians John Randolph and Robert Pleasants freed several hundred enslaved people in the late 1700s and early 1800s. Such courageous people, by small currents, worked against the Virginia culture, just like Edward Coles.[69] Coles once asked Bishop Madison, "Is it right to do what we believe to be wrong because our forefathers did it?"[70] "Histories of emancipation in American show that it was difficult but possible to give [the enslaved] freedom. These stories add weight to the costly failures by so many [Founding Fathers and common citizens alike] who were witness to and aware of the inhumanity of slavery and did not act."[71] Edward Coles did act, and he made a difference.

Notes to Edward Coles: Making a Difference

1. Kurt E. Leichtle and Bruce G. Carveth, *Crusade against Slavery: Edward Coles, Pioneer of Freedom* (Carbondale, IL: Southern Illinois University Press, 2011), 4.
2. Leichtle and Carveth, *Crusade against Slavery*, 9.
3. Leichtle and Carveth, 12.
4. Leichtle and Carveth, 14.
5. Leichtle and Carveth, 14.
6. Leichtle and Carveth, 14.
7. Leichtle and Carveth, 14.
8. Suzanne Cooper Guasco, *Confronting Slavery: Edward Coles and the Rise of Antislavery Politics in Nineteenth-Century America* (DeKalb, IL: Northern Illinois University Press, 2013), 27.
9. Guasco, *Confronting Slavery*, 27.
10. Guasco, 26.
11. Leichtle and Carveth, *Crusade against Slavery*, 22.
12. Leichtle and Carveth, 22.
13. Leichtle and Carveth, 23.
14. Leichtle and Carveth, 23.
15. Leichtle and Carveth, 18.
16. Leichtle and Carveth, 21.
17. Guasco, *Confronting Slavery*, 33.
18. Leichtle and Carveth, *Crusade against Slavery*, 25.
19. Leichtle and Carveth, 40.
20. Leichtle and Carveth, 40.
21. Leichtle and Carveth, 62.
22. Leichtle and Carveth, 35.
23. Leichtle and Carveth, 43.
24. Leichtle and Carveth, 43.
25. Leichtle and Carveth, 44.
26. Leichtle and Carveth, 44.
27. Leichtle and Carveth, 45.
28. Quoted in Leichtle and Carveth, *Crusade against Slavery*, 45.
29. Leichtle and Carveth, *Crusade against Slavery*, 47.
30. Quoted in Leichtle and Carveth, *Crusade against Slavery*, 47.
31. Leichtle and Carveth, *Crusade against Slavery*, 47-48.
32. Quoted in Leichtle and Carveth, *Crusade against Slavery*, 48.
33. Quoted in Leichtle and Carveth, *Crusade against Slavery*, 48.

34. Leichtle and Carveth, *Crusade against Slavery,* 221n.
35. Leichtle and Carveth, 51.
36. Leichtle and Carveth, 58.
37. Leichtle and Carveth, 59.
38. Quoted in Leichtle and Carveth, *Crusade against Slavery,* 69-70.
39. Leichtle and Carveth, 70.
40. Leichtle and Carveth, 70.
41. Leichtle and Carveth, 89.
42. *Crusade against Slavery,* 77.
43. Guasco, *Confronting Slavery,* 231.
44. Guasco, 128.
45. Guasco, 79.
46. Leichtle and Carveth, *Crusade against Slavery,* 74.
47. Leichtle and Carveth, 77.
48. Leichtle and Carveth, 78.
49. Leichtle and Carveth, 84.
50. Leichtle and Carveth, 87.
51. Leichtle and Carveth, 90.
52. Guasco, *Confronting Slavery,* 94.
53. Guasco, 101.
54. Leichtle and Carveth, *Crusade against Slavery,* 108.
55. Leichtle and Carveth, 114.
56. Guasco, *Confronting Slavery,* 115.
57. Leichtle and Carveth, *Crusade against Slavery,* 118.
58. Guasco, *Confronting Slavery,* 131.
59. Guasco, 146.
60. Guasco, 135.
61. Guasco, 148.
62. Leichtle and Carveth, *Crusade against Slavery,* 170.
63. Leichtle and Carveth, 170.
64. Leichtle and Carveth, 190.
65. Leichtle and Carveth, 190.
66. Guasco, *Confronting Slavery,* 232.
67. Guasco, 203.
68. Leichtle and Carveth, *Crusade against Slavery,* 208.
69. Leichtle and Carveth, 209.
70. Guasco, *Confronting Slavery,* 30.
71. Leichtle and Carveth, *Crusade against Slavery,* 109-110.

Lincoln's Legacy

For years our family has had the eight volumes of *The Collected Works of Abraham Lincoln* on our bookshelves in the living room. Published by the Abraham Lincoln Association organized in 1945, these volumes contain unpublished writings and speeches of Lincoln, but also letters, memorandums, drafts of speeches, endorsements of candidates, newspaper reports, and assignments to his administration and for the Civil War. These are not history texts per se, but historic markers.

Contemplating human unhappiness as he saw slavery on board the steamboat *Lebanon* on its way to Springfield, Illinois in 1841, Lincoln recorded these words: "A gentleman had purchased twelve Negroes in different parts of Kentucky and was taking them to a farm in the South. They were chained six and six together. A small iron clevis was around the left wrist of each, and this fastened to the main chain by a shorter one at the convenient distance, from the others so that the Negroes were strung together precisely like so many fish upon a trout-line. In this condition they were being separated forever from the scenes of their childhood, their friends, their fathers and mothers, and brothers and sisters, and many of them, from wives and children, and going into perpetual slavery where the lash of the master is proverbially more ruthless and unrelenting than any other...and yet...they were the most cheerful and apparently happy creatures on board...God... renders the worst of human conditions tolerable, while he permits the best to be nothing better than tolerable."[1]

In a powerful speech in Edwardsville, Illinois in 1858, titled "A House Divided," Lincoln also said: "When you have succeeded in dehumanizing the Negro; when you have put him down, and made it forever impossible for him to be but as the beasts of the field; when you have extinguished his soul, and placed him where the ray of hope is blown out in darkness like that which broods over the spirits of the damned, are you quite sure the demon which you have roused will not turn and rend you?"[2] "Our defense is in the preservation of the spirit which prizes liberty as the heritage of all men, in all lands, everywhere."[3]

The legacy of Abraham Lincoln rests in his preservation of the Union of the United States. Abolishing slavery was a by-product of this endeavor. Imagine the consequences for the United States today if the nation had been separated into a North Country and a South Country with slavery tagging along.

After some eighty years of slavery in the United States, Lincoln wanted the issue settled before new territories such as Kansas, Nebraska, Missouri, and Arkansas were added to the Union. He seriously objected to extending slavery into free territories. He put it this way: "I think that if anything can be proved by natural theology, it is that slavery is morally wrong."[4] Thereupon, Lincoln began his arguments to preserve, protect, and defend the Union.

First, Lincoln reviewed the Ordinance of 1787 that declared slavery or involuntary servitude (except as punishment for a crime) should never exist in the territory north and west of the Ohio River, including Ohio, Indiana, Illinois, Michigan, and Wisconsin. But a rapidly growing population drew Western states under scrutiny about slavery. Even though the slave trade was prohibited in 1808, slaveholders were moving enslaved people west to settle into new territory. The Missouri Compromise of 1820 did not resolve the issue of slavery, and legal historian Paul Finkelman, among others, has suggested that it should be called "The Appeasement of 1850" since it "more accurately describes the uneven nature of the agreement."[5] The legislation gave the North the territories of Iowa and Nebraska as free states and gave the South Missouri and Arkansas as slave states. Lincoln spoke vociferously against this development: "All legislation that recognized and tolerated [slavery's] extension, has been associated...with compromises...showing that it was something that moved forward, not by its own right, but its own wrong."[6] Lincoln thought that a union of states could not stand united on unresolved principles.

Second, Lincoln declared that a union could not have a division in social status between the free and the enslaved. In a speech in New Salem, Illinois in 1832, when he campaigned for representative to the General Assembly, he referred to his social standing: "I was born and have ever remained in the most humble walks of life. I have no wealthy or popular relations to recommend."[7] But as your representative, "I shall be governed by the will of the people if I know their will or for all others, do what my own judgement teaches me best advances their interests."[8] Lincoln made clear that the true philosophy of our government is that Congress should represent all opinions and principles, and the will of the majority should be carried out.[9]

Third, in 1854, Lincoln fully understood the power of states' rights. States had the right to regulate their own affairs within their own borders, but they did not have rights in federally owned territory. The federal government at this point owned and protected vast expanses of land in the West. Only states having a constitution with specific laws governing their population could become Union members. Thus, a person enslaved upon soil that belonged to the federal government was a federal issue, not a states' rights issue. States' rights and government rights had to be resolved to preserve the Union.

Fourth, in the debates between Stephen Douglas and Lincoln in 1858, Douglas argued for the right of states to declare whether their citizens wanted to be a free state or a slave state. Lincoln refuted this claim and said that politicians were political hypocrites before the world "by fostering Human Slavery and proclaiming ourselves, at the same time, the sole friends of Human Freedom."[10] Humans could not be free if they were enslaved. Civilized nations considered the slave trade and murder great wrongs. Lincoln wondered why the institution of slavery should stand on the side of freedom, on a soil that is free.[11]

Fifth, Lincoln pointed out that there is no allusion to slavery in the Constitution, as it would never exist in a "National Charter of Freedom."[12] In declaring that "All men are created equal," the Declaration of Independence was broad enough to include the whole human family, including Negroes. But the United States was not granting the enslaved the inalienable rights of "life, liberty, and the pursuit of happiness." Perhaps the framers of the Constitution thought slavery was a necessity for agriculture. At the time, the three-fifths clause was necessary to convince the South to accept the

Constitution. The framers emphasized the "principle of liberty," not liberty, so that all signers could agree, even those who were enslavers. In a speech in 1856, Lincoln complained that "slavery is looked upon by the light of dollars and cents."[13] If slavery increased in the new territories, it would increase the value of the enslaved by 50 percent.[14] Their stolen labor, knowledge, and skills were economically valuable, but morally indefensible.

Sixth, Lincoln believed that without laws, the government could not secure and protect citizens. Reverence for the law was a "political religion" of the nation. While Congress had the power to abolish the institution of slavery, it could not authorize powers to the territories outside the Union. Lincoln argued that the slave trade was never legislated by law; it existed because of the worth of millions of dollars in "property rights."

Lincoln delivered a powerful speech in Springfield, Illinois in 1858. "A House Divided" addressed Lincoln's major question for the nation: Shall we have slave states or not? He argued that there are "sacred rights of self-government" in the United States. "I do not understand how the privilege one man takes of making a slave of another...is any part of 'self-government.'"[15] Furthermore, "I think the true magnitude of the slavery element in this nation is scarcely appreciated by anyone..., both in and out of Congress... nor is it confined to politics alone. Presbyterian assemblies, Methodist conferences, Unitarian gatherings, and single churches...are wrangling and cracking, and going to pieces on that same question."[16] Lincoln believed that the government could not endure permanently half slave and half free. "A house divided against itself cannot stand!"[17]

Lincoln's stance was not popular in the South. As stated previously, Lincoln never advocated that slavery be abolished in those states where it already existed. He made this emphatically clear, especially when he became president. He maintained, however, that slavery should not be allowed to extend into United States territory that was already legally free.

Lincoln believed the southern people were not responsible for slavery, but it was an institution that was hard to abandon. "If slavery did not exist, [the South] would [probably] not introduce it."[18] But in 1860, the South had a great financial interest in slavery while the North would not gain any money by restricting it. "Turning to the South, we see a people who...boast of being free [in the nation] but keep their fellow beings in bondage."[19]

Lincoln was elected president of the United States on November 6, 1860 and took office on March 4, 1861. In the interim months, he was burdened with the imminent secession of the South from the Union. He declared that "the Federal Union must be preserved."[20] He appealed more and more for divine guidance at this vexing time.

In his first inaugural address as president on March 4, 1861, Lincoln declared, "I will preserve, protect, and defend the Union. In doing this there needs no bloodshed or violence; and there shall be none unless it be forced upon the national authority."[21] Why would we want "the destruction of our national fabric, with all its benefits, its memories, and its hopes"? "The mystic chords of memory...will yet swell the chorus of the Union...by the better angels of our nature.... Intelligence, patriotism, Christianity, and a firm reliance on Him, who has never forsaken this favored land."[22] Thereupon, a divided nation entered the Civil War.

Imagine for a moment if Lincoln had not preserved the Union and two separate countries emerged from the conflict. No national policy or identity would unite the country. Contention between North and South would have intensified as potential trade barriers between the two nations would have caused shortages of food and raw materials. The two divided nations would be diminished and weaker on the world's stage. Some of those in the new nation of the South would have maintained their practice of enslaving Black people. Freedom and liberty for each individual would not have existed there.

Perhaps our current juncture in American history in 2020 is like that of 1861: a decision needs to be made to unify our nation. A politically and socially polarized nation cannot stand forever. The dangerous inequalities between the affluent, the middle class, and the poor are pulling us apart. One can only hope that current political and social problems can be settled amicably and we can remain a united nation without recourse to a new Civil War.

Notes to Lincoln's Legacy

1. *The Collected Works of Abraham Lincoln,* ed. Roy P. Basler, vol. I (New Brunswick, NJ: Rutgers University Press, 1953), 260.
2. *The Collected Works of Abraham Lincoln,* ed. Roy P. Basler, vol. III (New Brunswick, NJ: Rutgers University Press, 1953), 95.
3. *Collected Works,* vol. III, 95.
4. *The Collected Works of Abraham Lincoln,* ed. Roy P. Basler, vol. IV (New Brunswick, NJ: Rutgers University Press, 1953), 3.
5. Michael Landis, "A Proposal to Change the Words We Use When Talking about the Civil War," *Smithsonian Magazine,* September 9, 2015, https://www.smithsonianmag.com/history/proposal-change-vocabulary-we-use-when-talking-about-civil-war-180956547/.
6. *The Collected Works of Abraham Lincoln,* ed. Roy P. Basler, vol. II (New Brunswick, NJ: Rutgers University Press, 1953), 245.
7. *Collected Works,* vol. I, 8-9.
8. *Collected Works,* vol. I, 48.
9. *Collected Works,* vol. II, 2-3.
10. *Collected Works,* vol. II, 242.
11. *Collected Works,* vol. II, 245.
12. *Collected Works,* vol. III, 78.
13. *Collected Works,* vol. II, 365.
14. *Collected Works,* vol. II, 365.
15. *Collected Works,* vol. II, 452.
16. *Collected Works,* vol. II, 452.
17. *Collected Works,* vol. II, 452.
18. *Collected Works,* vol. III, 14.
19. *Collected Works,* vol. II, 368.
20. *Collected Works,* vol. IV, 157.
21. *Collected Works,* vol. IV, 266.
22. *Collected Works,* vol. IV, 266.

Sojourner Truth: A Life, a Symbol

During the nineteenth century in the United States, many citizens of the North believed that they were morally superior to the enslavers of the South, "as though their own section remained innocent of involuntary servitude or slavery."[1] They were self-righteous in comparing their legacy to that of the South. However, slaves born in New York before 1799 were bound subjects—until the state formally emancipated them in 1827. In Ulster County, New York, 3,220 Black people lived in bondage in 1800.[2] Thirty to sixty percent of Dutch farmers and other New York state households owned two to seven slaves.[3]

Isabella Baumfree, who later renamed herself Sojourner Truth, was born into this Northern system of slavery around 1797 in Ulster County, although "no one wrote down or kept information of where or when she was born because no one who could write anticipated that an enslaved baby would become an American legend."[4] But she did become a legend. At the age of nine, she was torn from her family and sold for $100 to the Neely family.[5] One year later, at the age of ten, she was sold to the Schrivers, a family of innkeepers. In 1809 at age twelve, Truth was sold for $175 to a Dutch parishioner, John Dumont, in whose household she lived until she was thirty. In 1815 she was forced to marry Thomas, also enslaved by Dumont, by whom she had five children.[6] "Love" for an enslaved person was a luxury; "attachment" was the key to having someone as a partner. According to an 1809 law, enslaved people could marry in New York and own property (without the legal title to the land), and they could not be forcibly separated from their families.[7] In the Dumont household, Truth was beaten and sexually abused. She learned the Dutch language, and later learned to speak English with a New York accent "that made her English so remarkable."[8]

Free Black people in New York were discriminated against, so they lived in a few poor wards in New York City, not economically solid areas like Harlem and Brooklyn. In 1817, New York passed a law to emancipate in 1827 all slaves born before 1799; Dumont freed Truth in 1827.[9] At the age of thirty, Truth left her family to declare her independence. She took only her baby Sophia with her. She became a live-in helper for the wealthy Whiting household in New York City. "She seems to have existed in a world entirely separate from that of Black male institutions like the Phoenix Society, from the fledgling antislavery movement that men also dominated" in the 1830s and 1840s.[10] Her main acquaintance was David Ruggles, a Black abolitionist and author of *National Anti-Slavery Standard*. "Notable black men worried about the oppression of all black people in New York City, but they held traditional ideas about women's proper place."[11] If men had been aware of Truth's existence, they would have been appalled "by this nontraditional Black woman who was a powerful, middle-aged, unlettered, preaching woman."[12] "Her religious unorthodoxy would have struck the leading Colored men as something to be hidden.... Prominent Black ministers and citizens also would have deplored Isabella's lack of interest in abolitionism."[13] Instead, Truth "heeded the voice of the Holy Spirit"; the life of the spirit attracted her.[14]

In 1827 in New York State, Truth was free, but for the previous two years her son Peter had been enslaved in Alabama by a Mr. Fowler. To recover her son, she received free legal counsel from two Dutch lawyers who entered her case to a grand jury. After a traumatic year of anxiety for Truth, Peter was returned to his mother and she took him to New York City. "Peter was covered with scars from head to toe, and his lacerated back was as rough as a wash barrel," mourned Isabella. He had been "whipped, kicked, and beaten, not yet seven years old.... A man who would abuse a Black child so cruelly could murder someone white, even one of his own, especially a woman."[15] Through this trauma, Isabella declared that slavery was never ordained by God. She received comfort from the holy scriptures that were read to her, since she was illiterate. Furthermore, she believed that slavery perpetuated a slave mentality: lack of confidence and independent thought, personal indignation, a sense of one's insignificance, a desire to please the powerful, and finally, bitterness and anger within one's soul.[16] She attempted to overcome these problems in her life and become master of her own fate.

In New York City, Truth joined the John Street Methodist Church. Between 1828 and 1832, Truth and Peter lived with the Latourette family, fervent Christians. At prayer meetings which anyone could attend, Truth was welcomed by women from the Presbyterian, Dutch Reformed Baptist, and Methodist churches. She visited prisons and the poor in the city. She was exposed to abolitionists such as Arthur Tappan, a religious philanthropist and leading abolitionist by 1830.

Truth established herself as an antislavery feminist. She attracted other Black women as she pursued her ambition to become a preacher. She "took pride in fashionable clothing" but wore plain clothes as "a means of distancing herself from the female lower classes whose loud dresses announced their lowly status."[17] She worked hard for her wages and finally was able to purchase furniture and save some money. Other talents were noted by Gertrude Dumont, daughter of the Dumont family: "She was an excellent dancer and a good singer," with a rich and powerful voice.[18] She established herself "as a powerful and moving preacher."[19] In the early 1830s, Truth started her public career. "Her physical stature, fervor, eloquence, and singing were making her reputation."[20]

Staying in the Latourettes' home between 1828 and 1832 crucially influenced the course of Truth's life in New York. She saw herself as the equal of the women she now encountered. "She knew that in the Holy Club she was associating with people more privileged than she, ...and she extended their superior level of education to their attainment of holiness."[21] Whereas Isabella had been illiterate as an enslaved person, she had friends read to her. Thereupon, the scriptures came alive to her by a gradual, often unconscious, process of osmosis.

"During Isabella's years in New York City, insult constantly fouled the lives of the Black poor, and even educated and respectable Colored gentlemen ran up against bigotry on a regular basis."[22] Arthur Tappan began a crusade "to ameliorate the condition of the free people of color in the North, who were nearly everywhere and nearly always despised. In the wake of the abolition of slavery, persecution and exclusion of Blacks became the rule in the North...in big cities...[which] in the 1830s and 1840s held the largest concentration of African Americans in the United States."[23] In New York City, streetcars refused to take Black passengers; public accommodations were not open to Black people; Black parents were barred from public schools. James McCune Smith, a medical doctor trained in Scotland, was not allowed to enter the New York Academy of Medicine. Northern Black people, on personal and political levels, suffered from the transition from slavery to freedom by "violent assault and legal harassment." White commoners and elites regularly used the n-word to refer to a Black person. Even in the late 1860s "when officially sanctioned segregation and disfranchisement ended in the North, discriminatory habits held on."[24]

On June 1, 1843, Truth quit New York City as the Holy Spirit directed her on Pentecost Day. She said she was "fleeing" a "wicked city" in the biblical imagery of fire and brimstone.[25] Truth marked her rebirth in 1843 by changing her name to "Sojourner Truth." She had "a long-standing preoccupation with truth."[26] She was secure in the integrity of her word. "Sojourner" is appropriate for a first name because it means "impermanence"—without a "home" all her life. But as a Sojourner, "she saw her mission as lecturing to the people, testifying and exhorting them to 'embrace Jesus and refrain from sin.'"[27]

In her Pentecostal rebirth and her departure from New York City, Sojourner Truth fell into the Adventist movement known as Millerism. "Some fifty thousand Millerites in the Northeast expected the world to end in the Jewish year that began in 1843."[28] "In racial terms, the Millerite movement resembled the company Truth usually kept, being mostly white, but heterogeneous...rich and poor, educated and untutored, Black and white."[29] Millerism appealed to Black Americans throughout the nineteenth century because the "starkness of racial injustice made the need for God's judgment all the more imperative."[30] In her messages, Sojourner Truth expressed ambivalence toward the doctrine of the Millerites who enjoined fanaticism and extremism. She agitated many members but reintroduced a sense of proportion. Ministers "admired Truth's thinking and the very fact that she was willing to argue with [Millerites] and contest their monopoly on Christian wisdom."[31] "Truth distrusted any mediation between herself and God, whether trained and paid ministers, anyone who presumed to interpret the Bible for her."[32] Hearing the scriptures read to her enticed her to find her own meaning in them, not what others thought they meant. The voice of the Holy Spirit gave her authority to speak and act accordingly. Millerites conceded that her views on divine revelation were proof of "her energy and independence of character."[33]

Millerites welcomed Truth into their homes and recommended her as a speaker for meetings where a diversity of views evolved. At this time, Truth had a "commanding figure and dignified manner," and her "singular and sometimes uncouth modes of expression" were never ridiculed. She became a "great favorite" adored for her "remarkable gift in prayer, and still remarkable talent for singing."[34] She became famous for captivating an audience with "the aptness and point of her remarks, frequently illustrated by figures the most original and expressive."[35] In Springfield, Massachusetts, Truth opened a "third great chapter in her life. After thirty years in slavery, fifteen years of making herself free through the power of the Holy Spirit, Sojourner Truth now launched the career of antislavery feminism."[36]

Truth preferred communal living, so she moved to a cooperative community in Northampton, Massachusetts, where lectures were exchanged for simple living quarters. Here, she said, the Northampton Association of Education and Industry gave her "accomplished literary and refined persons" with whom to associate. She was offered the same "equality of feeling," "liberty of thought and speech," and "largeness of soul."[37] This utopian community in 1840 provided Truth with an education in the lofty principles of economics, women's rights, freedom of expression, and the abolition of slavery.[38] Lecturers included prominent American reformers: William Lloyd Garrison, president of the American Anti-Slavery Society; Frederick Douglass, journalist and statesman; Wendell Phillips, pillar of antislavery and labor reform; and Sylvester Graham, health evangelist. Truth was able to live in a non-racial, classless, open-minded, dynamically intellectual place. She was assigned work in the laundry for $1.50 per week.

Sojourner Truth became a memorable character. She commanded respect for her singing, working, and speaking. According to George R. Stetson, she had "a tall imposing figure (5' 11"), a strong voice, and a ready wit."[39] The Northampton Association provided Truth an introduction to antislavery reformers such as John Humphrey Noyes, James Boyle, Giles Stebbins, David Ruggles, and Basil Dorsey, who shared their belief with Truth in abolitionism, women's suffrage, and spiritualism.

Frederick Douglass had little in common with Truth except race and a touch of Methodism.[40] Whereas Douglass preached against slavery in the African Methodist Episcopal (A.M.E.) Church, Sojourner Truth, as a preacher and a woman, would never have been able to become an A.M.E. minister. Douglass associated illiteracy with enslavement.[41] Emancipation through reading and writing, he believed, was a model of a well-educated leader. He saw Truth as "a genuine specimen of the uncultured [N]egro, who cared very little for elegance of speech or refinement of manners."[42] Douglass, however, admitted that her success was acquired through wisdom and wit. Her ideas may have appeared in odd forms, but her insights were of interest to white audiences who perhaps needed her message. In addition, her singing was unforgettable. Olive Gilbert, to whom Truth dictated her autobiography, writes, "All who have ever heard her sing [a] hymn will probably remember it as long as they live…, in her most animated moods, in the open air, with the utmost strength of her most powerful voice."[43]

When the Northampton Association dissolved in 1846, Truth was adrift and longed for her own home. To earn money, she dictated her autobiography—*Narrative of Sojourner Truth, a Northern Slave*—in 1850 to Olive Gilbert. The book sold for 25¢ per copy for a 128-page, soft-covered edition.[44] From the proceeds, Truth was able to get a mortgage on a home on Park Street in Florence, Massachusetts. She discharged the mortgage in 1854 and at last owned her own house free and clear at the age of fifty-seven.[45] As a middle-aged woman, she was "a mixture of brightness and shadow…with the energy of a naturally powerful mind—the fearlessness and child-like simplicity of one untrammeled by education or conventional customs…. She is a singing evangelist whose religion is joyous, optimistic, and at times ecstatic. She trusted in God, and from him she looks for good, and not evil."[46] But when facing the twilight of her years, Truth felt apprehension and distrust in her personal life.[47]

The three great chapters in Sojourner Truth's life were slavery, evangelism, and antislavery feminism. At the first, she considered her enslaved family as a chapter in her life. The second chapter spun out of Methodism, Millerites, and the Northampton Association—all of which nurtured her spiritual vitality. In the third chapter she was surrounded by abolitionists, feminists, spiritualists, and other leading intellectuals of American reform. In 1844, Truth gave her first antislavery speech in Northampton. In 1845, she spoke at the American Anti-Slavery Society meeting in New York City. Between 1845 and 1850, she attended and addressed large women's rights meetings. At a women's convention in Seneca Falls, New York, in 1848, Truth met Elizabeth Cady Stanton, Lucretia Mott, and Amy Post (who would play a large role in Truth's later life). Since women "speakers" were snubbed as "promiscuous in character," it was rare for an evangelical preacher like Truth to appear before a mixed public crowd.

Reporting on a women's rights meeting in 1850 in Worcester, Massachusetts, a newspaper wrote that, although Truth's "skin was dark and her outward appearance 'uncomely,' [she] spoke primarily as a preacher.... She said women set the world wrong by eating the forbidden fruit, and now she was going to set it right. She said Goodness [was] everlasting.... But Evil... had an end. She expressed great reverence for God, and faith that he will bring about his own purposes and plans."[48] In her remarks, Truth said little about antislavery politics because she did not know about politics as well as faith in God. But issues such as the Compromise of 1850 were becoming extremely political at the time. It was hard for Northerners to ignore slavery after the Southern enslavers threatened to move Negroes west into New Mexico and Utah. Political repercussions opened a decade of conflict about slavery: the fate of fugitives from slavery; the Kansas-Nebraska Territory; the formation of antislavery political parties; the Dred Scott decision; and John Brown's raid.

In this conflict, Truth, a reform-minded woman, was invited to the Ohio Women's Rights Convention in Akron, Ohio in 1851. The meeting propelled her into a dominant role as a competent, experienced, antislavery feminist. Moderators Jane Swisshelm and Frances Gage disagreed over whether African Americans belonged in women's rights meetings. "Swisshelm had no interest in poor and Black women's most pressing concerns."[49] At this convention, men were included in the discussion about the position on equal rights for women. As a powerful, popular speaker, Sojourner Truth turned the tide in an angry debate between feminists and conservative ministers with this now-famous speech:

> Well, children, where there is so much racket there must be something out of kilter. I think that 'twixt the Negroes of the South and the women at the North, all talking about rights, the white men will be in a fix pretty soon. But what's all this here talking about?

> That man over there says that women need to be helped into carriages, and lifted over ditches, and to have the best place everywhere. Nobody ever helps me into carriages, or over mud-puddles, or gives me any best place! And ain't I a woman? Look at me! Look at my arm! I have ploughed and planted, and gathered into barns, and no man could head me! And ain't I a woman? I could work as much and eat as much as a man—when I could get it—and bear the lash as well! And ain't I a woman? I have borne thirteen children, and seen them most all sold off to slavery, and when I cried out with my mother's grief, none but Jesus heard me! And ain't I a woman?
>
> Then they talk about this thing in the head; what's this they call it? (Intellect someone whispers.) That's it, honey. What's that got to do with women's rights or Negro's rights? If my cup won't hold but a pint, and yours holds a quart, wouldn't you be mean not to let me have my little half-measure full?
>
> Then that little man in black there, he says women can't have as much rights as men, 'cause Christ wasn't a woman! Where did your Christ come from? Where did your Christ come from? From God and a woman! Man had nothing to do with Him.
>
> If the first woman God ever made was strong enough to turn the world upside down all alone, these women together ought to be able to turn it back, and get it right side up again! And now they is asking to do it, the men better let them.
>
> Obliged to you for hearing me, and now old Sojourner ain't got nothing more to say.[50]

The Boston *Liberator* reported, "The power and wit of this remarkable woman convulsed the audience with laughter."[51] What is significant in this speech is Truth's use of the Bible to argue for women's rights. Truth was reborn with the vision and voice of the Holy Spirit as a woman and an evangelical preacher. Her friend Marius Robinson, who transcribed and published her speech in the *Anti-Slavery Bugle,* reported that "her powerful form, her whole-souled earnest gestures, and... her strong and truthful tones" affirmed her platform against slavery and for women's rights.[52] "She demands rights for women by virtue of her own physical equality with men.... Intelligence can be measured quantitatively. Mental capacity [for women] is her basic knowledge.... She compares man's absence from the creation of the savior to man's role in the present antislavery and women's rights agitation."[53] In Akron, Ohio, in 1851, Truth was clearly saying what needed to be said. As a highly respected figure, she was an important voice for women's equality.

The punitive, cruel Fugitive Slave Act of 1850 turned the country into the enemy of Black people in the 1860s.[54] An enslaver could swear a Black person was his property and seize the fugitive from slavery whose "testimony was not admissible in court, and he or she lacked the right to trial by jury."[55] In 1857, the United States Supreme Court in the Dred Scott decision declared that Americans of African descent were ineligible for citizenship. Indeed, Truth described herself as a citizen. To people in a Black church in New York City in 1853, she preached cleanliness and economic independence, not vengeance.[56] She encouraged Black people to become sharecroppers on Pennsylvania farms where they could prosper. "Abolitionists were fond of implicating orthodox Christianity in the moral economy of slavery. The regular ministry and conventional churches tolerated slaves and slavery."[57] In fact, Truth declared that "the sale of slave children…paid for the training of ministers of the gospel."[58] "She spoke of sinful whites and vengeful Blacks, but her humor let her listeners exempt themselves. They did not hear wrath against whites, but against the advocates of slavery…. Truth's audience… wanted to love this old Black woman who had been a slave, [but] found it difficult to fathom the depths of her bitterness."[59] From this point, Sojourner Truth began to condemn the institution of American slavery.

Fear and anger dogged Truth at nearly all white antislavery meetings. She grew increasingly angry and let her anger show. She said, "Black people were a great deal better than the white people had brought them up…. The white people owed the Colored race a big debt, and if they paid it all back, they wouldn't have anything left for seed."[60]

While Sojourner Truth traveled and lectured in relative obscurity, the Civil War altered everything.[61] Lincoln's preliminary Emancipation Proclamation of September 1862 accepted Black men into the Union Army and "Black people suddenly rose in the national consciousness…. The subject of 'the Negro' exploded in the popular press."[62] Truth started discussing the war and championing the Union cause. But she faced legal trouble as a Black woman. In Steuben County, Indiana, she boarded a carriage for a parade to the courthouse where she warned crowds that the Confederacy was arming Black people to fight against the Union. She declared she would "fly to the battlefield" and nurse and cook for the Massachusetts troops, "*her boys,*" and punch a blow if needed.[63] Truth was arrested because Indiana, which was sympathetic to the Confederate cause, prohibited people of African descent from entering the state.[64] She was released after ten days. Truth had lectured earlier in Indiana without incident, but now racial prejudice showed its face. She said, "It seems that it takes *my* black face to bring out *your* black hearts; so it's well I came. You are afraid of my black face because it is a looking glass in which you see yourselves."[65]

Thereafter, she volunteered her services to Black troops, especially those in Battle Creek, Michigan, where she was living, and in Detroit, Michigan. She addressed segregated audiences and settled on a mission for Black soldiers and freed people, especially in Washington, D.C. and Massachusetts. By the end of the Civil War, "about 186,000 men, or a tenth of the Union Army, were Black, serving mostly in segregated infantry regiments with white officers."[66] In essence, the ambivalence about Truth's race lasted a lifetime, even though many of her associates in adult life had been educated, middle-class, white people.[67] Throughout the war, however, she retained her "unimpeachable moral character" and continued to embrace feminism and maintain an antislavery stance.[68]

After the Emancipation Proclamation in 1863, Washington, D.C. became the "land of freedom—the capital of a nation waging war on Southern institutions."[69] In partisan politics, Sojourner Truth had made speeches in support of Lincoln during his reelection campaign and then was honored by his welcome to shake his hand at a meeting in 1864 in Washington, D.C., during which Lincoln made "gestures of civility that whites rarely offered to Blacks at the time."[70] Truth announced, "I am proud to say that I never was treated with more kindness and cordiality...."[71] She gave him her photograph; he signed Truth's autograph book.

Freed people sought refuge in the District of Columbia beginning in 1861. The Fugitive Slave Act of 1850 still remained in force. An estimated 25,000 refugees ended up in camps and became an economic burden. Deplorable, crowded conditions in the camps were caused by failures of the government. Truth, from 1864 to 1865, worked in refugee camps for the National Freedman's Relief Association. Audiences accepted her preaching as a Black woman but also her legal advice as an agent for employment. She proclaimed all this work was her duty.

Even after emancipation and the repeal of the Black codes, racial discrimination still prevailed in Washington. In March 1865, a federal law ended segregation on streetcars, so Truth knew her rights. She tried entering a streetcar but was "dragged several feet because the conductor would not wait for her to mount."[72] In another incident, the conductor passed her by, pretending not to see her, but she raised her hand and shouted, "I want to ride!"[73] The conductor stopped the streetcar and growled, "Go forward where the horses are, or I will throw you out."[74] She refused to be cowed, for she knew the laws. Later, another conductor wrenched her right arm when he tried to remove her from the streetcar. She recorded the conductor's number and had him arrested and convicted of assault and battery.[75]

In May 1867, Susan B. Anthony invited Sojourner Truth to a meeting of the American Equal Rights Association in New York, and Elizabeth Cady Stanton welcomed Truth as her houseguest. During the convention, Truth did not share the same opinions as those of the two giants of women's suffrage. First, Stanton and Anthony believed that emancipation had destroyed slavery, but Truth stressed the fragility of the Fourteenth Amendment. Second, Truth defended the political rights of men but questioned Stanton's defense of rich, southern white women and pointed out that Stanton rarely spoke of Black women of the South. Truth warned the Stanton-adoring audience, "I came from another field—the country of the slave."[76] Third, Stanton and Anthony supporters prioritized the right to vote of white women over the rights of Black men, but Truth pointed to the weaknesses of Black men as an argument for Black women's suffrage.[77] Truth did not want Black men to become dominant over Black women in financial matters, for example. In a further difference with Stanton and Anthony, Truth declared that "what women needed was the vote, but Black women needed it even more, having less education and a more limited choice of jobs. '[W]ashing,' she said, 'is about as high as a Colored woman gets.'"[78] Fifth, Truth's appearance in court three times revealed the fact that "in the courts women have no right, no voice; nobody speaks for them."[79] Finally, Truth believed Stanton was a woman of wealth, status, and privilege who did not understand "a poor working woman...who knew the life at the bottom of the economic ladder."[80] In 1851, Truth spoke about her right to equal remuneration for labor. Essentially, Stanton said she would not trust Black men to make laws for her. She preferred that enfranchised educated people serve first instead of ignorant, poverty-stricken, vice-prone individuals.[81]

By the time Truth had spoken her words to the Equal Rights Convention, Susan B. Anthony acknowledged to the audience that Truth was a symbol of slavery. One of Truth's fingers had been chopped off by a cruel enslaver in a moment of anger.[82] "Truth stood for both Blacks and women."[83] Unfortunately, Stanton supported education and property rights as prerequisites for voting. Truth, in contrast, "distinguished wisdom from education and worth from wealth."[84] At best, Truth established herself openly in the presence of Stanton and Anthony, even though she repudiated their position that Black male suffrage endangered woman's suffrage.

After the Civil War, Sojourner Truth turned her attention to the salient issue of woman suffrage. Black male suffrage was granted through the Fourteenth and Fifteenth amendments ratified between 1865 and 1870. "Southern politics demanded Black male suffrage, and Black male suffrage galvanized feminists."[85] Truth stood beside Elizabeth Cady Stanton and Susan B. Anthony even if there were differences. Now that Black men had advanced, why hadn't women been granted the vote? Women's suffrage communities sought the blessings of Sojourner Truth who had advanced women's rights with her rhetoric for all women. Watching freed men voting in the District of Columbia, Truth felt it was unfair to women. She believed that Black suffrage was necessary to sustain emancipation. "During the presidential Reconstruction in 1865 to 1866, Southern states passed Black codes that virtually reproduced slavery. In 1866, a wave of terrorism swept the South. White supremacists murdered and raped Black Republicans and their supporters in Memphis and New Orleans.... Violence in the South was demonstrating that emancipation, of itself, would not transform southern society."[86] Further, Black women could not be given the vote until white women were also enfranchised. Truth represented Black female authenticity; she insisted that Black women were women, and therefore, that women's issues were as much their concern as the concern of white women. She felt that woman suffrage should mean the same thing to women of all races.[87]

Sojourner Truth died on November 26, 1883, at the age of eighty-six. Her family—Diana Corbin, Elizabeth Boyd, and Sophia Schayler—were poor and illiterate domestic servants who could not "memorialize their famous mother."[88] Two daughters died in "the county poorhouse as objects of private charity."[89] Lack of financial resources and illiteracy often left Black families in "homebound obscurity."[90] A dedicated friend of Truth, Frances Titus, "laid the cornerstone of Truth's memory" in one great labor of love: the 1870s and 1880s editions of the *Narrative of Sojourner Truth*. In 1875, Titus republished Olive Gilbert's 1850 *Narrative* together with excerpts from the "Book of Life," Truth's scrapbooks. The complete repertoire of Sojourner Truth's life is recorded in manuscripts, journals, letters, newspapers, and photographs. In the prose of other people, "Truth seemed usually to abide by herself, an isolated Black presence among a mass of genteel, reformist whites."[91] She was a shining light in the antislavery movement, and she promoted women's rights and Pentecostal spirituality.

Above all, Sojourner Truth was an iconoclast, breaking the belief in the institution of slavery. Besides, she was a woman, a feminist, and a long-suffering "breaker" of bondage. Humbled by illiteracy but possessing formidable courage and moral character, she inspired many audiences. Presidents of the United States even made her feel welcome. William Still, a Black friend of Truth's, said that she "dauntlessly [faced] the most intelligent and cultivated audiences to advance the interests of the slave."[92] The American Woman Suffrage Association remembered Truth as a native genius, "one of the most remarkable women of the age.... She has rare natural gifts; a clear intellect; a fine moral intuition and spirited insight, with much common sense."[93] John W. Cromwell published a volume in 1914 with this account: When an aspiring Frederick Douglass once confronted an audience, "Sojourner Truth rose in the audience and, stretching forth her arms in a shrill voice exclaimed, 'Frederick, is God dead?' The effect was electrical.... The house was changed to one of hope and assurance."[94] Hallie Q. Brown related another vignette: As Brown was leaving Truth's house one day after a visit, Truth said, "'I isn't goin' to die, honey. Ise goin' home like a shootin' star.'"[95]

Sojourner Truth's strength continued through the Civil War, but in the mid-1870s "a serious illness paralyzed her entire right side and left her legs with gangrenous ulcers that never healed completely."[96] A woman doctor, Sallie Rogers, and a veterinarian restored her ability to walk, so she went on the lecture tour again in 1880.[97] She rarely left Michigan where she lived, but she reached thousands. She described God as "a great ocean of love" and said, "We live and move in him as the fishes in the sea, filled with his love and spirit, and his throne is in the hearts of his people...."[98]

The author Nell Irvin Painter concludes her book about Sojourner Truth with these thoughts:

> As a slave, Truth had been abused, like millions of her counterparts in bondage. Women who have been enslaved and beaten are far more likely to appear depressed than to project intriguing strength of character. They tend to fade from memory rather than make an indelible impression. The legacy of abuse helps explain why Truth's success on the antislavery lecture circuit was unique among women who had actually been enslaved.
>
> Truth in public was extraordinary as an ex-slave woman, and her vitality needs an explanation. The key lies in Truth's refashioning herself over long years of adult life and through access to uncommon sources of power. Relying on the gifts of the Holy Spirit and a remarkable network of abolitionist, feminist and spiritualist supporters, she healed the fear and insecurity embedded in her wretched childhood.... She was a forceful, indefatigable speaker for political causes that needed the strength and the body she brought to them.[99]

Notes to Sojourner Truth: A Life, a Symbol

1. Nell Irvin Painter, *Sojourner Truth: A Life, A Symbol* (New York: W. W. Norton & Co., 1996), 10.
2. Painter, *Sojourner Truth*, 6.
3. Painter, 6.
4. Painter, 11.
5. Painter, 13.
6. Painter, 14.
7. Painter, 19.
8. Painter, 7.
9. Painter, 20.
10. Painter, 69.
11. Painter, 71.
12. Painter, 71.
13. Painter, 71.
14. Painter, 72.
15. Painter, 35.

16. Painter, 17.
17. Painter, 43.
18. Painter, 43.
19. Painter, 43.
20. Painter, 45.
21. Painter, 46.
22. Painter, 63.
23. Painter, 63.
24. Painter, 64.
25. Painter, 74.
26. Painter, 75.
27. Painter, 74.
28. Painter, 79.
29. Painter, 81.
30. Painter, 87.
31. Painter, 86.
32. Painter, 86.
33. Painter, 86.
34. Painter, 87.
35. Painter, 87.
36. Painter, 87.
37. Painter, 89.
38. Painter, 92.
39. Painter, 95.
40. Painter, 96.
41. Painter, 97.
42. Painter, 98.
43. Quoted in Painter, *Sojourner Truth,* 105-106.
44. Painter, *Sojourner Truth,* 11.
45. Painter, 112.
46. Painter, 112.
47. Painter, 112.
48. Painter, 115.
49. Painter, 123.
50. Version of speech in Pamela J. Annas and Robert C. Rosen, eds., *Literature and Society: An Introduction to Fiction, Poetry, Drama, Nonfiction,* 3rd ed (Upper Saddle River, NJ: Prentice Hall, 2000), 566.
51. Painter, *Sojourner Truth,* 128.
52. Painter, 125.

53. Painter, 127-128.
54. Painter, 132.
55. Painter, 132.
56. Painter, 136.
57. Painter, 137.
58. Painter, 137.
59. Painter, 138.
60. Painter, 137.
61. Painter, 151.
62. Painter, 157.
63. Painter, 180.
64. Painter, 180.
65. Painter, 181.
66. Painter, 182.
67. Painter, 181.
68. Painter, 181.
69. Painter, 200.
70. Painter, 204.
71. Painter, 206.
72. Painter, 210.
73. Painter, 210.
74. Painter, 210.
75. Painter, 211.
76. Painter, 226.
77. Painter, 227.
78. Painter, 227.
79. Painter, 227.
80. Painter, 227.
81. Painter, 228.
82. Painter, 229.
83. Painter, 229.
84. Painter, 230.
85. Painter, 221.
86. Painter, 222.
87. Painter, 224.
88. Painter, 258.
89. Painter, 253.
90. Painter, 252.
91. Painter, 252.

92. Painter, 249.
93. Painter, 249.
94. Painter, 264.
95. Painter, 265.
96. Painter, 248.
97. Painter, 249.
98. Quoted in Painter, *Sojourner Truth,* 249.
99. Painter, *Sojourner Truth,* 178.

John Steinbeck's Humanistic Legacy

In March 2001, the John Steinbeck Centennial Convention at Hofstra University on Long Island discussed the contribution that John Steinbeck made to humanism. His writing during the Great Depression in the United States passionately engaged with the social and political currents of his time. "The humanitarian concerns were the underpinning of a life that included notoriety and celebrity. Steinbeck was attacked by the Right for his depiction of the plight of migrant workers and by the Left for his stand on the Vietnam War."[1] He connected with humanity on a profound level by advocating that each of us should be our brother's and sister's keeper.

Steinbeck follows the central tenet of modernist humanism in his book *To a God Unknown,* where he pleads for humans to be true to one another. In *The Log from the Sea of Cortez,* he describes an expedition with Ed Ricketts to the Sea of Cortez where they study marine life. He contends that we are part of the whole universe, but we are responsible for it all. His interrelated humanistic messages dwell on Christian sacrifice, America's self-conception (dream or myth), and humanity's relationship with the earth and the ecosystem. According to M. Kathryn Davis, Steinbeck was aware that "the Chicago ecologists who effectively shaped Ricketts' scientific understanding believed that morality could be discerned in nature and that the theory of succession in plant and animal communities offered seminal lessons for human society."[2] In fact, *The Grapes of Wrath* "is not merely about historical injustice or social failure…, but it is a complete [re-examination] of humanity's relationship with the earth," from the parched earth of Oklahoma to the abundantly green, fertile pastures of California.[3] The turtle's struggle to get across the road is a parable of the struggle of the Okies driving across the United States to California.

In his works, Steinbeck is sympathetic to the poor, the dispossessed, the displaced, the inarticulate, the handicapped, bums, prostitutes, alcoholics, laborers, farmers, and ordinary people who are unrecognized and unappreciated. *Tortilla Flat,* for example, portrays with sympathetic gaiety a houseful of drifters, outcasts, lazy alcoholics, and bums who are doing good but protesting conventionality. *Of Mice and Men* portrays Lennie, the mentally handicapped individual who depends entirely on his caretaker, George. It is a story of human beings voluntarily accepting responsibility for others. The novel *In Dubious Battle* depicts destitute labor union sympathizers fighting for human rights and a decent salary in the midst of violence and degradation. *The Pearl* portrays a peasant's drive for wealth that ends in tragedy and disappointment. And, of course, the classic masterpiece *The Grapes of Wrath* depicts the Okies, victims of the Dust Bowl who suffered as farm laborers. In all these examples, Steinbeck expresses humanistic values. According to Jackson Benson, Steinbeck claimed "that even with the pressure of modern life, individualism and materialism, it is still possible for human beings to understand and have compassion for one another."[4]

Steinbeck's humanistic legacy exemplifies itself most fully in his preparation for writing *The Grapes of Wrath.* He was a skillful, objective observer and "a caring man, but also very detached."[5] He had to be detached to some degree to visit the squatter camps in California and to see the appalling scene at Weedpatch where thousands of people camped, destitute and desperate, starving and sick, spiritually squelched, wallowing in the rain and mud. These hearty souls had formerly been farmers, sharecroppers, and small businessmen, mainly from Arkansas, Texas, Kansas, Colorado, and Oklahoma. They had had pride in themselves and their work, but because of the Great Depression they were reduced to slaves in the agricultural empire of California. Their unrefined speech, their ragged clothes, and their lethargic manner identified them as "poor whites…, primitive, rural, backwoods [trash]" of the industrial society.[6] They were classified as "animals"—dirty, untrustworthy, uncivilized people dispensable to society. In reality, they were proud, hard-working people who had to accept charity because they were starving physically, mentally, and spiritually.

In California during 1935, according to Jackson Benson in *The True Adventures of John Steinbeck,* there were an estimated 300,000 to 400,000 migrants scheduled to pick peas, but the crop was ruined by rain, so many tens of thousands could not find work. Those adults who did get hired earned 12 to 26 cents per day; children who picked cotton earned 20 or 25 cents per day. Families paid $1.00 per month for a shack. Because they were required to buy all supplies at company stores that charged high prices, farm workers went in debt to the companies, which deducted the cost of purchases from their pay.[7] In his article "Starvation under the Orange Tree," Steinbeck records an outrageous act of revenge upon these migrants. Agricultural growers dumped carloads of oranges and poured kerosene over them to punish workers who had struck for higher wages. The hungry thousands stood in awe as this fruit was destroyed.

In 1936, Congress was hostile to the idea of housing these displaced immigrants in California, so they refused to allocate adequate funds for the purpose of establishing sanitary government camps. One health official in California's Madeira County spread information to the Agricultural Association that migrants were immoral, lazy people, incapable of being absorbed. Farm owners deliberately made life difficult for them in order to induce them to leave.[8] By 1937, the population of migrants had been reduced to 70,000; most had either died or returned to their home state.[9] Apathy describes the society's response to these people. Growers had all the power locally and statewide until 1939, when the Democrat Culbert Olson became California's governor.[10] Steinbeck saw the treatment of migrants as a social injustice.

During this time, Steinbeck met a camp administrator, Tom Collins. Together they toured squatter and labor camps, talking with the people and surveying conditions from Bakersfield to Arvin, California. Steinbeck and Collins listened to migrants recount their endless problems. The camp dwellers lived in paper box homes and stood in mud and rain through terrible times. Children had measles, whooping cough, mumps, pneumonia, and throat infections. Sick parents and children were separated when quarantined. Babies lacked mother's milk; many died at birth. Out of frustration, a man beat his wife. Collins and Steinbeck lingered among these migrant workers, ate with them, and gave them sympathy. Both "had a knack for getting close to ordinary people and winning their confidence."[11]

Both Collins and Steinbeck believed in democratic rule through democratic institutions, even within the camps. They insisted that all should have security, voting rights, and recourse to justice through the rule of law. Steinbeck hated the abuses of capitalism; he saw agricultural businesses profit from the exploitation of human beings. Rather than being concerned with developing an elaborate political theory, he focused on the damage society inflicts on individuals. As Steinbeck saw it, the common people were blessed with old-time American virtues of perseverance, a work ethic, and a belief in justice. A formal religion was of little use to them. Once clean and educated, these good people were capable of restoring their dignity and leading stable lives. Collins called these people "the salt of the earth." He and Steinbeck wanted human beings to become good neighbors who were "responsive to each other's need" and "responsible citizens in a democratic society that was responsive to the general welfare."[12]

In preparation for writing *The Grapes of Wrath*, Steinbeck took extensive notes, and Collins supplied him with numerous detailed reports and statistics. The Associated Farmers of California, a group representing the interests of farm owners, denounced *The Grapes of Wrath* as "a pack of lies," but it was hard to refute the depictions of migrants' experiences in the novel, for Steinbeck had observed the truth firsthand and told it as it was. After returning home to Monterey Bay to begin writing the novel, Steinbeck was in the depths of anger and anguish over many months. "It threatened to incapacitate him as an artist.... He wanted to lash out against the suffering and injustices that he had seen.... He struggled for many months with the temptation to satirize and attack those, who through their greed and indifference, made such widespread suffering possible.... He wasn't able to write *The Grapes of Wrath* until he was able to contain his anger—and that took almost two years."[13]

Steinbeck offered to edit Collins' material for publication, but in place of this he wrote a series of seven articles titled "The Harvest Gypsies" for *The San Francisco News*. These articles reported to the public the suffering of migrant workers and the injustices they faced in California. In other humanitarian pursuits, he gave money to help migrants in camps raise pigs for food and restore their farm roots. Also, he contacted charitable organizations to obtain books to send to the children in the camps. Furthermore, he wrote a magnificent collection of accounts to the government, the public, and the California Agricultural Association about the social problems that he described as "a bomb ready to explode." These articles "would make one of the greatest and most authentic and hopeful human documents I know," writes the biographer Jackson J. Benson.[14] Unfortunately, when the La Follette Senate Committee began hearings in 1939 about conditions of California's migrant farm workers—and referenced material in *The Grapes of Wrath* and Steinbeck's articles—Steinbeck was harshly attacked by businesspeople and some politicians and newspapers. Additionally, some Congressmen denounced the film version of *The Grapes of Wrath* as political propaganda. Steinbeck shunned all this publicity, but he held fast to his depiction of human suffering at the hands of tyrants because he had documents to prove it.

In a letter that appeared in *The San Francisco News* in 1938, Steinbeck set forth his basic humanistic philosophy for the working class in the United States: "Every effort I can bring to bear is and has been at the call of the common working people to the end that they may eat what they raise, wear what they weave, use what they produce, and in every way and in completeness share in the work of their hands and their heads.... I am actively opposed to any man or group who, through financial or political control of the means of production and distribution, is able to control and dominate the lives of workers."[15]

Steinbeck wanted to change the system that oppressed the poor, but he was primarily a storyteller, not a social reformer. In fact, when he received money for his novels, he did not give most of it away to support social causes; instead, he bought a large ranch and then moved to New York City where he no longer seemed concerned with the issues facing the downtrodden. When he was young in the 1930s, he crusaded for disenfranchised workers and "extolled a social group's capacity for survival in a hostile economic world."[16] As a writer, Steinbeck depicted fanatics, eccentrics, the mentally impaired, rascals, the lonely, the ugly, and the ridiculous. Furthermore, he recognized that the world was full of cruelty, fierceness of expectancy, and greed.[17] But when Steinbeck moved east to New York City in 1950, he left behind the California he knew and the people he depicted. "He had lost contact with the only setting he could properly use for a novel."[18] Absorbed into the middle class, he no longer had the impulse to write about the working class. In New York City, he turned from others to himself, enjoying money, fame, material possessions, and famous friends. The great issues of social justice never again filled his creative imagination. He became a displaced writer who was detached from the culture of the working class.

By 1956 at the age of 54, Steinbeck was friendly with a couple at the newsstand in New York, the bartender, and the neighborhood characters. In Sag Harbor, he liked to converse with people at the local hardware store and with locals and shopkeepers on Main Street. But these people never fueled his creativity like the California farm workers had. When Steinbeck looked inward instead of outward toward others, his work lost its theme of community spirit.

Toward the end of his life, Steinbeck wrote a series of essays on *America and Americans*. He claimed that in the United States of the 1960s, morality, integrity, and honesty were breaking down. He felt that Americans were losing the ability to tell the difference between good and bad. Corporations showed shame only when they got caught; students cheated on exams. He lamented, "Ethics, morals, codes of conduct are the stern rules which in the past we needed to survive."[19] Steinbeck believed that the "highest qualities of humans are their courage, their willingness to sacrifice for others, and their capacity for love."[20]

The Greek philosopher Protagoras defined humanism as an approach to faith, thought, and action that assigns an overriding interest to human beings rather than a supernatural being. According to Jack Mendelsohn, Bertrand Russell said, "Humanist faith sprung ultimately from an admiration of two human qualities: kindly feeling and veracity."[21] For Russell, veracity meant accuracy, observation of truth, and conformity to fact. In his writing, Steinbeck believed that he had a conversation with his audience. What some people find in religion, a writer may find in his or her craft.[22] *The Grapes of Wrath* is a testament to Steinbeck's humanism, and his works are the legacy of an enlightened human being. Certainly, a thread of compassion runs clearly through all his writing. In Steinbeck's words, "Perhaps we will have to inspect [human beings] as a species, not with our usual awe at how wonderful we are, but with the cool and neutral attitude we reserve for all things save ourselves."[23]

Notes to John Steinbeck's Humanistic Legacy

1. Cover of Jackson J. Benson, *The True Adventures of John Steinbeck, Writer* (New York: Penguin, 1984).
2. M. Kathryn Davis, "Edward F. Ricketts: Man of Science and Conscience," *Steinbeck Studies* 15, no. 2 (2004): 16.
3. Davis, "Edward F. Ricketts," 17.
4. Jackson J. Benson, *Looking for Steinbeck's Ghosts* (Las Vegas: University of Nevada Press, 2002), 218.
5. Benson, *Looking for Steinbeck's Ghosts,* 49.
6. Benson, *True Adventures,* 334-335.
7. Benson, *True Adventures,* 335.
8. Benson, *True Adventures,* 336-337.
9. Benson, *True Adventures,* 336.
10. Benson, *True Adventures,* 336.
11. Benson, *True Adventures,* 344.
12. Benson, *True Adventures,* 345-346.
13. Benson, *True Adventures,* 346.
14. Benson, *True Adventures,* 348.
15. John Steinbeck, *Working Days: The Journals of "The Grapes of Wrath" 1938-1941,* ed. Robert DeMott (New York: Viking Penguin, 1989), 152.
16. Robert DeMott, introduction to *Working Days: The Journals of "The Grapes of Wrath" 1938-1941,* by John Steinbeck (New York: Viking Penguin, 1989), xlvi.
17. Steinbeck, *Working Days,* 17.
18. Benson, *The True Adventures,* 608.
19. John Steinbeck, *America and Americans and Selected Nonfiction,* ed. Jackson J. Benson and Susan Shillinglaw (New York: Viking, 2002), 398.
20. Steinbeck, *America and Americans,* 456.
21. Jack Mendelsohn, *Being Liberal in an Illiberal Age: Why I Am a Unitarian,* 2nd ed. (Boston: Skinner House Books, 2006), 127.
22. Steinbeck, *America and Americans,* 162.
23. Steinbeck, *America and Americans,* 392.

Tuesdays with Morrie

In his memoir *Tuesdays with Morrie,* Mitch Albom illustrates human relationships at their prime in an exchange between himself and a terminally ill professor, Morrie Schwartz. In the fourteen weeks of lessons on each Tuesday that Morrie gives to Mitch, Morrie instills wisdom about living and dying. In essence, Morrie's meditations fill each lesson with the propensity for living.

Mitch was a sociology student in Morrie's classes at Brandeis University. At graduation, he promised Morrie that he would keep in touch, but he had not kept his promise for sixteen years until he saw Morrie interviewed on television and felt chagrined for breaking a promise. Mitch had become a very successful sportswriter and sports broadcaster. His life had been so fast paced that he waited for seven years after first meeting his girlfriend Janine to ask her to marry him. But Tuesdays spent with Morrie for fourteen weeks caused a stunning awakening in Mitch and helped him see his life differently.

In this true story, the reader is deeply filled with pathos when observing Morrie's courage to face death from ALS (amyotrophic lateral sclerosis) and his wisdom to overcome bitterness. ALS, also known as Lou Gehrig's disease, is "a brutal, unforgiving illness of the neurological system," similar to an "insidious decay."[1] Miraculously, however, the mind is not directly affected by the disease. Morrie says, "To know you're going to die, and to be prepared for it at any time. That's better. That way you can actually be more involved in your life while you're alive. Am I doing all I need to do? Am I being the person I want to be?"[2]

In these last lessons that Morrie teaches each Tuesday, Mitch finds insights for living, not dying. These insights are a sweet, gentle tribute to aging, speaking to a busy, successful young man. Mitch mentions that "sitting in [Morrie's] presence was almost magically serene."[3] Morrie never asks God for endurance, courage, or freedom from pain, and he doesn't refer to God, the Bible, salvation, or heaven. His philosophy is attuned to Unitarian Universalist philosophy and principles. He was born Jewish but became an agnostic when he was a teenager. "He enjoyed some of the philosophies of Buddhism and Christianity, and he still felt at home, culturally, in Judaism. He was a religious mutt...and the things he was saying in his final months on earth seemed to transcend all religious differences. Death has a way of doing that."[4]

Morrie shows a Unitarian view when he states, "Once you learn how to die, you learn how to live."[5] Living and dying "respect the interdependent web of all existence of which we are a part." However, Morrie admits that "some mornings I cry and cry and mourn. I'm angry and bitter. It doesn't last long and I say, 'I want to live.'"[6] In saying this, Morrie believes that living is earth-oriented, not heaven-oriented. Somehow Morrie could take his impending death on earth and teach others how to live abundantly on earth. Morrie's belief in an earth-centered tradition encourages human beings to celebrate the sacred circle of life and instructs them to live in harmony with nature.

Morrie says to Mitch, "You know, Mitch, now that I'm dying, I've become much more interesting to people."[7] Ted Koppel interviewed Morrie twice on the TV news program Nightline. Morrie states, "Now that I'm suffering, I feel closer to people who suffer than I ever did before."[8] "Maybe death is a great equalizer, the one big thing that can finally make strangers shed a tear for one another."[9] "I may be dying, but I'm surrounded by loving, caring souls. How many people can say that?"[10] Morrie's philosophy is centered on relationships with his family and friends rather than with God, but the reader is aware of spirituality in all that Morrie says. A family is not just about love, but "letting others know there's someone who is watching out for [you]."[11] "Invest in a human family. Invest in people... Build those you love and those who love you.... You need others to survive."[12] While dying, Morrie claims, you have more time for silent meditation and friendships. "Make room for some spiritual things."[13]

One's spiritual security comes from "knowing that your family will be there watching out for you. Nothing else will give you that. Not money. Not fame."[14] "Money is not a substitute for tenderness, and power is not a substitute for tenderness.... When you need it most, neither money nor power will give you the feeling you're looking for, no matter how much of them you have."[15] "You can't substitute material things for love or for gentleness or for tenderness or for a sense of comradeship."[16] Morrie advises Mitch to give service to other human beings: "I don't mean money, Mitch. I mean your time. Your concern. Your storytelling. It's not so hard."[17] "By giving to other people is what makes me feel alive. Not my car or my house. Not what I look like in the mirror. When I give my time [and listen], when I can make someone smile after they were feeling sad, it's as close to healthy as I ever feel."[18]

Day by day Morrie realizes his infirmities. When he couldn't push the brakes on his car, he stopped driving. When his legs became unsteady, it became impossible to walk and dance. When he couldn't undress to go swimming, it ended his privacy. When he couldn't teach any more, it ended a chapter in his life. But Morrie's commitment to "living with death's shadow" allowed him to propose "bite-sized philosophies": "'Accept what you are able to do and what you are not able to do'; 'Accept the past as past, without denying it or discarding it'; 'Learn to forgive yourself and to forgive others'; 'Don't assume that it's too late to get involved.'"[19] Live involved in the universe around you. For example, Morrie could not go outside and walk in the garden, but he could look out the window, and when the window was open, he could feel the wind blowing and hear it rustle in the trees. "I am drawn to nature like I'm seeing it for the first time," like a spiritual development.[20]

A clear principle of Morrie's philosophy is: "Love wins. Love always wins."[21] "So many people walk around with a meaningless life. They seem half-asleep, even when they're busy doing things they think are important. This is because they're chasing the wrong things. The way you get meaning into your life is to devote yourself to loving others, devote yourself to your community around you, and devote yourself to creating something that gives you purpose and meaning."[22] This reminds one of the principle that good works are the natural product of a good faith, the evidence of an inner grace that finds completion in social and community involvement. During the Vietnam War, Morrie gave all the male students As to keep them in school and defer them from the draft.

On the subject of love, Morrie contends that "the most important thing in life is to learn how to give out love, and to let it come in."[23] "If you don't have the support and love and caring concern that you get from a family, you don't have much at all. Love is so supremely important."[24] As the poet Auden wrote, "Love each other or perish."[25] The important questions "have to do with love, responsibility, spirituality, awareness."[26] "Love is when you are as concerned about someone else's situation as you are about your own."[27] "Dying," Morrie contends, "is only one thing to be sad over, Mitch. Living unhappily is something else."[28] Morrie was "fighting time to say all the things he wanted to say to all the people he loved."[29]

At this point in his life, Morrie did not care much for material things. His simple pleasures came from visits with his friends, especially Mitch, e-mails, phone calls, and writing and receiving letters—all human contacts. He cultivated such habits early in life that sustained him to the end. He wasted no time watching TV sitcoms or movies of the week. Instead, he visited with people, wrote letters, ate, looked at nature, danced in his mind, and kept abreast with the news. He states, "Because I'm dying, is it strange not to care what happens in this world?"[30] When singing, laughing, and dancing were impossible, he was sad. He had little breath for singing; when he laughed, he choked on the phlegm; and for dancing, Morrie said, "ALS is like a lit candle; it melts your nerves and leaves your body a pile of wax."[31]

Morrie warns Mitch that "the culture we have does not make people feel good about themselves...you have to be strong enough to say if the culture doesn't work, don't buy it. Create your own. Most people can't do it. They're more unhappy than me...even in my current condition."[32] But "I've had a good life."[33] "Mitch," Morrie says, "the culture doesn't encourage you to think about things until you're about to die. We're so wrapped up with egotistical things, career, family, having enough money, meeting the mortgage, getting a new car, fixing the radiator when it breaks—we're involved in trillions of little acts just to keep going. So we don't get into the habit of standing back and looking at our lives and saying, Is this all? Is this all I want? Is something missing?"[34]

"We've got a form of brainwashing going on in our country," Morrie sighs. "Do you know how they brainwash people? They repeat something over and over. And that's what we do in this country. Owning things is good. More money is good. More property is good. More commercialism is good.

More is good. More is good. We repeat it—and have it repeated to us—over and over until nobody bothers to even think otherwise. The average person is so fogged up by all this, he has no perspective on what's really important anymore."[35] The most important lesson in life is connecting to one another through compassion and love.

Morrie contends that "there's a big confusion in this country over what we want versus what we need.... You need food, you want a chocolate sundae.... You don't need the latest sports car, you don't need the biggest house. The truth is, you don't get satisfaction from those things. You know what really gives satisfaction?... Offering others what you have to give."[36] "I feel sorry for your generation.... In this culture, it's so important to find a loving relationship with someone because so much of the culture does not give you that. But the poor kids today, either they're too selfish..., or they rush into marriage and then six months later, they get divorced.... They don't know who they are themselves—so how can they know who they're marrying?"[37]

"People are only mean when they're threatened,...and that's what our culture does. That's what our economy does. Even people who have jobs in our economy are threatened, because they worry about losing them. And when you get threatened, you start looking out only for yourself. You start making money a god. It is all part of this culture."[38] "If you're surrounded by people who say 'I want mine now,' you end up with a few people with everything and a military to keep the poor ones from rising up and stealing it."[39] You have to work at creating your own values in your own culture.[40]

Morrie has two grown sons: Rob, a journalist in Tokyo, and Jon, a computer expert in Boston. He says, "Whenever people ask me about having children or not having children, I never tell them what to do.... I simply say [that] there is no experience like having children.... If you want the experience of having complete responsibility for another human being, and to learn how to love and bond in the deepest way, then you should have children."[41]

"Aging is not just decay, you know. It's growth. It's more than the negative that you're going to die, it's also the positive that you understand you're going to die, and that you live a better life because of it."[42]

Morrie makes these basic guides known:

- Accept what you are able to do, not what you can't do.
- Accept the past and hang on to whatever traditions you can.

- Learn to forgive yourself for all the things you didn't do and all the things you should have done.
- It's never too late to be involved with life on earth.

The wisdom that Morrie expresses to Mitch does not connect to biblical verses, creeds, parables, or God's will. Instead, four liberating convictions are juxtaposed with Morrie's lessons. These are found in Jack Mendelsohn's book, *Why I Am a Unitarian*:

First, I am life that wills to live in the midst of all life that wills to live.

Second, separating the essential from the nonessential is what I call being spiritual.

Third, power, ethically understood, is the ability to achieve moral purpose.

Finally, to be spiritual is to offer thanks for the privilege of being.

Notes to Tuesdays With Morrie

1. Mitch Albom, *Tuesdays with Morrie* (New York: Broadway Books, 1997), 1.
2. Albom, *Tuesdays with Morrie*, 81.
3. Albom, 36.
4. Albom, 82.
5. Albom, 82.
6. Albom, 21.
7. Albom, 32.
8. Albom, 50.
9. Albom, 51.
10. Albom, 36.
11. Albom, 92.
12. Albom, 157.
13. Albom, 84.
14. Albom, 92.
15. Albom, 125.
16. Albom, 125.
17. Albom, 126.
18. Albom, 128.
19. Albom, 18.

20. Albom, 84.
21. Albom, 40.
22. Albom, 43.
23. Albom, 52.
24. Albom, 91.
25. Albom, 91.
26. Albom, 175.
27. Albom, 178.
28. Albom, 35.
29. Albom, 12.
30. Albom, 50.
31. Albom, 9.
32. Albom, 35-36.
33. Albom, 37.
34. Albom, 64-65.
35. Albom, 124-125.
36. Albom, 126.
37. Albom, 148.
38. Albom, 154.
39. Albom, 156.
40. Albom, 156.
41. Albom, 93.
42. Albom, 118.

PART 3

Reflections on American Society and Politics

The Costs of Giving

Giving is one way to show care for others, but it also has potential costs for the giver and the recipient. First, one risks embarrassment and disappointment if one's gift is rejected, perhaps because the color is wrong, it's too pretentious to wear, or it's the wrong size. Second, a recipient might misunderstand the motives of a giver. I know someone who once gave an expensive ring to a widow friend, and that ended their friendship. Third, one might invest time, energy, thought, or money into creating a gift, only to be unable to actually give it to the intended recipient. Fourth, giving money to charities can hamper one's ability to meet the needs of one's own family. My father gave generously to the Church of the Brethren and to Manchester College in my hometown, but I saw my mother sacrifice to help make ends meet—she sewed our clothes and boarded chickens and labored in a huge garden to provide extra food for the family.

Fifth, some people endanger their own health by donating a kidney or a portion of their liver to someone else. In recent years, it has become more common for people to donate an organ to a total stranger. That is what "altruistic" kidney donors Harold Mintz and Christine Karg-Palreiro did in the early 2000s. Karg-Palreiro said, "Giving a kidney is the coolest thing I've ever done, and if I had a spare, I'd do it again."[1] Similarly, in 2003, Zell Kravinsky, a philanthropist who has given more than $30 million to Ohio State University and the Centers for Disease Control and Prevention, donated a kidney to a total stranger. He later announced that he would consider donating his other kidney, even at the cost of his own life: "What if I was a perfect match for a dying scientist who was the intellectual driving force behind a breakthrough cure for cancer or AIDS or on the brink of unlocking the secrets of cell regeneration?...I'd be a schnook not to give it to him.... He could save millions of lives, and I can't."[2] In another case in 2003, Teddy Mocibob donated 60 percent of his liver to his ailing wife Elena, justifying it by saying, "I would not go through this pain for fun. But what else could I do? I could not just lose her."[3]

In an essay titled "A Modest Proposal to Destroy Western Civilization as We Know It: The $100 Christmas," Bill McKibben brings attention to how giving handmade gifts at Christmas—despite imposing costs on ourselves and the overall economy—can bring more joy to the holiday. McKibben describes going into the woods in his snowshoes, choosing a balsam fir, and bringing it home to decorate with popcorn and cranberries. Then his family makes their Christmas gifts—such as walking sticks, spicy chicken sausage, baked goods, snapshot calendars, and knit scarves—or they provide someone a service, like stacking firewood for an uncle. While this holiday practice is pretty radical because it hurts the consumer spending-driven economy, it reduces environmental harm from production of paper, plastic products, and batteries. McKibben defends his different kind of gift-giving: "We felt cheated by the Christmas we were having—so rushed, so busy, so full of mercantile fantasy and catalog hype.... We wanted more joy [in the season]."[4]

The most enlightening book that I have read on generosity and why it is necessary to give is *Rambam's Ladder*. Author Julie Salamon describes eight different forms of giving, from least to most virtuous, on what she calls the "Ladder of Charity": (1) "to give begrudgingly"; (2) "to give less to the poor than is proper, but to do so cheerfully"; (3) "to hand money to the poor after being asked"; (4) "to hand money to the poor before being asked, but risk making the recipient feel shame"; (5) "to give to someone you don't know, but allow your name to be known"; (6) "to give to someone you know, but who doesn't know from whom he or she is receiving help"; (7) "to give to someone you don't know and to do so anonymously"; and (8) "to hand someone a gift or a loan, or to enter into a partnership with him or her, or to find work for them, so that the individual will never have to beg again."[5]

Salamon admired her parents for their belief in universal humanity. She grew up in one of the poorest counties in Ohio, in a rural town in Appalachia where her father was the only doctor. He never refused a patient who could not afford to pay. As an adult, Salamon moved to Manhattan and now serves as a board member of the Bowery Resident's Senior Center, which offers meals and social services to elderly homeless people. In *Rambam's Ladder*, Salamon recounts the generosity of Paolo Alavian, an Iranian immigrant who owns four restaurants in the Manhattan area, after 9/11. On that fatal day, Alavian's wife called and asked him to take their three-year-old daughter to nursery school. He replied, "No, I'm too busy." Suddenly, his wife began screaming into her cell phone, "Look at this idiot airplane flying very low downtown." Alavian went outside and was transfixed as the Twin Towers collapsed. Immediately, he ran to the dentist's office next door to get face masks to distribute. The next day he invited relief workers to drop into his restaurants for free food. The restaurants served 416 people and donated $76,000 to the 9/11 relief fund. September 11 changed Alavian's perception of himself, his place in the world, and his responsibility to others.

Unfortunately, notes Salamon, major charities such as United Way and the Red Cross have recently been engulfed in scandals. Some nonprofit organizations have paid high salaries to their CEOs while giving relatively little to charity. Salamon claims that when philanthropy becomes big business, often depersonalized, it is stripped of spiritual content and meaning. "Most companies," she writes, "in the name of corporate responsibility, now give money to get something back—improved image, political currency, shareholder goodwill—or to cover the chairman's obligation to cronies."[6] Nevertheless, a few companies make charity the centerpiece of their activities. Newman's Own, founded by Paul Newman, "gives away 100 percent of after-tax profits to charities benefitting affordable housing, the arts, education, and disaster relief."[7]

How does an ordinary person giving a dollar compare to the Bill and Melinda Gates Foundation, which has already given out more than $40 billion to improve health care for the world's poorest children? Where is the profound connection between obligation and fulfillment? Salamon states that to give unbegrudgingly is to be a human being, to be involved in a community. Charity should have its own power and be a catalyst for political action.

In the United States, religious organizations have usually been the biggest recipients of charitable donations; in 2019 they received 29 percent of total giving (mostly from individuals).[8] People also give to others in non-money ways, such as by donating blood, volunteering to supervise after-school sports, taking care of a neighbor's pet, and giving emotional support to parents, grandparents, and friends. "Caring behavior" is motivated from within each individual by a genuine identification with the needs of others. Salamon believes that giving can be a way of involving ourselves in the process of being alive—of making our brains light us with quiet joy. She believes that the highest rung in the "Ladder of Giving" is rooted in a sense of responsibility to help others become self-sufficient, self-confident, and self-motivated.

Giving should not be an afterthought, what nations do to promote their self-interest or repair the damage they've inflicted on people, or what individuals do to calm the guilt resulting from their excesses and indifference. What we give to one another is a measure of our conscientiousness and common humanity.

Notes to The Cost of Giving

1. Stephanie Strom, "Ideas & Trends: Extreme Philanthropy; Giving of Yourself, Literally, to People You've Never Met," *New York Times*, July 27, 2003. https://www.nytimes.com/2003/07/27/weekinreview/ideas-trends-extreme-philanthropy-giving-yourself-literally-people-you-ve-never.html.
2. Stephanie Strom, "An Organ Donor's Generosity Raises the Question of How Much Is Too Much," *New York Times*, August 17, 2003. https://www.nytimes.com/2003/08/17/us/an-organ-donor-s-generosity-raises-the-question-of-how-much-is-too-much.html.
3. Richard Pérez-Peña, "Gift from a Loving Husband: Part of Himself," *New York Times*, August 2, 2003. https://www.nytimes.com/2003/08/02/nyregion/gift-from-a-loving-husband-part-of-himself.html.
4. Bill McKibben, "A Modest Proposal to Destroy Western Civilization as We Know It: The $100 Christmas," *Mother Jones*, November 1, 1997.
5. Julie Salamon, *Rambam's Ladder: A Meditation on Generosity and Why It Is Necessary to Give* (New York: Workman Publishing, 2003).
6. Salamon, *Rambam's Ladder*, 30-32.
7. Salamon, *Rambam's Ladder*, 30.
8. National Philanthropic Trust, "Charitable Giving Statistics," accessed April 3, 2021. https://www.nptrust.org/philanthropic-resources/charitable-giving-statistics/.

Equality in the Declaration of Independence

The Declaration of Independence of 1776 is a political document ostensibly based on equality: "We hold these truths to be self-evident, that all men are created equal, that they are endowed by their Creator with certain inalienable Rights, that among them are Life, Liberty, and the Pursuit of Happiness." That is, political equality equals political empowerment for each human being. God grants human beings equal power on earth. In declaring freedom from the tyranny of Britain, the creators of the Declaration claimed that British Americans were equals of the British.[1] Of course, the signers did not believe in full equality. At the time, only white men with property had equal voting power in the political system, while white women and children, free Black people, Indigenous people, and the enslaved had few rights. And the leaders responsible for composing the Declaration were "reputable" men, not ordinary, equal citizens.

In July 1774, Thomas Jefferson drafted a series of guides for independence from Britain for approval by the First Continental Congress. In the following year, on June 26, 1775, Jefferson was assigned to continue drafting "The Declaration of the Causes and Necessity of Taking Up Arms." He presented this draft to the Committee of Five: Richard Henry Lee, representative of the South; John Adams, representing the North; Benjamin Franklin; Roger Sherman, a Puritan; and Robert Livingston, a lawyer. With revisions, this document was sent to the fifty-five members of the Second Continental

Congress who wrangled and quarreled over its contents. Those who wrote and then signed the Declaration on July 4, 1776, generally believed that democracy was a system that would work for the common good. God was edited in and slavery was edited out in harmony with the philosophy of the time.[2] However, equality of health, happiness, liberty, and education was a sham because many people in society did not have equal power.

In the Declaration of Independence, the American colonists justified their break with Great Britain by stating that it was necessary "to assume among the powers of the earth, the separate and equal station to which the Laws of Nature and of Nature's God entitle them." Southern segregationists later perverted the meaning of the Declaration's phrase "separate *and* equal" when they established the "separate *but* equal" principle.[3] Individual states dictated that many people, such as the enslaved, be segregated and kept in dependency instead of being equal. The dark clouds of inequality hovered over American society for decades when the "separate but equal" principle enforced racial segregation in public services and facilities. But today, drawing on the Declaration's phrase "separate and equal" means stressing freedom from domination but with mutual respect.[4]

According to Danielle Allen, author of *Our Declaration,* it is difficult to reconcile the thought "that Jefferson could write words as powerful as those condemning slavery for his first draft of the Declaration, yet also be a slaveholder."[5] Like many others who helped craft the Declaration, he took actions in his private life that conflicted with some of the principles he enunciated in public life. He eventually removed the words condemning slavery from the final version.

The Declaration of Independence is such a revered document in American history that Americans want to believe it created the foundation for equality. But Stephen M. Caliendo, author of *Inequality in America,* and Joseph E. Stiglitz, Nobel Prize winner in Economic Sciences in 2001 and author of *The Price of Inequality: How Today's Divided Society Endangers Our Future,* contend that inequality in the United States today is incompatible with the nation's founding values of "life, liberty, and the pursuit of happiness" and the belief that "all humans are created equal." In fact, the writers of the Declaration created a system of inequality in which "a small minority has a disproportionate power over the majority."[6] In 1776, wealthy landowners and enslavers codified their economic and political power over the majority of ordinary citizens. "Unequal property leads to unequal political power."[7]

By 2015, the class structure in the United States was comparable to that during the time of the Founding Fathers, in that an upper class used its wealth to consolidate power. Economic inequality today reinforces political inequality, according to the French economist Thomas Piketty in his book *Capital in the Twenty-First Century*.[8] Similarly, Michael Thompson notes, "Any political community that suffers severe [inequality] is in danger of losing its democratic character."[9] Many Americans are evidently unconcerned with growing inequality; it was not a major issue for political candidates in the 2014 congressional elections. According to John Kenneth Galbraith in *The Affluent Society*, concern with inequality as an economic issue was declining even in 1998.[10] He observes that, in the absence of fear, violence, and alarm in society, "inequality is more easily accepted."[11] Notably, many political figures in Congress are millionaires or billionaires, and most are much wealthier than the average American citizen. They often make policy changes and laws that benefit themselves, their elite friends, and their family. Political analyst Allan Ornstein declares that "we are witnessing the rise of a new aristocratic class, based on wealth and power, far worse than the European model our Founding Fathers sought to curtail."[12] Thus, Americans seem to be accepting an oligarchic or a plutocratic form of government. Paul Krugman warned in an op-ed on April 6, 2015 in *The New York Times*, "Elections determine who has the power, not who has the truth."[13]

The dazzling optimism of the Declaration leads people to believe that they have as much power as any other citizen to fight against abusive political leaders and laws that bolster inequality. That is, many Americans assume that a democracy based on equal rights for all produces "good governments," protects the rule of law, and promotes justice, security, peace, and happiness. The creators of the Declaration may have believed in equality for all in principle, but in reality they protected slavery, deracinated Native Americans, and silenced women and children of all races. In an op-ed in *The New York Times* on February 23, 2015, columnist Charles M. Blow states, "'All men are created equal' is an exquisite idea, but one that wasn't fully embraced when the words were written. We, the American people, have pushed this country to consider that clause in the broadest possible interpretation for hundreds of years."[14]

Dedicated to a belief in our Declaration, Americans are committed to the belief in equality. But we have so many inequalities, especially linked to economics. In his book *The Price of Inequality,* Joseph Stiglitz points to a few:

- Inequality in health based on income.
- Inequality of education. (Many children lack access to pre-school. There is a wide gap between test scores of rich and poor students. It costs some $450,000 to put a student through Harvard.)
- Inequality of income. (CEO pay is vastly disproportionate to the minimum wage.)
- Inequality of housing. (The cost of housing in urban areas is out of the reach of ordinary citizens.)
- Inequality in justice. (The ability to protect one's rights in the legal system depends on one's race, gender, and income.)[15]

Stiglitz states that "globalization is surely a contributing factor in the growing inequality."[16] He further says that something is wrong with the moral compass of modern capitalism when some people can, with impunity, skirt the law, shape laws on their behalf, take advantage of others, and play unfairly when necessary.[17] In essence, capitalism promotes winners, some of whom are not very admirable. Americans should be unwilling to accept the status quo, but do we have power to change the landscape? According to Timothy Noah in his book *The Great Divergence,* "The worst thing we can do…is to get used to [inequality]."[18]

Here is some of what Americans have gotten used to:

- "Between 1987 and 2013, the number of billionaires rose from 140 to 1,400."[19]
- In 2014, the top 10 percent of Americans owned 81 percent of all stocks.[20]
- Since 1981, the top 1 percent has increased their incomes by 224 times while the bottom half has increased theirs by 7 percent.[21]
- In 2000, 16,000 families earned 50 percent of all national income.[22]
- In 2009, nearly half of all members of the U.S. Congress were millionaires.[23]

- In 2009, the 400 wealthiest Americans earned $97,000 per hour—double that of 1992—indicating that economic inequality is rising very fast.[24]
- In 2010, only 13 percent of board members at America's top corporations were women.[25]
- In 2014, the top 10 percent of Americans owned 75 percent of the nation's wealth.[26]
- In 2010, the unemployment rate among Black people was twice as high as that among white people.[27]
- In 2015, five million persons of color lived within 1.8 miles of a hazardous waste facility.[28]
- By 2012, the percentage of the U.S. workforce that was unionized had shrunk to 9.3 percent.[29]

Joseph Stiglitz claims that inequality in the United States is higher than in any other advanced industrialized country. "We are now approaching the level of inequality that marks dysfunctional societies," he observes.[30] Whereas the level of inequality stabilized in the United States from 1870 to 1914 and from 1950 to 1970, the financial sector grew faster in the 1980s than in any other period in U.S. history.[31] Greed festers in inequality, and collective action for the common good languishes. When a minority group holds too much power, policies tend not to benefit the majority.[32] When the equality enshrined in the Declaration breaks down, we get an increase in deviant investment behavior, corporate takeovers, distorted tax reform, and poverty. Inequality disempowers workers and weakens their morale. The government also underinvests in education and infrastructure. In this "Second Gilded Age" in the twenty-first century, speculation, instability, and excesses in the financial sector eat away at democracy.[33]

Inequality also erodes Americans' sense of fair play and their belief in equal opportunity. When communities become segregated, they are unable to respect each other as equals. Unsurprisingly, low-paid workers begin to question the work ethic. The middle class invests less in Wall Street and goes deeper into debt. According to Thomas Piketty, "No matter how justified inequalities of wealth may be initially, fortunes can grow and perpetuate themselves beyond all reasonable limits and beyond any possible rational justification in terms of social utility."[34] Furthermore, he writes, "The wealth hierarchy is not just about money; it is also a matter of honor and moral values."[35] According to economist Paul Krugman, in his op-ed in *The New York Times* on February 23, 2015, "As for wages and salaries, never mind college degrees—all the big gains are going to a tiny group of individuals holding strategic positions in corporate suites or astride the crossroads of finance. Rising inequality isn't about who has the knowledge; it's about who has the power."[36]

In early America, "unequal property leads to unequal political power," states Michael Thompson in his book *The Politics of Inequality*.[37] The creators of the Declaration and the Constitution knew that ownership of property enhanced their positions of leadership. The larger the tract of land one owns, the more important one becomes to the society. Enslavers often inherited large tracts of land and held large numbers of people captive as their property. With the benefit of the Constitution's three-fifths compromise, the South wielded great power in Congress for many years. Likewise, those now who own most of the wealth, stocks, and resources of the United States have immense political power. Property owners of today are similar to the property owners at the time the Declaration was signed. "Power follows property."[38]

In my opinion, the problem of inequality is deep. Without a sense of fairness, decay sets in. Democracy is threatened. It becomes hard to ensure the "worth and dignity of each human being." Some in society do not have an equal claim to "life, liberty, and justice." When narrow self-interest denies the majority its equal rights, human selfishness and greed will permeate the power structures of a country.

Individualism is a social theory advocating for the liberty, rights, and independence of an individual who pursues his or her interests rather than the common or collective interests. Benjamin R. Barber assails this theory in an op-ed in *The New York Times* on July 29, 2002: "Within the United States, we foolishly think we possess a private liberty that allows us to work and prosper individually, not together or in conformity with a social contract."[39] Senator Elizabeth Warren substantiates Barber's critique of individualism in a speech she delivered on the campaign trail in 2011: "There is nobody in this country who got rich on their own. Nobody.... You moved your goods to market on roads the rest of us paid for; you hired workers the rest of us paid to educate; you were safe in your factory because of the police forces and the fire forces that the rest of us paid for. You don't have to worry that someone will seize everything in your factory; you built a factory and it turned into something terrific, or a great idea. God bless. Keep a big hunk of it. But part of the underlying social contract is, you take a hunk of that and pay forward for the next kid who comes along."[40]

So, how do we realize the promise of equality?

Thomas Piketty believes that the level of inequality in the United States is moving higher than in any other society at this time, anywhere in the world.[41] To reverse this trend, he advocates for much higher taxation of capital. A capital tax would promote financial transparency by clarifying who owns what assets,[42] and it would be more progressive than a tax on income.[43]

Timothy Noah believes that Americans can increase equality if they do the following: levy higher taxes on corporations; tax capital income; decrease government bureaucracy; provide preschool education to every child; impose price controls on colleges and universities; reregulate Wall Street; limit the action of banks; and revive the labor movement so that businesses can no longer "treat their least powerful employees as poorly as they can get away with."[44]

As an important part of the American heritage, the Declaration of Independence will continue to shape our conception of equality. Equality inspires a commitment to serving others.

Notes to Equality in the Declaration of Independence

1. Danielle Allen, *Our Declaration: A Reading of the Declaration of Independence in Defense of Equality* (New York: Liveright Publishing, 2014), 119.
2. Allen, *Our Declaration*, 75.
3. Allen, 124.
4. Allen, 124.
5. Allen, 156.
6. Stephen M. Caliendo, *Inequality in America: Race, Poverty, and Fulfilling America's Promise* (Boulder, CO: Westview Press, 2015), 19.
7. Michael J. Thompson, *The Politics of Inequality: A Political History of the Idea of Economic Inequality in America* (New York: Columbia University Press, 2007), xiv.

8. Thomas Piketty, *Capital in the Twenty-First Century*, trans. Arthur Goldhammer (Cambridge, MA: The Belknap Press of Harvard University Press, 2014), 20.
9. Thompson, *The Politics of Inequality*, 4.
10. John Kenneth Galbraith, *The Affluent Society* (Boston: Houghton Mifflin Co., 1998), 68.
11. Galbraith, *The Affluent Society*, 71.
12. Allan Ornstein, *Class Counts: Education, Inequality, and the Shrinking Middle Class* (Lanham, MD: Rowman & Littlefield, 2007), 150.
13. Paul Krugman, "Economics and Elections," *New York Times*, April 6, 2015.
14. Charles M. Blow, "Who Loves America?" *New York Times*, February 23, 2015.
15. Joseph E. Stiglitz, *The Price of Inequality: How Today's Divided Society Endangers Our Future* (New York: W. W. Norton and Co., 2013), 104-222.
16. Stiglitz, *Price of Inequality*, 80.
17. Stiglitz, *Price of Inequality*, 46-47.
18. Timothy Noah, *The Great Divergence: America's Growing Inequality Crisis and What We Can Do about It* (New York: Bloomsbury Press, 2012), 195.
19. Piketty, *Capital*, 433.
20. Noah, *Great Divergence*, 177.
21. Caliendo, *Inequality in America*, 41.
22. Piketty, *Capital*, 23.
23. Caliendo, *Inequality in America*, 206n.
24. Stiglitz, *Price of Inequality*, xi.
25. Caliendo, *Inequality in America*, 42.
26. Paul Krugman, "Our Invisible Rich," *New York Times*, September 29, 2014.
27. Caliendo, *Inequality in America*, 125.
28. Caliendo, *Inequality in America*, 130.
29. David Cay Johnston, *Divided: The Perils of Our Growing Inequality* (New York: The New Press, 2014), 248.
30. Stiglitz, *The Price of Inequality*, 27.
31. Piketty, *Capital*, 231.
32. Stiglitz, *Price of Inequality*, 104.
33. Stiglitz, *Price of Inequality*, xxxiii.
34. Piketty, *Capital*, 443.
35. Piketty, *Capital*, 509.

36. Paul Krugman, "Knowledge Isn't Power," *New York Times*, February 23, 2015.
37. Thompson, *Politics of Inequality*, 26.
38. Thompson, *The Politics of Inequality*, 74.
39. Benjamin Barber, "A Failure of Democracy, Not Capitalism," *New York Times*, July 29, 2002.
40. Elizabeth Warren, *A Fighting Chance* (New York: Metropolitan Books, 2014), 215.
41. Piketty, *Capital*, 265.
42. Piketty, 518.
43. Piketty, 532.
44. Noah, *Great Divergence*, 189.

Forgotten Souls

Even before the Covid-19 pandemic, "forgotten souls" living in small-town America and Rust Belt cities were fighting for their dignity. In Hunts Point, New York, 40 percent of the residents live below the poverty level. In Portsmouth, Ohio, most of its once-thriving industries are gone and opioid abuse is widespread. In Prestonsburg, Kentucky, a poor white community of 3,500, there are many churches but few jobs. Black people struggle to find good schools, homes, and jobs. In Bakersfield, California (the city whose "Okies" John Steinbeck depicted in *The Grapes of Wrath*), a high percentage of residents do not have a college degree. The city of Gary, Indiana is filled with rusted factories, empty lots, and abandoned buildings. These crumbling towns and cities are in crisis, facing unemployment, broken homes, pain, drugs, humiliation, and anger.

In his 2019 book *Dignity*, Chris Arnade writes about the people he met in these cities and towns and other parts of "back-row America." Many of the "forgotten souls" he interviewed—often in drug houses and McDonald's restaurants—wanted to talk to someone "who wasn't trying to save them, didn't scold them, and didn't judge them."[1] Facing problems seemingly too big to solve, many individuals turn to drugs, alcohol, or suicide to ease the pain. According to Arnade, "We pretend that the addicted take drugs because of bad character, not because it's one of the few good ways they have to dull the pain of not being able to live good lives on the economy we've created for them."[2]

In the 1940s, people with only a high school education could find jobs in factories and build a life with health care, a pension, and a decent, stable salary. But presently, the path to a decent job and a middle-class standard of living is not available for many people. According to political philosopher Michael Sandel, today's educated, credentialed elites devalue the contributions of those without colleges degrees.[3] There is less chance today than in previous decades that if you work hard, your dignity and social esteem will rise.

Arnade provides glimpses of the forgotten people he met, including the following:

- James, who grew up in Portsmouth, Ohio, started drinking as a teenager, then started abusing heroin and prescription opioids. Since being evicted from their home, he and his family have lived in a shed behind the house of a friend. When Arnade met James, he was pushing a shopping cart with his kids, collecting cans and bottles to sell. His wife was standing along the roadside with a sign, "Homeless Hungry Anything Helps."[4]
- Jen was carrying a one-year-old in her arms when Arnade met her in Portsmouth, Ohio. Her mother was an addict with mental illness. At age fourteen Jen ran away from home to avoid abuse and was placed in a foster home. She has had seven children, only three of whom are still alive. By age twenty-four she began using Vicodin and heroin, and eventually she fell into sex work.[5]
- In Youngstown, Ohio, Bruce was dragged into drugs while his friends went off to college. While serving three years in prison for burglary, he found religion and got sober. He said, "Islam saved my life."[6]
- Beauty, a young woman from Oklahoma who was born in a prison hospital, started street sex work at the age of sixteen. She ended up in Hunts Point, New York, where she was controlled by a series of pimps who beat her and cheated her. She smoked "strawberry smack," satisfied homeless boyfriends, and served five months at Rikers Island prison.[7]
- Takeesha, a forty-seven-year-old homeless woman whom Arnade met in Hunts Point, was sexually abused in foster care and began using heroin at age thirteen, when she also had her first baby. Asked to describe herself, Takeesha said, "I am a prostitute, a mother of six, and a child of God."[8]

After three years of listening to stories of addiction, poverty, and pain in small towns and blighted cities in America after the election of Donald Trump, Arnade asks, "What are the solutions? What can we do differently, beyond yell at one another? I don't know.... We all need to listen to each other more."[9] National problems and differences were so big, so structural, and so deep in 2020 that legislation and policy could not offer solutions. Some of the people Arnade met found it hard to leave their oppressive hometown, partly because they would lose connections with friends, family, and the community. Lives are messy and complicated. But Arnade also discovered warm, welcoming communities in which people are helping each other. He was amazed "how resilient people can be, how a community can thrive anywhere even amid pain and poverty."[10] He stresses that those whom we have forgotten also value community, happiness, friendship, pride, and dignity.

"Those of us in the front row," writes Arnade, "have a special obligation to listen because we presently are the in-group."[11] "We are the ones who get paid well in money and status because we claim to know what is best. We are the ones who asked to be in control.... We moved from our hometown to have a larger voice in shaping our country. Have we fixed the ugly racism, sexism, and inequality?"[12] Similarly, *The New York Times* columnist Thomas Friedman argues that we need to understand the sense of hardship and humiliation that many Americans feel: "The poverty of dignity explains so much more behavior than the poverty of money."[13] And Michael Sandel provides a penetrating reminder to meritocratic elites in the United States who have disdain for and prejudice against those who are less educated: "Appreciating the role of luck in life can prompt a certain humility: There, but for an accident of birth, or the grace of God, or the mystery of fate, go I. This spirit of humility is the civic virtue we need now. It is the beginning of the way back from the harsh ethic of success that drives us apart."[14]

Notes to Forgotten Souls

1. Chris Arnade, *Dignity: Seeking Respect in Back Row America* (New York: Sentinel, 2019), 16.
2. Arnade, *Dignity,* 17.
3. Michael J. Sandel, "The Consequences of the Diploma Divide," *New York Times,* September 5, 2020.
4. Arnade, *Dignity,* 43.
5. Arnade, 49.
6. Arnade, 113.
7. Arnade, 88-90.
8. Arnade, 7.
9. Arnade, 282.
10. Arnade, 7.
11. Arnade, 283.
12. Arnade, 283.
13. Thomas L. Friedman, "Who Can Win America's Politics of Humiliation?" *New York Times,* September 9, 2020.
14. Sandel, "The Consequences."

Individualism and Others

Benjamin Franklin uttered the phrase "God helps those who help themselves," yet 75 percent of Americans believe that the phrase comes from the Bible. This uber-American idea of divinely blessed individualism, "a notion at the core of our current individualist politics and culture," is counter-biblical.[1] Few ideas could be further from the message to love one's neighbor as oneself. Those who help themselves to whatever is available—money, property, land, advantage, privilege—inaugurate selfishness and greed. Instead, individuals should seek to feed the hungry, quench the thirsty, clothe the naked, welcome the stranger, and visit the prisoners of fate.

"The judgment of who is deserving [or who needs it]—as opposed to what is more effective is at the heart a moral one," states Patricia Cohen in a news analysis in *The New York Times* on May 8, 2017.[2] Ben Carson, the housing secretary of the Trump administration, commented in May 2017, while touring publicly subsidized housing in Columbus, Ohio, "We are talking about incentivizing those who help themselves."[3] That is, he stressed the need to distinguish between "the really needy" and those "too indolent to help themselves."[4]

How well do Americans help themselves? UNICEF reports that the United States ranks 36th of the 41 wealthy nations in childhood poverty. In 2018, 16 percent of all American children lived in poverty.[5] The United States comes in nearly last among rich countries in measures of childhood nutrition, infant mortality, and access to preschool.[6] The United States has a high infant mortality rate, although, according to the Centers for Disease Control and Prevention, it declined from a rate of 6.75 infant deaths for every 1,000 live births in 2007 to 5.79 per 1,000 in 2017. The United States Department of Agriculture reported that "the number of households that were 'food insecure with hunger'" rose more than 26 percent from 1999 to 2003.[7] Incidentally, according to Bill McKibben, America is the most violent rich nation on the earth with a murder rate four or five times that of our European peers.[8] We are the only Western democracy that still sanctions capital punishment. Half of our marriages end in divorce. McKibben highlights the disconnect between a claim to be a Christian nation and a reality for Americans that doesn't look very Christian.

Furthermore, how do Americans help themselves concerning climate change? In an article in *The New York Times* on April 23, 2017, titled "The Planet Doesn't Have Time for This," environmentalist Bill McKibben warns the United States that "we have only a short window to deal with the climate crisis or else forever lose the chance to thwart truly catastrophic heating.... The species that go extinct as a result of the warming won't mostly die in the next four years, but they will die.... We're right now breaking the back of the climate system."[9]

How do Americans help themselves spiritually? The American society is the "most spiritually homogenous rich nation on earth," according to Laurie Goodstein, a former national religion correspondent for *The New York Times* in an article in 2012.[10] Yet, a study by the Pew Forum on Religion and Public Life found that white Protestants have steadily been leaving churches for the last forty years. Whereas 7 percent of American adults claimed no religion forty years ago, in 2012, 15 percent made that claim. One in five are atheists, agnostic, or "nothing." One-third of young people in the United States are unaffiliated with a church. Nevertheless, the unaffiliated young still "run the soup kitchens and they build the houses for Habitat for Humanity," according to a New Jersey pastor.[11] Many Millennials visualize an alternative creed for serving others.

McKibben notices many megachurches preaching a new creed that matches the culture of "God helps those who help themselves." Pastors focus relentlessly on you and your needs: Your self-improvement, your self-esteem, your self-confidence, your self-obsession with oneself. These self-help issues thrive in sermons about "how to discipline your children, how to reach your professional goals, how to invest your money, how to reduce your debt."[12] *Publishers Weekly* even characterized one megachurch pastor's book as "a treatise in how to get God to serve the demands of self-centered individuals."[13] Yes, indeed, humans need to take care of themselves, be responsible, and survive. Authors of these "how to" books present perfectly sensible advice, but they may be ignoring the need to focus on *others*. When the fixation with self-improvement and self-esteem infuses our culture, Americans forget the spiritual references that make sense for a progressive world in which we think of *others*. We are losing the vital cultural belief that "you shall love your neighbor as yourself."[14] Such a radical notion to love the poor person, the sick person, the naked person, the hungry person is "a call for nothing less than a radical, voluntary, and effective reordering of power relationships, based on the principle of love."[15] We should love the neighbor in the next pew; love the neighbor far away; love the one who is in poverty or weakened by hurricanes; visit people hospitalized; give counsel to grieving souls. We need to make our human connections to others visibly important. Instead of following the conservative, individualistic, Ayn Randian notion of taking "responsibility" simply for ourselves, we must collectively take responsibility for ensuring that *others* have Social Security and health insurance. We need to push back against the notion that "God only helps those who help themselves."

Consider Alabama, where 90 percent of the population in 2002 identified as "Christian." Under the state's regressive tax code in 2002, the wealthy paid 3 percent of their income in state and local taxes but the poorest Alabamians paid 12 percent.[16] The governor proposed a tax hike to increase funding for the state's school system. He argued that it was the Christian duty to look after the poor more carefully. However, in 2003, 68 percent of the population of the state voted against the tax hike.[17] "The opposition was led...by the state's wealthiest interests but also by the Christian Coalition of Alabama."[18] The president of the coalition argued that taxing the rich at a higher rate than the poor "results in punishing success.... When an individual works for their income, that money belongs to the individual."[19] Claiming that individual income is totally one's own to keep is essentially asserting that citizens are not required to share wealth through taxation for the common good of an entire society.

How do individual Americans fulfill their social contract? In an op-ed entitled "The Social Contract" in *The New York Times*, economist Paul Krugman states that people who assume they are exempt from the social contract that applies to everyone paying their fair share are selfish.[20] He also notes that for taxing purposes in the United States, inherited and invested wealth are valued higher than wages and salaries. Six out of the ten wealthiest Americans have inherited their wealth rather than being entrepreneurs. Eighty percent of households in the United States have income solely from wages and salaries. Finally, Krugman believes that the affluent, on average, are less likely to exhibit empathy toward the interests of the poor.[21] Indeed, the rich cling to the individualistic idea that "God helps those who help themselves."

The novelist-philosopher Ayn Rand, who has unfortunately had significant influence in American politics and business, espoused a radical version of individualism. President Trump named Rand his favorite writer and *The Fountainhead* his favorite novel. Secretary of State Rex Tillerson has cited *Atlas Shrugged* as a favorite work.[22] "In business, Rand's influence has been especially pronounced in Silicon Valley where her overarching philosophy [is] 'that man exists for his own sake, that the pursuit of his own happiness is his highest moral purpose, that he must not sacrifice himself to others, nor sacrifice others to himself.'"[23]

Given our current desires as consumers, it is hard to depart from selfishness in American culture. However, many people still manage to invest in worthy causes. Locally, many participants in civic life support preservation of parks, the environment, and social services, volunteer for Meals on Wheels or soup kitchens, defend the ethical treatment of animals, and support local businesses. "When Americans hunger for selfless love, [but] are fed only love of self, they become hungry."[24]

David Brooks, a columnist for *The New York Times,* writes that when self-obsession occurs, it fosters narrowness, prejudice, and moral arrogance; it closes off "the dynamic creativity of a living faith."[25] We need to immerse ourselves more deeply into friendships with diverse individuals with different believers and atheists, liberals and conservatives. We need to tolerate differences among us. Accepting this mysterious truth about humans, we are bound in love of ourselves *and* of others.

Notes to Individualism and Others

1. Bill McKibben, "The Christian Paradox: How a Faithful Nation Gets Jesus Wrong," *Harper's Magazine*, August 2005.
2. Patricia Cohen, "On Health and Welfare, Moral Arguments Can Outweigh Economics," *New York Times*, May 8, 2017.
3. Cohen, "On Health."
4. Cohen, "On Health."
5. Children's Defense Fund, *The State of America's Children 2020* (Washington, DC: Children's Defense Fund, 2020). https://www.childrensdefense.org/wp-content/uploads/2020/02/The-State-Of-Americas-Children-2020.pdf.
6. McKibben, "The Christian Paradox."
7. McKibben, "The Christian Paradox."
8. McKibben, "The Christian Paradox."
9. Bill McKibben, "The Planet Doesn't Have Time for This," *New York Times Sunday Review*, April 23, 2017.
10. Laurie Goodstein, "Study Finds That the Number of Protestant Americans Is in Steep Decline," *New York Times*, October 10, 2012.
11. Goodstein, "Study Finds."
12. McKibben, "The Christian Paradox."
13. McKibben, "The Christian Paradox."
14. McKibben, "The Christian Paradox."
15. McKibben, "The Christian Paradox."
16. McKibben, "The Christian Paradox."
17. McKibben, "The Christian Paradox."
18. McKibben, "The Christian Paradox."
19. McKibben, "The Christian Paradox."
20. Paul Krugman, "The Social Contract," *New York Times*, September 23, 2011.
21. Paul Krugman, "Privilege, Pathology, and Power," *New York Times*, January 1, 2016.
22. James B. Stewart, "Tough Times for Disciples of Ayn Rand," *New York Times*, July 14, 2017.
23. Stewart, "Tough Times."
24. McKibben, "The Christian Paradox."
25. David Brooks, "The Benedict Option," *New York Times*, March 14, 2017.

Integration

In the article "Skin Deep" in *National Geographic*'s April 2018 special issue on race, Elizabeth Kolbert provides an account of Samuel Morton, a prominent scientist of the first half of the nineteenth century who propounded a theory that people can be divided into five races according to the shape of their skulls and "distinct characteristics."[1] Each of the races in the "divinely determined hierarchy" supposedly corresponded to a separate act of creation.[2] Whites (Caucasians) were "the most intelligent of the races." One step down were East Asians (Mongolians)— "ingenious" creatures "susceptible of cultivation." In third place were Southeast Asians. Native Americans came fourth, and at the bottom of the hierarchy were Blacks (Ethiopians) destined for slavery.[3] Unfortunately, writes Kolbert, "We still live in Morton's legacy: Racial distinctions continue to shape our politics, our neighborhoods, and our sense of self."[4] Nevertheless, says biotechnologist Craig Venter, with our modern understanding of DNA we must conclude that "the concept of race has no genetic or scientific basis."[5] Race is a "human construction" of different groups.[6]

In fact, homo sapiens emerged in Africa and then dispersed throughout the continents, undergoing genetic mutations over the centuries. For example, at high altitudes oxygen is scarce, so mutations among people in the Ethiopian highlands helped them cope with the rarified air.[7] As migrants dispersed they reached Australia 50,000 years ago; they settled in Siberia 45,000 years ago; 15,000 years ago they reached South America. Assuredly, we need "new ways of thinking about human diversity."[8] If we want integration, it would help to recognize that humans all started out in the same form.

In an op-ed titled "Integration Now or Forever" in *The New York Times* on March 30, 2018, David Brooks points to a study revealing that "three-quarters of American whites have no close nonwhite friends."[9] Of course, "many people support racial integration in the abstract but don't want to do the things integration would require. Some see integration as a sentimental notion not connected to immediate concern. Others have accepted the idea that birds of a feather flock together and always will."[10] Therefore, we have become "a racially divided nation," complacent about the way it is. Brooks believes that "racism is America's great sin, and if this isn't given continual progress to combat it, the nation becomes ugly to itself."[11] Progress toward integration is a moral necessity.

Historically, Americans have been segregated in their cities, schools, marriages, and churches, but Brooks sees some encouraging signs of change. "American neighborhoods have become steadily more integrated. Northern and Midwestern cities like Milwaukee and New York are still very segregated but Southern and Western cities like Atlanta; Louisville, Kentucky; Dallas; and Las Vegas have made strides."[12] He notes that "racial integration in schools does produce better student outcomes."[13] Although in 1967 only 3 percent of Americans married outside their race or ethnicity, by 2018, 17 percent did. In the past, Sunday morning was the most segregated hour in America, but today one in five churchgoers is in an integrated congregation.[14] Finally, how many of us are part of an organization that lets us meet once a week with people who are different from those in our own group?

I live a segregated life in a neighborhood in the northwest section of Delaware, Ohio, where very few Black families live. (A Black family lived in the house next to us for two years. The father was a Provost at Ohio Wesleyan University. Unfortunately, they built a high row of hedges between their property and ours, and we chatted only intermittently.) Children don't walk down my street to attend elementary school; only occasionally do a few nonwhite high school students walk past my house. In fact, at this time I don't have a single Black friend. I have Black acquaintances at the local Democratic Party headquarters where I volunteer as a secretary, but I never invite them for lunch, dinner, or a visit. Furthermore, no Black people attend worship services at the Delaware Unitarian Universalist Fellowship that I belong to. I don't know of any Black-owned businesses in downtown Delaware as of 2020. For over thirty years, the city had a shoe repair shop whose Black owner gave excellent service, but the shop is now gone. In fact, the Black population in Delaware has decreased over the years.

In essence, over the sixty years I have lived in Delaware, the only Black people I have known well have been three African American women. Ms. Alfreda Bonner facilitated a bus service that my husband and I used to attend opera performances in Cincinnati. Mrs. Randolph befriended our family and ironed for me and provided other help during the ten years when I had four children. She even gave us meals. The other dear person, Louise James, provided domestic help for me, but she also shined sunlight on our whole family. Louise was a devoted friend until her death. I visited with her four children. I wrote a short biography of her. Since Louise passed away, I have had no other meaningful relationships with Black people in my community.

The responsibility for the lack of interracial relationships lies with me. If this issue is important to me, I need to initiate friendships through social avenues in my community, joining interracial activities at the Unity Community Center, volunteering for work duties in the Center, mentoring individuals, and encouraging diversity in housing in the northwest section of Delaware where I live. Therefore, I have taken some small steps. In the spring of 2018, I twice attended Sunday worship service at the Zion African Methodist Episcopal Church on Washington Street in Delaware. On one occasion I had lunch after the service with members of this church. I found a friendly atmosphere, accompanied with warmth, a hug, and cordial words. Soon after I registered to tutor at the Center, which is a block away from the church. As a volunteer, I tutored a Black student during the year of the pandemic. During this opportunity to tutor, I had many chances to interact with a racially diverse group of personnel. In addition to these contacts, a friend and I attended an interracial Christmas dinner for residents of homes built by Habitat for Humanity. Though these small steps might not make a big difference, I have begun to make friends. I find myself seeking change.

I have had the opportunity to know well a number of young people from different parts of the world. In the mid-1970s my family and I hosted for a year an AFS high school student, Marcos, from Brazil; we also boarded Ohio Wesleyan University students in our home from Jordan, Japan, Tunisia, The Netherlands, and Pakistan. I taught English as a Second Language at Ohio Wesleyan University and Ohio Dominican College, so I interacted with many students of color. However, I have never participated in a civil rights march or a protest against racial injustice in the United States.

Notes to Integration

1. Elizabeth Kolbert, "Skin Deep," *The Race Issue,* special issue of *National Geographic,* April 2018, 30.
2. Kolbert, "Skin Deep," 30.
3. Kolbert, 30.
4. Kolbert, 31.
5. Kolbert, 31.
6. Kolbert, 41.
7. Kolbert, 35.
8. Kolbert, 41.
9. David Brooks, "Integration Now and Forever," *New York Times,* March 30, 2018.
10. Brooks, "Integration Now."
11. Brooks, "Integration Now."
12. Brooks, "Integration Now."
13. Brooks, "Integration Now."
14. Brooks, "Integration Now."

Intolerance

The winds of intolerance sweep over every individual at some point in his or her life. Trying to be tolerant, an individual may tolerate or endure pain and anger. He or she may tolerate the ideas, opinions, and practices of others that are different from one's own. With a liberal, undogmatic viewpoint, we should be able to resist animosity toward others. But in some circumstances, intolerance supersedes our congenial intentions to be tolerant. An unwillingness to accept, respect, or endure what seems abnormal, insensitive, disrespectful, bigoted, unreasonable, or racist hinders tolerance to listen. Each of us can show intolerance internally. Whether or not one actively resists the ugly ideas and practices of others depends on one's conscience, the energy to fight, the available resources, the money to litigate an issue, and the constraints of loyalty, the law, and political affiliations. However, many ordinary individuals have activated their intolerance of injustices simply by being activists or refusing to tolerate situations harming human beings. When intolerable situations arise in the course of time affecting human beings, change must be made if at all possible.

There are numerous examples in American history when citizens decided to no longer abide in some terrible situations, policies, or ideas. Intolerance of polio, which marred the lives of thousands of children, pushed scientists to conduct research for a vaccine that would eliminate this disease. When the Great Depression paralyzed the economy, we ultimately could not tolerate the conditions depriving citizens of their right to secure a livelihood. The government massively expanded its role in the economy to reverse the social devastation, despite conservative resistance. During the McCarthy era, with its Red Scare and accusations against many citizens, people like Senator Ralph Flanders of Vermont and Senator Prescott Bush of Connecticut denounced McCarthyism and worked to end the campaign against freedom of thought.

Rosa Parks, a seamstress at a Montgomery Fair department store, refused to give up her seat to a white passenger in a bus on December 1, 1955. She would no longer countenance unequal rights under the law. Women long denied their rights changed the horizon in the suffrage movement that created the Nineteenth Amendment: "The right of citizens of the Unites States to vote shall not be denied or abridged in the United States or by any state on account of sex." After the Civil War, the passage of the Fourteenth Amendment in 1868 gave former slaves birthright citizenship and equal rights under the Constitution. Also, the Fifteenth Amendment granted voting rights to African American men in 1870. But tolerance of the KKK continued; Jim Crow laws came into effect in 1890; a separate but equal principle was established in 1896; and school segregation laws appeared in 1954. Not until the Civil Rights Act was signed in 1964 did we firmly establish our intolerance of these kinds of practices in national legislation.

In *The Soul of America,* Jon Meacham writes, "The best of the American soul envisions a creed of love, grace, godliness, and generosity versus racism, hatred, fear, and cruelty."[1] "The soul is the vital center, the core, the heart, the essence of life."[2] Presidents have the responsibility to open up the soul of citizens. "Leadership is the art of the possible, [whether] generosity can triumph over selfishness in the American soul."[3] "The better presidents do not cater to such forces [as mobs]; they conquer them with a breath of vision that speaks to the best of our soul."[4] Article II, Section 3 of the American Constitution states that the president "shall take Care that the Laws be faithfully executed." Laws become the avenue to the soul of America.

Meacham believes that the soul of America has survived many crises, and it will survive the crisis we face today, too. The American soul is more than the American Creed. "There is a significant difference between professing adherence to a set of beliefs [liberty, freedom, equality] and acting upon them [as Martin Luther King Jr. did]. The war between the ideal [honesty, truth, justice] and the real [fraud, corruption, lies], between what's right and what's convenient, between the larger good and personal interest is the contest that unfolds in the soul of every American.... Our fate is contingent upon which element—that of hope or that of fear—emerges triumphant."[5]

Meacham compares the present national struggle with the past national struggle under the leadership of President Lincoln. "Lincoln, who gave us the image of our better angels..., was a president who understood people, and when it came time to make decisions, he was willing to take the responsibility and make those decisions no matter how difficult they were."[6] Such an example of a principled president stands in stark contrast to the character of the current president—Donald Trump. "A president's vices and his virtues matter."[7] According to many Americans, not since 1861 has the American soul been so damaged by the undermining of our democracy and the rule of law.

If "we are determined to take our country back,"[8] Meacham urges us to personally engage in these ways:

- ENTER THE ARENA to become "a political addict hooked on every twist and every turn, and every tweet."[9] Pay attention, express your opinion, and cast your ballot. In other words, live up to the obligations of citizenship in a republic.
- RESIST TRIBALISM by following the advice of Eleanor Roosevelt: "It is not only important but mentally invigorating to discuss political matters with people whose opinions differ radically from our own."[10]
- RESPECT FACTS and DEPLOY REASON so that you don't reflexively support only "one side or the other without weighing the merits of a given issue."[11]
- FIND A CRITICAL BALANCE in thoughts. In 1789 Thomas Jefferson wrote, "Wherever the people are well informed, they can be trusted with their own government.... Whenever things get so far wrong as to attract their notice, they may be relied on to set them to rights."[12] Meacham contends, "To announce that there must be no criticism of the president, right or wrong, is not only unpatriotic and servile, but is morally treasonable to the American public."[13]
- KEEP HISTORY in MIND as a frame of reference. In the 1880s, the English jurist and historian James Bryce warned us of a president who "might be a tyrant, not against the masses, but with

> the masses."[14] In his Gettysburg Address, Lincoln stated that the survival of a Union was worth "blood and toil and treasure."[15] No struggle seemed more important, and none nobler in the human cause than a battle to save the Union.

Seemingly, many people believe struggling to change or save an endangered, democratic nation is imperative. Intolerance of a dangerous administration "cannot adequately address and measure what's gone wrong with the American soul and what we can do about it."[16] Meacham fails the reader by giving too much assurance that we have survived worse times than these, so we can survive this crisis unscathed, no matter how damaged our institutions have become. To convey the profound depth of the crisis in which we are embroiled, we must deliver change through the enforcement of laws, a sympathetic Congress, and the will of the people. U.S. Representative Elijah Cummings stated this point emphatically in August 2018: "We are in a fight for the soul of our democracy."[17]

Intolerance may lead us to "enter the arena" of change even here in Delaware, Ohio. Change can come by writing letters to the editor of a newspaper; by voicing our opinions on radio, television, and social media; by addressing postcards for a candidate (recently, twenty people one evening wrote a message and addressed 600 postcards on behalf of a candidate); by canvassing in neighborhoods; by sponsoring a home gathering to discuss issues; by attending rallies and marching for a cause; and by supporting the work of organizations with which we agree. Intolerance of a president's administration may be the gravity to pull the American soul toward change.

Hope becomes our creed. "The United States, through its sporadic adherence to its finest aspirations, is the most durable experiment in pluralistic republicanism the world has known."[18] The American ideal is inclusiveness. In this, "our best instincts will carry the day against our worst."[19] Meacham states that in the twenty-first century, the United States is "freer and more accepting than it has ever been."[20] Americans can learn from the past "that perfect should not be the enemy of good. That compromise is the oxygen of democracy."[21] That hope must bring us to the moral utility of history. Harry Truman once observed, "The country has to awaken every now and then to the fact that the people are responsible for the government they get.... And when they elect a man in the presidency who does not take care of the job, they've got nobody to blame but themselves."[22]

Notes to Intolerance

1. Jon Meacham, *The Soul of America: The Battle for Our Better Angels* (New York: Random House, 2018), 237.
2. Meacham, *The Soul of America*, 7.
3. Meacham, 258.
4. Meacham, 260.
5. Meacham, 7.
6. Meacham, 271.
7. Meacham, 258.
8. Meacham, 5.
9. Meacham, 266.
10. Meacham, 267.
11. Meacham, 268.
12. Meacham, 269.
13. Meacham, 269.
14. Meacham, 271.
15. Meacham, 272.
16. Sean Wilentz, "Hard Times," review of *The Soul of America: The Battle for Our Better Angels*, by Jon Meacham, *New York Times Book Review*, June 10, 2018.
17. Michelle Goldberg, "The End of Impunity," *New York Times*, August 8, 2019.
18. Meacham, *The Soul of America*, 258.
19. Meacham, 258.
20. Meacham, 258.
21. Meacham, 259.
22. Meacham, 265.

Millennials

Millennials "are bringing a new ideology that Americans have not seen in this country for a long time: a dynamic and refreshing form of good ol' fashioned American pragmatism."[1] "It's a powerful theory that describes how we create truth in our lives and how we should act."[2] Any attempt to box all seventy-eight million Millennials into one category is impossible; they have a wide variety of behaviors and cognitive patterns that defy stereotyping.[3] In general, however, they are America's "most stubborn optimists" with an "unshaken confidence" that they can change America and the world.[4] But this new generation is not flawless.

According to Elizabeth Olson in *The New York Times* article "Write Grandma a What?" published on March 16, 2006, today's young people may never again in their lives put pen to paper to write a personal letter. It simply takes too much time in their fast-paced lives. Economically, printed greeting cards and stationery are a dwindling business. Although traditional hand-written letters make individuals take time to think deeply about what they want to say, how they want to say it, and what impact their letters could have on the people receiving them, Millennials keep in touch with family and friends quickly and easily through email, Twitter, Facebook, texting, and cell phones. Ninety percent of Millennials are social media users.[5] Technology lets them send personal messages with the magical touch of their fingers. They look to Google, "Internet experts," blogs, apps, Alexa, and Siri for answers to any questions they may have. They feel empowered with digital media, even though it is filled with information from unverified and unreliable sources. For example, in his op-ed column titled "Social Media:

Destroyer or Creator?" in *The New York Times* on February 3, 2016, Thomas Friedman warns about the dangers of social media. First, people tend to believe social media rumors that confirm their biases. Second, people gravitate to opinions consistent with their own views and block out contradictory opinions. Third, "Because of the speed and brevity of social media, we are forced to jump to conclusions and write sharp opinions in one hundred forty characters about complex world affairs." And finally, people using social media tend to talk "at each other instead of talking with each other." Undoubtedly, however, technological savvy has immeasurably changed the culture for Millennials.

Millennials never knew a world without technology or the media to empower them. They have been so steeped in digital technology that some critics believe they do not have polished communicative skills. First, they are constantly texting and checking their Facebook entries instead of having fact-to-face conversations requiring instant responses. Furthermore, in their online communications they are prone not to filter what they write.[6] They speak their minds more freely. Self-expression is one of their highest values. Secondly, the digitally wired Millennials write abbreviated and misspelled words for speed and efficiency, but their messages can lack clarity and be misunderstood. Effective writing is clear and direct. The text of any message must master the depth of the material being presented and not meander aimlessly searching for the point.[7] Clear writing delivers the nuance and impact and understanding of a message that is necessary in the workplace. Millennials also need clear messages for social and community solidarity if they want to change the world. The fact is, many Millennials think quick access to information is everything, but they need more context and explanation in a digital communicative world.

Morley Winograd and Michael Hais interviewed a member of Generation X (someone born between 1965 and 1981) who said, "I work with several Millennials and they are difficult. They lack the basic communication skills necessary for face-to-face interaction and often cannot write a complete sentence. They have a hard time accepting that they might be wrong about anything and have little regard for the experience and expertise of others. The narcissism of this group is unbelievable."[8] This narcissistic attitude and the lack of respect for others can create tensions in the workplace between experienced workers and novice workers. Millennials are confident and capable individuals who want to contribute ideas and make changes, which can make them seem arrogant.[9] As the most educated generation in American history, they are impatient to use their talents to create a more moral world. Eighty-five percent of Millennials in one study "resented their unused potential" and believed that "they can do anything" if their talent is recognized.[10] However, Millennials are not cognizant of the fact that experienced workers have known many hardships and failures. Furthermore, Millennials did not experience the suffering of the Great Depression; however, they did experience the effects of the Great Recession of 2007-2009. Critics say that Millennials are a generation of "self-important, entitled, indecisive individuals."[11] Winograd and Hais quote Glenn Beck, the conservative radio and television host, as complaining: "[Millennials] don't give a crap about anyone but themselves because they're special, look at all the trophies they won.... You can live like they live in France...; countries have whole sections of floors dedicated to people who just sit in an office and do nothing because the state won't let them fire them.... That's where we're headed."[12]

In the workplace, Millennials work hard with passion and purpose, but they may work differently. For example, their idea is not to work in cubicles but arrange workers in the shape of an O with glass walls and open spaces. Also, they want flexible work hours to maintain a work-life balance, especially if they have children. Millennials are a "melting pot of go-getters... breaking down barriers" that have been too traditional.[13] They want speedier outcomes. They are impatient to work their way up in a business. They believe that they have potential for senior level management within two years. Some experienced workers may misunderstand Millennials, who often have a casual, informal approach. First, Millennials speak their minds freely. Second, they prefer casual clothes, whether or not it's appropriate for a certain situation. Third, Millennials do not like lectures, either in class or in the workplace. Their attention span is geared to digital time. Fourth, Millennials want to achieve consensus in the workplace, in society, in government, and in business, but this goal of consensus is not possible in a partisan climate. Finally, with their "spirit of service," Millennials want to help those in need.[14] Thereupon, Millennials are a hearty generation of energetic, creative, skeptical agents who have a "concrete hunger for order, security and stability," even though they have lost faith and trust in the government, corporations, banks, universities, and churches.[15]

For their 2011 book *The Millennials: Connecting to America's Largest Generation,* Thom and Jess Rainer interviewed 1,200 Millennials. Though Millennials are well educated and diverse, they are the least religious generation in modern American history.[16] They are more agnostic about God,[17] but those who are religious usually believe in one god.[18] Seventy-five percent are not involved in any established church; they are leaving traditional churches.[19] Six percent are Evangelical; six percent are atheists; eight percent are agnostic; and fourteen percent have no religion. Sixty-seven percent rarely or never read the Bible; sixty-five percent rarely or never attend religious services; only twenty-four percent are active in church activities.[20] Fifty percent claim they pray once a week; thirty-eight percent rarely or never pray; and sixty-five percent identify as Christian.[21]

Millennials are leaving established American churches because they consider many of them to be too bound to traditional creeds, too divisive, and not inclusive enough.[22] Furthermore, Millennials are well aware of moral failures and scandals involving church leaders, and they view business leaders as often unethical.[23] However, seventy-five percent of Millennials define themselves as "spiritual."[24] Instead of obeying the dictates of established churches, they want independence. Thirty-four percent do not believe in an afterlife.[25] Only twenty-five percent believe the Bible is the written word of God.[26] For the future, they want and expect more cultural and religious diversity in the mainstream of American religious life.[27] Finally, seventy-five percent of Millennials recognize that God created the universe and rules the world.[28]

Millennials are a major segment of the U.S. population; they want to shape the future of the world.[29] It behooves the public to pay attention to this generation. One Millennial, Mark Zuckerberg, Chief Executive of Facebook, commented, "The biggest risk is not taking any risk.... In a world that is changing really quickly, the only strategy that is guaranteed to fail is not taking risks."[30] For Millennials, sometimes doing things "extraordinary and worthwhile means doing things others will consider crazy," even radical.[31] But Millennials yearn to "chase our dreams, to create something worthwhile and valuable that will outlive us."[32] They claim they will never give up trying to make the world a better place.[33]

Because Millennials "think in images from digital technology more than words," they communicate less and less through books, magazines, and newspapers.[34] They are also usually less attached to political parties, which means they have lower voter turnout than Baby Boomers and Gen Xers. Generally speaking, they profess to be highly independent and can solve their own problems, but eighty-five percent turn to their parents for advice and guidance.[35] Fifty-two percent of Millennials want to be good parents even more than having a successful marriage.[36] Thirty-five percent of women 25 to 29 years old and twenty-two percent of women 30 to 34 years old who had babies in 2012 were not married.[37] As stated in Fromm and Vidler, "It's the abandonment of the idea that marriage has anything to do with children."[38] Besides, older generations may have conflicts with Millennials over the role of women, gay rights, abortion, and stay-at-home Dads; the younger generation has these things figured out. Millennials support labor unions (78 percent) and believe that the government must provide food and shelter for every citizen (69 percent). They think the government must provide a health care system for every American (80 percent); they want an inclusive society with economic equality, and they support the right of same-sex marriage (85 percent).[39] Millennials bring a new ideology into the culture of the United States; they may embrace a new understanding of the role, responsibility, and power of government. This new generation wants to remake America and the world.

Notes to Millennials

1. Jeff Fromm and Marissa Vidler, *Millennials with Kids: Marketing to This Powerful and Surprisingly Different Generation of Parents* (New York: American Management Association (AMACOM), 2005), 16.
2. Fromm and Vidler, *Millennials with Kids*, 16-17.
3. Thom S. Rainer and Jess W. Rainer, *The Millennials: Connecting to America's Largest Generation* (Nashville, TN: B & H Publishing Group, 2011), 1-2.
4. Paul Taylor, *The Next America: Boomers, Millennials, and the Looming Generational Showdown* (New York: PublicAffairs, 2014), 20.
5. Katy Steinmetz, "*Help! My Parents Are Millennials*," *Time*, October 26, 2015.

6. Morley Winograd and Michael D. Hais, *Millennial Momentum: How a New Generation Is Remaking America* (New Brunswick, NJ: Rutgers University Press, 2011), 148.
7. Lee Caraher, *Millennials and Management: The Essential Guide to Making It Work at Work* (Brookline, MA: Bibliomotion, Inc., 2015), 6.
8. Winograd and Hais, *Millennial Momentum*, 147.
9. Caraher, *Millennials and Management*, 26.
10. Rainer and Rainer, *The Millennials*, 168.
11. Winograd and Hais, *Millennial Momentum*, 29.
12. Winograd and Hais, *Millennial Momentum*, 29.
13. Stace Ferreira and Jared Kleinert, eds., *2 Billion Under 20: How Millennials Are Breaking Down Age Barriers and Changing the World* (New York: St. Martin's Press, 2015), 2.
14. Winograd and Hais, *Millennial Momentum*, 267.
15. David Brooks, "The Self-Reliant Generation," *New York Times*, January 8, 2016.
16. Rainer and Rainer, *The Millennials*, 47.
17. Rainer and Rainer, 23.
18. Rainer and Rainer, 243.
19. Rainer and Rainer, 55.
20. Rainer and Rainer, 236.
21. Rainer and Rainer, 232, 235.
22. Rainer and Rainer, 244.
23. Rainer and Rainer, 118.
24. Rainer and Rainer, 47.
25. Rainer and Rainer, 233.
26. Rainer and Rainer, 244.
27. Rainer and Rainer, 208.
28. Rainer and Rainer, 243.
29. Ferreira and Kleinert, *2 Billion*, 2.
30. Ferreira and Kleinert, 65.
31. Alex Jeffrey, "Find Your Gift, Give Your Gift!" In *2 Billion Under 20: How Millennials Are Breaking Down Age Barriers and Changing the World*, ed. Stacey Ferreira and Jared Kleinert (New York: St. Martin's Press, 2015), 137.
32. Jeffrey, "Find Your Gift," 139.
33. Zoe Mesnik-Greene, "What's a Smile Worth to You?" In *2 Billion Under 20: How Millennials Are Breaking Down Age Barriers and Changing the*

World, ed. Stacey Ferreira and Jared Kleinert (New York: St. Martin's Press, 2015), 106.

34. Winograd and Hais, *Millennial Momentum,* 186.
35. Winograd and Hais, 120.
36. Fromm and Vidler, *Millennials with Kids,* 12-13.
37. Fromm and Vidler, 12-13.
38. Fromm and Vidler,13.
39. Winograd and Hais, *Millennial Momentum,* 37, 54.

Truth

American traditions and institutions protect us in our daily lives. Institutions seem inherently fragile at this time and require careful tending. "In America today, they are under serious stress," according to Michael V Hayden, a former director of the Central Intelligence Agency.[1] The Enlightenment ideals of the seventeenth century "that value experience and expertise, the centrality of fact, humility in the face of complexity, the need for study and a respect for ideas" are threatened.[2]

In 2016, the Oxford English Dictionary named "post-truth" its Word of the Year. The term is an adjective "relating to or denoting circumstances in which objective facts are less influential in shaping opinion than appeals to emotion and personal belief."

According to Hayden, "Intelligence becomes an academic exercise if it is not relevant and useful."[3] Intelligence should constitute objective reality. Reality and truth must be evidence-based. The historian Timothy Snyder contends that "to abandon facts is to abandon freedom. If nothing is true, then no one can criticize power because there is no basis upon which to do so.... Post-truth is pre-fascism."[4] Traditionally, we have relied on truth-telling institutions to protect us as a matter of national security. We must "preserve the commitment and ability of our society to base decisions on our best judgment of what constitutes objective reality."[5] The end of intelligence is the end of truth.

In March 2018, the *Washington Post* reported that Donald Trump had made more than 2,400 false or misleading claims since becoming president. By November 4, 2020, the *Post*'s Fact Checker database had raised the number of false or misleading claims made by President Trump to 29,508. Even some intelligent individuals—not just fanatics and conspiracy theorists—believe that Trump's "alternate truths" might be true. Some doubt the falsehoods while others tolerate them because they admire Trump, see political benefits from post-truth rhetoric, or have become desensitized to dishonesty.

Trump once circulated a concocted story that Japan drops bowling balls on American cars to test their safety. Many people accept false stories like this one because it could *possibly* be true or because the story fits with a much broader narrative that they think is plausible. In an experiment conducted by Daniel A. Effron, a professor of organizational behavior at London Business School, 2,783 Americans of all political stances were asked to read a series of claims that they were told (correctly) were false. "All the participants were asked to rate how unethical it was to tell the falsehoods."[6] Half the participants were asked "to imagine if the falsehoods could have been true if circumstances had been different." The results of this experiment "show that reflecting on how a falsehood could have been true did cause people to rate it less unethical to tell, but only when the falsehood seemed to confirm their political views."[7] "Post-truth" exists when "facts are less influential in shaping opinion than emotion and personal beliefs."[8]

According to Effron, "In this time of 'fake news' and 'alternative facts,' commentators worry that people with different political orientations base their judgments of right and wrong on entirely different perceptions of reality. My research suggests an additional concern: Even when partisans agree on the facts, they can come to different moral conclusions about the dishonesty of deviating from those facts. The result is more disagreement in an already politically polarized world."[9] I guess we can blame humans for being able to imagine *what might have been.*

Notes to Truth

1. Michael V. Hayden, "The End of Intelligence," *New York Times,* April 29, 2018.
2. Hayden, "The End of Intelligence."
3. Hayden, "The End of Intelligence."
4. Quoted in Hayden, "The End of Intelligence."
5. Hayden, "The End of Intelligence."
6. Daniel A. Effron, "Why Trump Supporters Don't Mind His Lies," *New York Times,* April 29, 2018.
7. Effron, "Why Trump Supporters."
8. Hayden, "The End of Intelligence."
9. Effron, "Why Trump Supporters."

PART 4

Literature

Shelley's Anonymous Monster: The Power of Names in an Ordered Universe

Why didn't Mary Shelley in her novel *Frankenstein* give a name to the Monster she described as a "wretch," "abhorred devil," "vile insect," "demon," and "fallen angel?" She could have assigned him a name based on his creator, Victor Frankenstein, or a name whose original meaning in some precursor to a contemporary language expressed a characteristic of the Monster (like Matthew, from Hebrew, denoting a "gift of God"). Instead, Shelley left the Monster without a symbolic representation of himself or any identity even among all other Monsters, despite his having power and a unique personality.

In ancient times, Herodotus said there were nameless people among outcasts and slaves. The Monster is certainly an outcast and a slave to his own destiny. According to Leonard Ashley in his book *What's in a Name?*, people must have a name to distinguish them from all others.[1] Parents usually pass their family name down to their offspring and add a given name. But was Frankenstein willing to attach his family name to a Monster made from body parts collected from corpses? Monster Frankenstein? Frankenstein, Junior? A surname can be given to a descendent of some notable. But was Frankenstein a notable scientist, or a selfish egotist trying to defy the odds of life after death? Does Frankenstein become a father to the Monster and want to claim the Monster as his son? A surname can represent an occupation such as Miller, Baker, or Carpenter. But what was the future occupation for the Monster? A name might identify the town in which one resides, like John of Lincoln which would become John Lincoln. But where does the Monster reside? He is forced to roam the countryside without social acceptance in any town. A name can endear a person to someone else. But Frankenstein didn't want a close bond with the Monster; he wanted it out of his life. If Frankenstein didn't want to claim the Monster, why didn't he give the Monster a codename such as Victory, Dasher, Ultra, or Peacemaker so as to conceal the Monster's identity? Most likely, Harold Bloom states, Frankenstein flees his responsibility to name the Monster because he "never achieved a full sense of another's existence."[2] Frankenstein simply did not know what to call his horrendous creation. He was not proud of "it." Therefore, he slandered this creature with a nameless identity.

A well-chosen name can bring prosperity, popularity, or power. It can confer untold social and psychological benefits for a lifetime. In his research, Ashley confirms that an individual with a well-chosen name tends to go through life better adjusted and more successful than someone with an undesirable name. However, the Monster was not a human being; he was a collection of deadly attributes. According to Ashley, Frankenstein, a scientist and modern Prometheus, had "overstepped the bounds of conscience."

Mary Shelley also had reasons for not granting her character Victor Frankenstein permission to name the Monster. First, Shelley sensed "the spirit of modern times" and evoked "the threat of 'science run amok.'"[3] She saw how scientists were glorified for trying to create life after death, and by refusing to give a human name to a life-like creation, she condemned as irrational the endeavors of these scientists. Instead, she wanted to illuminate and elevate the human condition.

A second reason Shelley might not have assigned a name to the Monster is that she wanted to cast his misdeeds as a tragedy of a human soul, caused by the abandonment of his Creator. By denying him a name or identity, she indicts society's cruelty to a human form deprived of dignity, compassion, love, and humanness. In his commentary "On Frankenstein," written in 1817 before Mary Shelley published *Frankenstein* in 1818, Percy Shelley states this key moral theme in his wife Mary's novel: "Treat a person ill, and he will become wicked.... Divide him, a social being, from society, and you impose upon him the irresistible obligations—malevolence and selfishness. It is thus that, too often in society, those who are best qualified to be its benefactors... are branded by some accident with scorn, and changed, by neglect and solitude of heart, into a scourge and curse."[4]

Third, Mary Shelley reflects on her own family influences and responsibilities to a newborn. To name her children was an act of love and humanness, even though only one child survived. She carefully chose the names of each of her newborns. During the time she was writing *Frankenstein*, she became "hideously mixed" with death and life because of the death of her mother and the death of her newborn children. Her novel in the early nineteenth century "would suggest that a woman's desire to write and a man's desire to give birth would both be capable only of producing monsters."[5]

As Anne K. Mellor states in her essay "Possessing Nature: The Female in Frankenstein," Victor Frankenstein performed a "rape of nature" and a "miscarriage of technology" because he eliminated the female's biological function and her source of cultural power. Frankenstein denies "the value of female sexuality."[6] Domestic affection was natural for Shelley, not an unnatural reproduction that produced a freak, a gigantic structure eight feet tall with watery eyes, a shriveled complexion, and straight black lips. Not to name the Monster shows Shelley's revulsion at the inhumanity of excluding parents' loving affection for a newborn. Shelley's point is made succinctly: Frankenstein is a monster himself for not naming and acknowledging his only child.

In the August 31, 2003 edition of *The New York Times,* Michael Kimmelman wrote an article entitled "Finding Comfort in the Safety of Names." Really, what's in a name? "Its power is palpable but mysterious. Without thinking, we say we know someone when we know his name.... We react to names that resemble ours.... We look for something of ourselves.... When the World Trade Center was attacked...it's a safe bet that many of the 5,200 submissions interpret that as some kind of list of names. By aesthetic and social consensus, names are today a kind of reflexive memorial impulse, lists of names having come almost automatically to connote 'memorial.'...So now the memorial becomes a literal cemetery, with the oldest form of human identification, names...."[7] Indeed, the memorial to a nameless Monster is Frankenstein, the connotation of which is "evil."

Notes to "Shelley's Anonymous Monster: The Power of Names in an Ordered Universe"

1. Leonard R. N. Ashley, *What's in a Name?: Everything You Wanted to Know* (Baltimore, MD: Genealogical Publishing Co., 1989), 32.
2. Harold Bloom, *The Ringers in the Tower* (Chicago: University of Chicago Press, 1971), 125.
3. Walter James Miller, "Foreword: The Future of Frankenstein," in *Frankenstein,* by Mary Shelley (New York: Signet Classic, 2000), vi.
4. Mary Shelley, *Frankenstein,* ed. J. Paul Hunter, Norton Critical Edition (New York: W. W. Norton, 1996), 186.
5. Barbara Johnson, "My Monster/My Self," in *A World of Difference* (Baltimore, MD: Johns Hopkins University Press, 1987), 152.
6. Anne K. Mellor, "Possessing Nature: The Female in *Frankenstein*" in *Frankenstein,* by Mary Shelley, ed. J. Paul Hunter, Norton Critical Edition (New York: W. W. Norton, 1996), 279.
7. Michael Kimmelman, "Finding Comfort in the Safety of Names," *New York Times,* August 31, 2003.

PART 5

The Writings of Scott Russell Sanders

The Force of Spirit

In *The Force of Spirit*, Scott Russell Sanders describes the world as "a whirl of time and energy." Through writing essays, he gathers together from that world what is essential to him and then tries to "discover something essential to the lives of others."[1] He seeks the "lightness, radiance, and wind-like subtlety" of "spirit." This "inescapable force" may be like the wind brushing across one's face, the solid handshake of a friend, the beat of one's heart, or even the call of the red-tailed hawk.[2] Wherever this spirit resides in humans and nature, it is a sacred force breaking through the surfaces of ordinary life. Surgeons find this spirit hiding in the open cavity of the chest when they repair a heart. Biologists trace it back to the evolutionary path of survival. The spirit points to an emotional center, a core of integrity, an indispensable power that dwells in "the beliefs we truly live by, the ones we'll die for, [which] are those we hold in our heart of hearts."[3]

This "power of the spirit" may sound too churchy, but believers trace it to a "breath of God."[4] Secularists might call it gravity, electromagnetism, or the energy of atoms. But humans are more than matter in motion. "Our fellowship with other creatures on earth is real."[5] Everything in Creation—whether the black-footed ferret, the elephant, the cardinal, the earth, the sun, or the galaxy—is a magnificent energy of the Spirit or Tao or God or some other holy source whom we want to honor. Wherever the force of the spirit flows, we feel something sacred. Spirit is the "current that lifts us into this life and bears us along and eventually lets us go."[6]

For certain individuals, "the force of the spirit" lies in the warning on a white barn that Sanders once saw in the countryside: the silhouette of a man hanging on a cross and the words "AT THE END THERE IS JUDGMENT!" In childhood on Sundays, Sanders heard these words: "He died for you." Many children remember on Sundays "singing hymns, memorizing Bible verses, listening to sermons, and learning that Jesus saves." With this in mind, Sanders states that, although his wife Ruth "still sings in a church choir and I sit in a pew on occasional Sundays..., neither of us any longer feels confident that the man on the cross will preserve us from annihilation, nor that he will reunite us with our loved ones in heaven. The only meetings we count on are those we make in the flesh. The only time we're sure of is right now."[7]

At one time, reading the Old Testament of the Bible dampened Sanders' spirit. God was so angry. He "threw Adam and Eve out of the garden, sent Cain off into the wilderness, drowned almost everything that lived, kept Moses from setting foot in the Promised Land, turned Lot's wife into salt, sucked Jonah into the belly of a whale, buried Job under a blizzard of misery, slaughtered whole tribes, burned cities, dried up crops, and shook the foundations of earth."[8] Only the Psalms delivered a soothing respite. The New Testament was more tolerable. At age twenty-one, Sanders recalls, "I realized that the Bible was a ramshackle anthology...bearing human stains on every page.... I realized that God was not a bearded man in the sky, neither Lord or Father, but...the source and urge of everything."[9] "The forces of the spirit" in the Bible lacked the radiance and lightness assigned to human and animal emotions.

To restore the power of the spirit, Sanders eschewed city living and moved into a log cabin he built in southern Indiana. His father had taught him carpentry, and he fulfilled his childhood dream of building his own home. He and Ruth bought five acres of land bordering a state forest where hawks and creeks and deer linger. The advice the audience gleans from Sanders is that we should make our work, whatever it is, a spiritual act. Doing jobs with shoddy materials or lackluster effort squander the earth's bounty.[10] "What you build ought to last, bearing up under rough weather and the abrasion of time...the work ought to give you...the pleasure of exercising your full strength and knowledge and skill."[11] Trees deserve to display their beauty, especially the grain of the wood that is revealed in bookshelves, furniture, and gleaming oak floors. "Most of the wood in our house...comes from species that grow in the forests near our home...like fragrant cedar, flamboyant sycamore and hickory, subtle white pine, elegant beech."[12] "Wood grain speaks to us of wildness, the push of sap from roots into the tips of branches, the stress of wind, the struggle for a place in the sun."[13] These are "the forces of the spirit" that fill life: push, stress, struggle.

Sanders notices that many of us devote ourselves to defending species like the whooping crane, the wolf, the monarch butterfly, the grizzly bear, and bull trout which are imperiled by our human sprawling. We even pay attention to our pets with "the passion and devotion that we usually reserve for people we love."[14] We feel a kinship with these pets that enlarge our senses. Even a red-tailed hawk has its fascination: its mating, its nest of sticks and evergreens, its soaring, its kiting maneuvers, its menu of all sorts of small reptiles, insects, and animals. "It is a celebrated killer of snakes."[15] The hawk's ways of dwelling in this world are a lesson to us; it reassures us that "we aren't alone in this feverish business of living and dying."[16] We strive to live moment by moment "more abundantly, more variously, more richly."[17] But our dilemma as a human species is to clarify how to be human, how to behave in harmony with nature, and never forget we have intelligence and emotions to discern the power of the spirit. It is a gift because it invites us to reach out to other species and learn what we can about their ways.[18] Their parallel lives of survival deserve our compassion and care. We should see other creatures "not as rivals nor prey but as fellow beings worthy of wonder and respect."[19] The lesson of the red-tailed hawk for Sanders was a moment of truth about himself: "I carry this bird inside me. I bear some sense of its hunger, its drive to reproduce, its needs, its keen gaze."[20] I pause to think how life rises, how it needs the subtleties of air, water, and food, and how science cannot explain "the forces of the spirit."

One particular winter Sunday, Sanders searched for a traditional Quaker meeting to regain the silence of his spirit. The North Meadow Circle of Friends gathered in a house at the intersection of Meridian and Sixteenth streets in Indianapolis. In his search for the meeting place, he used a phone in the International House of Pancakes. Diners had heaping platters of food, but he saw through the plate-glass window "a man slouching past on the sidewalk. He wore a knit hat encrusted with leaves, a jacket torn at the elbows to reveal several dingy layers of cloth underneath, baggy trousers held up with a belt of rope, and broken leather shoes wrapped with silver duct tape. His face was a color of dust. He carried a bulging gray sack over his shoulder, like a grim Santa Claus. Pausing at a trash can, he bent down to retrieve something, stuffed the prize in his bag, then shuffled north on Meridian into the slant of snow."[21]

"I thought how odd it was that none of the diners rushed out to drag him from the street into the House of Pancakes for a hot meal. Then again, I didn't rush out either. I only stood there feeling pangs of guilt, an ache as familiar as heartburn. What held me back?"[22] "I decided it was fear. He might be crazy...might be dangerous. He would almost certainly have problems greater than I could solve. And there were so many more like him, huddled out front of missions or curled up in doorways all over Indianapolis this bitterly cold morning. If I fed one person, why not feed two? Why not twenty? What would keep me from drowning in all that hurt?"[23] In his muddled guilt, Sanders felt that he should have fed this man instead of searching for a prayer meeting.

When Sanders arrived at the Quaker church, "there was celebration in the face of the woman who greeted me at the door.... From there I entered the former dining room, which had become the meeting room, and I took my seat on a wooden bench near the windows.... Before closing my eyes, I noticed that I was the ninth person to arrive.... The silence grew so deep that I could hear the blood beating in my ears. I tensed the muscles in my legs, balled up my fists, then, let them relax. I tried stilling my thoughts, tried hushing my own inner monologue, in hopes of hearing the voice of God."[24] Where were "the forces of the spirit?"

Sanders was attracted to Quakers, whom he saw as "homely and practical [mystics], less concerned with escaping to heaven than with living responsibly on earth."[25] Sadly, the Society of Friends has gradually been losing its spiritual energy. "It seems to be the fate of religious movements to lose energy over time, as direct encounters with the Spirit give way to secondhand rituals and creeds, as prophets give way to priests, as living insight hardens into words and glass and stone."[26] "It's no wonder that most religions put on a show, anything to fence in the wandering mind and fence out the terror... while tens of thousands of people [sit] through scripted performances in other churches...."[27] "Carrying on one's own spiritual search, without maps or guide, can be scary."[28]

"In the quiet of worship..., [Sanders] gradually sank into stillness, down below the babble of thought. Deep in that stillness, time let go its grip, the weight of muscle and bone slid away, the empty husk of self broke open and filled with pure listening.... A car in need of a muffler (outside) hauled me back to the surface of my mind. Only when I surfaced did I realize how far down I had dived. Had I touched bottom?"[29] "Refreshed, I took up the sack of my self, which seemed lighter than when I had carried it into this room."[30] "The force of the spirit" had possessed him in this silence.

"'The whole mechanism of modern life is geared for a flight from God,' wrote Thomas Merton. I have certainly found it so. The hectic activity imposed on us by jobs and families and avocations and amusements, the accelerating pace of technology, the flood of information, the proliferation of noise, all combine to keep us from the inward stillness where meaning is to be found. How can we grasp the nature of things, how can we lead gathered lives, if we are forever dashing about like water striders on the moving surface of a creek?"[31] Indeed, we turn to "the force of the spirit," the power of the spirit, to still our souls.

Notes to The Force of Spirit

1. Scott Russell Sanders, *The Force of Spirit* (Boston: Beacon Press, 2000), 3.
2. Sanders, *The Force of Spirit*, 3.
3. Sanders, 11.
4. Sanders, 15.
5. Sanders, 16.
6. Sanders, 18.
7. Sanders, 7.
8. Sanders, 24.
9. Sanders, 30.
10. Sanders, 70.
11. Sanders, 69.
12. Sanders, 41.
13. Sanders, 44.
14. Sanders, 147.
15. Sanders, 146.
16. Sanders, 148.
17. Sanders, 149.
18. Sanders, 149.
19. Sanders, 149.

20. Sanders, 150.
21. Sanders, 152.
22. Sanders, 152.
23. Sanders, 153.
24. Sanders, 154-155.
25. Sanders, 155.
26. Sanders, 158.
27. Sanders, 159.
28. Sanders, 160.
29. Sanders, 160.
30. Sanders, 161.
31. Sanders, 164.

Hunting for Hope

One summer Scott Russell Sanders took his seventeen-year-old son Jesse on a hiking/rafting/camping trip in the Rocky Mountains of Colorado. On the first day, he writes, "snowy peaks rose before me like the promise of a world without grief. A creek brim full of meltwater roiled along to my left, and to my right an aspen grove shimmered with new leaves. Bluebirds darted in and out of holes in the aspen trunks, and butterflies flickered beside every puddle, tasting the succulent mud. Sun glazed in new grass and licked a silver sheen along the boughs of pine."[1] Sanders is "hunting for hope" in the exigencies of nature. He yearns for answers to questions about the sorry state of the world, the bleak future.

Sanders' son and daughter and students at Indiana University would ask him if there was hope for the future. He states that they aren't searching for "assurances of pie in the sky, for magic pills or guardian angels, for stories ending happily ever after, but for real and present reasons to face the future with confidence."[2] Most young people are not facing depression, claims Sanders, for they are, as far as he can tell, "bright, healthy, stable, competent, and confident" individuals. "It is the earth they brood about, the outlook for life" on this planet.[3] Facing "ruined landscapes and ravaged communities and broken people" all around them, the students wonder if there is cause for hope.[4]

Sanders asserts that he finds optimism in the memories, images, hunches, and tales drawn from his ordinary life.[5] Thereupon, words are his power to overcome anxieties of despair: "I *do* live in hope, and this book is my effort to say as clearly as I can where that hope is grounded."[6]

Sanders had initially hoped that this trip to the mountains would help him discover the source of the strife he had with his teenage son. Feeling that the grievous fight between them ran deep, he wanted to find where the underlying anger hid, fed, and grew. Peace seemed impossible, but perhaps he could drag this demon into the light and look at it.[7]

In Big Thompson Canyon in Colorado, he had a chance to meet Jesse head on. Jesse began his accusations against his father with the following diatribe: "You ruin everything.... You hate everything that's fun. You hate television and movies and video games. You hate my music.... You hate billboards and lotteries and developers and logging companies and big corporations. You hate snowmobiles and jet skis. You hate malls and fashions and cars.... You look at any car and all you think is pollution, traffic, roadside crap. You say fast-foods are poisoning our bodies and TV is poisoning our minds. You think the Internet is just another scam for selling stuff. You think business is a conspiracy to rape the earth.... But that's the *world.* That's where we've got to live. It's not going to go away just because you don't approve. What's the good of spitting on it?"[8]

After Sanders retorted, "I don't spit on it. I grieve over it." Jesse continued, "What's the good of grieving if you can't change anything.... Your view of things is totally dark. It bums me out. You make me feel the planet's dying and people are to blame and nothing can be done about it. There's no room for hope. Maybe you can get by without hope, but I can't. I've got a lot of living still to do. I have to believe there's a way we can get out of this mess. Otherwise, what's the point? Why study, why work—why do anything if it's all going to hell?... We come to these mountains and you bring the shadows with you. You've got me seeing nothing but darkness."[9]

Stunned and hurt in the face of Jesse's caricature of his views, Sanders realized that he had passed on to his son an anguish over the world instead of hope. He had spoken about the demon called despair in one of Jesse's ears, while a chorus of voices had been saying in the other ear "that the earth is an inexhaustible warehouse, that the consumption is the goal of life, that money is the road to delight."[10] Sanders finally said to Jesse, "You're right. Life is meaningless without hope. But you're wrong to say I've given up. I don't think we're doomed. It's just that nearly everything I care about is under assault."[11]

Although accepting that Jesse needed to break free from his father's concerns, Sanders could not turn off his fathering mind as they roamed the landscape. Anyway, on this trip to the Rockies—far from calendars, cars, and television—Jesse didn't take orders from his father and his father didn't give orders. Sanders wondered what their relationship would be like when they left the measured, desirable atmosphere of wildness and returned to the real world.[12]

Human beings invent hope by statements about the future: spring will come, the drought will end, the fever will break. "All covenants, all vows, all prophesies are cast in the future tense," writes Sanders.[13] Of course, "the first condition of hope is to believe that you will have a future."[14] So, Sanders substitutes "despair of living" with "hope for living."

James Watt, Reagan's former secretary of the interior, once remarked publicly that there was no need to conserve the forests because God would be coming to judge us long before we could use up all those trees.[15] Likewise, an evangelical preacher told students to beware of reading any book except the Bible because the only future they need prepare for is the hour when God will divide the saved from the damned.[16] Marx viewed religion as the "opiate of the masses," a drug that "eases the ache of history by focusing on the hope in eternity."[17] And Nietzsche said, "Hope is the worst of evils for it prolongs the torment of [human beings]."[18]

Instead of being encouraged to nourish hope today in earth-grounded activities, human beings have been asked to wait for eternity for relief. "When *all* hope is projected beyond death into an afterlife, it becomes a form of despair," opines Sanders.[19] To base our lives on no hope is to take a narrow view of the possible here and now. Vaclav Havel, a former political prisoner in communist Czechoslovakia who was later elected president of his country, states that hope is not optimism: "It is an orientation of the spirit... that transcends the world that is immediate by experience."[20] Sanders believes that "those who seek a homeland only in paradise are unlikely to care for their actual homelands [and communities] in this world."[21] Instead, one needs to yearn and work for a better country to ease the world's grief.

Sanders keeps faith in the promise of earth's recovery. First, his hope lies in tangible sources such as trees, animals, clouds, limestone, mountains, human beings—in all those things that constitute *the wildness and holiness of all Creation*. "The more I learn about the natural world, from science and art and my sense, the more elegance, order and splendor I see."[22] Human beings find hope in the beauty and simplicity of nature. Creation is in constant motion, bringing new and complex forms into existence. This is the hope. Our life on earth passes in the blink of an eye when we consider the history of the universe. But we have learned how to sow seeds and even engineer new ones; we have learned "how to transplant trees and hearts, split infinitives and atoms, write sonnets, cure diseases, explore other planets, encode memory on silicon."[23] The comets and stars ignore the desolation we inflict on earth. Seeds and spores and eggs and sperms are "brimming with future lives of hope."[24]

Second, *human senses* keep us wild and clear. "Any child is a reminder that the rivers of our sense once ran clear. As [humans] grow older, the rivers may be damned, diked, silted up, or diverted, but as long as we live, [the senses] still run, bearing news inward through ears and eyes and nose and mouth and skin."[25] We can restore our senses, and they, in turn, will replenish us with hope. We ordinary men and women have desires that pull at us like magnets. And the sense of nostalgia for childhood can enliven us, just like seeing and hearing a child can give us hope that life goes on.

Third, the family is the grounded community of hope that most of us know. If we hear incessantly of war and rarely of peace, we may forget how much we need and nourish one another. When we become suspicious of every person we meet, fearing disappointment or the disaster of betrayal, we may withhold ourselves from love and friendship, from any sort of membership, and try going it alone. But that road leads to despair. To find hope, we need to travel in company, explains Sanders.[26] Many young students he teaches at Indiana University wonder how to find hope in committing themselves to any one person because they have already been wounded in battles at home. Sanders finds an answer from the farmer-poet Wendell Berry, who believes that family life—indeed, most deep personal connections—depend on the virtues of "trust, patience, respect, mutual help, and forgiveness—in other words the *practice* of love, as opposed to the mere *feeling* of love."[27]

A fourth grounding for Sanders' hope is *the gift of work*, its meaning and its delight. If we reserve strength to carry on the work we believe in, with people we love, in a place we cherish, what else do we need? "Everything depends on how we use our skills.... Masons and carpenters may build houses or gas chambers...; pilots may deliver mail or missiles;...chemists may purify aspirin or heroin; writers may compose sober histories or tabloid sleaze."[28] All in all, work balances what we add and what we subtract from the world. Within our minds and in our hands, we carry the power to bring about peace.

Finally, *hope is grounded in the simplicity of purpose* in our lives. Too often, to be hopeful means to expand, to grow, to progress. Cities and houses and budgets and waistlines keep swelling. Bigger is better. Sanders yearns to pare life down to the essentials—not always what we want, but what we need. He vows to live more simply. He suggests we give away what is excess, purchase only what we need, make room for silence, avoid television's blaring advertisements, and possibly go about town on a bicycle or on foot.[29] "The capacity for restraint based on knowledge and compassion is a genuine source of hope."[30]

Flying over Denver on their way back to Indiana, Sanders questions our blind faith that there will always be enough natural resources, that technology will make everything all right.[31] He points out that Americans have a constant "hankering for more.... Our devotion to perpetual growth now endangers the planet by exhausting resources and accelerating pollution and driving other species to extinction.... It harms the individual by encouraging gluttony, a scramble for possessions, and a nagging discontent even in the midst of plenty."[32] However, he is confident that "we can learn to seek spiritual rather than material growth."[33] This spiritual growth is nourished through art, music, literature, science, and useful work, and by sharing bread with others, having conversations, and encountering wildness. We can find beauty through our profound sense of how things ought to be.

At Thunder Lake in Colorado, Sanders vows he will do everything in his power to climb out of the shadows that his son says he has been lurking in. He believes he can learn to see issues more clearly. But when he returns home to electricity, money, clocks, blaring television, and Jesse's loud music, his nerves are racked; he has to find a way back to the sanity and clarity he found in the mountains. Hope arrives in a reconciliation with Jesse.

Sanders' hope does not rest in God as a gentle giant.[34] After all, the Creator in the Bible drowned a handful of people, kicked Adam and Eve out of the Garden of Eden, trapped a man inside a whale, urged one tribe to slaughter another one, killed every newborn son, and visited plagues on enemies.[35] So, Sanders turns to faith in science. He believes that the Creator within science is holy and worthy of our wonder, devotion, and love.[36]

After several years of living in hope, Sanders still hears Jesse's words ringing in his ears. However, at the age of fifty he cannot forget the darkness, suffering, and waste that he has witnessed. Sooner or later "all of us ground the hammer of suffering."[37] When we become vulnerable, we become more compassionate. But how do we face the tremendous problems of the universe? Surely, insists Sanders, "behind the turmoil and cruelty and loss, there is a mind, a being, a way of things."[38] A Creator transcends all wildness, beauty, art, and ideas. There is love, serenity, and wisdom in this enveloping presence. We honor the Creator by cherishing every parcel of Creation and accepting the gift of purpose in this universe.

Sanders lives in hope. Solving the world's problems seems overwhelming, but we can make changes in our own lives. We can let ourselves be guided by need more than want; we can become conservers rather than consumers. We can inhabit our communities rather than pass through them like tourists; we can slow down instead of rush; we can commit to our families more deeply. Being responsible citizens, we can support businesses in our community, inform ourselves of public matters, honor the necessity of government, and require representatives to govern well. "In order to live in hope, we needn't believe that everything will turn out well, but only that we hope to be on the right path."[39]

Rafting and camping in Big Thompson Canyon reaffirmed for Sanders the need to speak of hope. It renewed his courage to try to end the "clashing like swords" between him and his son.[40] He remembered that, at the start of his trip with Jesse in Rocky Mountain National Park, "I woke at first light, soothed by the roar of a river foaming on one edge of the campground, and I looked out from our tent to find half a dozen elk, all cows and calves, grazing so close by that I could see the gleam of their teeth. Just beyond the elk, a pair of ground squirrels loafing at the lip of their burrow, noses twitching. Beyond the squirrels, a ponderosa pine, backlit by sunrise caught the wind in its ragged limbs. The sky was a blue slate marked only by the curving flight of swallows."[41]

Notes to Hunting for Hope

1. Scott Russell Sanders, *Hunting for Hope: A Father's Journeys* (Boston: Beacon Press, 1998), 4.
2. Sanders, *Hunting for Hope,* 13.
3. Sanders, 1.
4. Sanders, 2.
5. Sanders, 2.
6. Sanders, 3.
7. Sanders, 5-6.
8. Sanders, 8-10.
9. Sanders, 8-10.
10. Sanders, 10.
11. Sanders, 10.
12. Sanders, 119.
13. Sanders, 20.
14. Sanders, 21.
15. Sanders, 25.
16. Sanders, 25.
17. Sanders, 25.
18. Sanders, 25.
19. Sanders, 24.
20. Sanders, 27.
21. Sanders, 27.
22. Sanders, 31.
23. Sanders, 31.
24. Sanders, 32.
25. Sanders, 44.
26. Sanders, 64.
27. Quoted in Sanders, *Hunting for Hope,* 71.
28. Sanders, *Hunting for Hope,* 99-100.
29. Sanders, 127.
30. Sanders, 132.
31. Sanders, 128.
32. Sanders, 130.
33. Sanders, 133.
34. Sanders, 156.
35. Sanders, 159-160.
36. Sanders, 164.

37. Sanders, 157.
38. Sanders, 162-163.
39. Sanders, 186-187.
40. Sanders, 176.
41. Sanders, 5.

Standing in Awe

Some people consider awe a tinge of power that surges through a human being. Some say it is an animalistic power that follows a bright thread of communion with God, Allah, The Great Spirit, or the Universal Mind. Perhaps Saints are perpetually aware of this force. Quakers describe moments of awe as "openings" that connect us to the divine. But for the rest of us, sudden glimpses of awe come only fitfully or suddenly, sometimes like lightning; other times they come like an upsurge of emotions or an awareness. In nature, according to the writer Scott Russell Sanders, "this holy shimmer at the heart of things" travels in a breeze, in the soil freshly turned, in skin, shells, feathers, leaves, bark, fur, and the light of the sun and moon and stars.[1] We might also describe the universe of awe as "a pulsing web," "a dance of energy," a mind thinking.[2] An individual standing in awe has to let the mind expand in the power of the universe and even in the perennial wisdom of religion.

In *A Private History of Awe*, Scott Russell Sanders traces his religious awakening, which started with his childhood education in the Baptist Church and matured after his education at Oxford University. Sanders recounts and explores the sense of awe he has experienced at different points in his life. He characterizes his awe as small awakenings, apprehensions, a sense of wonder mixed with dread, or a "rapturous, fearful, bewildering emotion."[3] The awe emerges from observing ordinary things such as Indiana limestone and clouds, and it is experienced when watching his granddaughter taking her first steps and spending time with his mother when she was 88 years old and suffering from Alzheimer's disease. He considers the blessedness of miracles such as a shiny apple, the sound of a cello, the fragrance of lavender, the flow of breath, the planet hurling through space, and the birth of his granddaughter Elizabeth. His awakening to the wisdom of religion is so Unitarian. He certainly is a perfect example of someone who respects the interdependent web of all existence for which humans are responsible.

When Sanders was seven, his family moved from Tennessee, where he was educated in the Baptist religion, to Dayton, Ohio, where his father helped make bombs ("the killing machines") at Ravenna Arsenal. The Bible stories he learned during childhood were better than war stories. Cain murdered Abel; David slayed Goliath with a slingshot and a stone; Jonah spent three days and three nights in the belly of a whale for disobeying God; "Solomon offered to settle a quarrel by sawing a baby in half"; "Joseph's brothers, driven by jealousy,...persuaded their father that his favorite son had been slain, then dumped Joseph into a well and left him to die"; God was angry and flooded Noah's Ark; Lot's wife hardened into a pillar of salt for turning her head to see her home; even Jesus died on a cross, but rose three days later.[4] "From one end of the Bible to the other," Sanders claims, "there were stiff-necked people crushed like bugs under the mighty hand of God."[5] So, the good news of the New Testament was welcome news. But this grand power of God at work in the world and the scary stories of preachers, Sanders says, fed his imagination.

As a child, Sanders began to wonder where to put his faith: in the Father, the Son, or the Holy Ghost. He saw the Father as "a moody, mighty king who lived in the sky and punished sinners" and the Son as "a kind man who walked barefoot on earth and forgave sinners."[6] He was taught that the Holy Ghost "came down from heaven into people's hearts and it bent the laws of nature to suit God's will."[7] None of these factions were in his textbooks at school. Sanders claims that he was more interested in his science books. He confirmed his scientific awe when he saw a feather lifted by the wind off of the windowsill; it was not God. Furthermore, tadpoles turned into frogs every spring without the help of Jesus. Ice, rain, and wind seemed more amazing than the Holy Ghost.[8]

By the age of twelve, when the Cold War was in full bloom, Sanders witnessed Sputnik being launched and understood that a nuclear war with Russia was possible. In addition, Sanders' father had a heart attack. According to Sanders, his father was an alcoholic and loved booze more than his family. At this point, "while I still prayed to God, the power I really counted on were the doctors, the scientists in the labs..., the slide rule in my desk, and the formulas in my textbooks. My faith in science had crowded out my faith in religion."[9] "I wanted to know about magnetism, migration, geology, subatomic particles, the periodic table of the elements, and about the Big Bang, nuclear fusion, and evolution, and a host of other fascinating things, not one of which appeared anywhere in the Bible."[10] Sanders felt awe at all these matters; however, he "couldn't decide which prospect was more frightening—facing a God who is mindful of every human act, facing a God who takes no notice of our puny lives, or facing a universe entirely empty of God."[11]

During high school, Sanders read the entire Bible, cover to cover, but it raised more questions than answers. In church he found that many Christians squeezed sacredness into one person: Jesus. But Sanders believed that Jesus was not himself God, but he "revealed a world saturated with divinity"...and renewed strength through time.[12] Sanders thought, "I sometimes wonder if all other animals, all plants, maybe even stars and rivers and rocks dwell in steady awareness of God."[13] Do humans set themselves apart from these other entities? Sanders wondered. How does one preach forgiveness and love while the Bible envisions God as intolerant and spiteful? "How can you love your enemies while preparing to exterminate them?"[14]

When Sanders entered Brown University in Providence, Rhode Island, he planned to major in physics and begin his estrangement from the church. Occasionally, he attended various denominations. He was appalled by the Apostles' Creed, which had no reference to bombings in Alabama, nuclear war, poverty, or any of the events of historic providence. It was only about Jesus. Sanders did not believe Jesus was the only one created by God or that Jesus had been born of a virgin or that he had risen from the dead.[15] The Apostles' Creed did not mention how humans should treat the poor, the sick, the weak, the mad, or the old (like his Mother). The creed said nothing about justice, healing, peacemaking, or compassion. "Left out entirely [from the creed] was any mention of how we should live, how we should treat one another, how we should deal...with the millions of other species on our planet."[16] "Nor did the creed convey anything of the awe I felt in the woods, along the stony creeks, or in the company of storms and stars."[17] Finally, Sanders could not bring himself to recite the Apostles' Creed. He believed that his private salvation was bound up in the universe and the fate of his neighbors and his family.

At the end of his sophomore year at the university (1965), Sanders took a literature course focused on Emerson, Thoreau, Hawthorne, Melville, and Whitman. He writes, "Unlike the authors of the Bible, [these writers] claimed no divine sanction for their insights, only the authority of their experience, imagination, and reflection" about nature and God.[18] A new era of awe in Sanders' life began when he read Thoreau's *Walden*. "Thoreau chased loons across the pond or traced the shapes of thawing mud or tracked the moon."[19] Thoreau proclaimed the soundest truth of reality. Sanders' awe arrived in "the power of language to map a life, to overcome distance to focus attention on what matters most; it signifies shaping an energy, intelligent and generous and inexhaustible."[20] Sanders recalled his awe when he looked out the window and saw tulips, rhododendrons, poppies, redbuds, and crab apples, and heard bird songs and running creeks. He marveled at the "intricate, exquisite life we behold all around us on this lowly planet."[21]

Some individuals think scientists lack a sense of awe in explaining emotions, that scripture cannot be trusted for scientific experimentation. Though stories and poems cannot be tested in laboratories, they can be tested in life experiences, according to Sanders.[22] At Brown, he decided to give up the study of science and physics, and instead, concentrate on literature. Thereupon, he and his wife Eva were granted scholarships at Harvard University, but they turned them down to pursue degrees at Oxford University. After four years, Sanders returned to the United States in 1971 and began teaching English Literature at Indiana University. One Sunday he attended a Methodist church in Indianapolis, Indiana, where he found that the minister "acknowledged no suffering at all except that of Jesus on the cross and it had no meaning for me."[23] He didn't mention the Vietnam War, assassinations, race riots, marches, sit-ins, or the millions of Americans living in poverty. Instead, the minister assured the congregation that they would be saved from grief by the salvation of Jesus Christ and that love required nothing except a belief in the saving power of Jesus. In this experience, Sanders recalls, "I was relieved when the benediction sent us...outside into the open air.... Christianity didn't seem to have changed; I had changed. I could no longer embrace a religion that ignored the power pulsing through everything—the prostitute on the corner, the civil rights marcher in jail, the starving child, the swallow, the river, the storm."[24]

In the fall of 1971, while the Vietnam War still raged, Sanders stood before a class of students at Indiana University. He believed that young people did not want to "teeter on the brink of despair," but hoped "that the world can be better—more peaceful, more generous, more just."[25] He felt that by putting a story or poem or play in their hands he could stop them from sliding into cynicism, open their minds and voices to the world's awesome wonders, and "renew their yearning for a life devoted to high ideals."[26]

Human beings "enter the world as warm and squirming bodies, empty of ideas and full of sensation"—hunger, sounds, images.[27] In contrast, while Sanders' mother was suffering from Alzheimer's disease, her world was full of sensations of fear, loneliness, and emptiness. In literature, Sanders claims, words "dice the world into pieces small enough for the mind to hold," but not spacious enough to accommodate awe.[28] Awe is an enlightenment that strikes in ordinary, earthy occurrences within reach of anyone who pays attention to universal pulses. If only we observe and feel and love its wondrousness.

Notes to Standing in Awe

1. Scott Russell Sanders, *A Private History of Awe* (New York: North Point Press, 2006), 26.
2. Sanders, *A Private History,* 5.
3. Sanders, 8.
4. Sanders, 49-51.
5. Sanders, 51.
6. Sanders, 97.
7. Sanders, 98.
8. Sanders, 99.
9. Sanders, 136.
10. Sanders, 99.
11. Sanders, 100.
12. Sanders, 166.
13. Sanders, 166.
14. Sanders, 184.
15. Sanders, 186.

16. Sanders, 187.
17. Sanders, 187.
18. Sanders, 202.
19. Sanders, 203.
20. Sanders, 161.
21. Sanders, 162.
22. Sanders, 204.
23. Sanders, 275.
24. Sanders, 276.
25. Sanders, 305.
26. Sanders, 306.
27. Sanders, 14.
28. Sanders, 13.

Writing from the Center

In the quest to live a meaningful, centered life in a world that seemed broken and scattered, Scott Russell Sanders, an author and conservationist, sought to understand his place in marriage, family, community, and Creation. He wanted a home territory where he could build a web of relationships with other people and share common experiences with them.[1] Sanders found this place in the Midwest countryside outside Bloomington, Indiana, where he settled in 1971 with his family and began his teaching career as an English professor at Indiana University. His writing is influenced by Midwest landscapes in which "skies... [are] filled with thunderstorms and red-tailed hawks, the creeks are bordered by limestone bluffs, the fields are planted in soybeans and corn, the woods are thick with grapevines and hickories."[2] Centering life and writing in a village made Sanders answerable to neighbors. He found that a village is stable and bound by love as well as duties such as caring for streets and fields. He became an inhabitant of a place, not just a passerby with no responsibility. This milieu led him to write about Midwest culture. Similarly, John Steinbeck wrote his most significant works by drawing on the culture of California.

Sanders wrote the book *Writing from the Center* in 1995 to explore those things that contributed to his search for a center: a "homogenized America," his heritage, his community, his religious faith, his work ethic, his appreciation for nature, and his capacity for writing. He wanted "to know where authentic writing comes from"—its "sources and conditions."[3]

First, Sanders discovered a wholeness in a "homogenized America." Even though the land in Ohio is different from Utah, and California is different from the New England states, the blurred regional boundaries speak with a wholeness of one nation. When looking for a sense of place, Sanders learned all he could about the soil, its platelets, the strokes of weather, the water supply, the seasonal drama of wind or pollen, the birds, beasts, insects, native plants, and the food chain.[4] His home in Indiana is far from the interstate highways and business franchises. Instead of constantly getting in and climbing out of cars, he rides a bicycle to work from his rural home. He urges us to develop a bioregional consciousness, which means "bearing your place in mind, keeping track of its condition and needs, and committing yourself to its care."[5]

Second, a part of Sanders' heritage centered his life and work. Basically, his essays focus on human beings, nature, and the earth. One day, holding two buckeyes that titillated in his hand reminded him of walks he took with his father at the Ravenna Arsenal in Portage County, Ohio. His father recognized all kinds of trees and their distinctive shapes, leaves, bark, and buds.[6] Within the forest adjacent to the arsenal, hundreds of deer roamed "in herds, in branches, in amorous pairs," but they were hunted for the sport.[7] As a young boy, Sanders grieved over their killing. In this arsenal area, farm ponds were polluted by TNT used in making bombs during World War II. "Gullies were choked with trash [from humans]."[8] This place hovered on the edge of destruction. Thirty years later, Sanders returned to this area in which he had grown up and saw a lone red-tailed hawk; it was a ghostly reminder of his alcoholic father that made Sanders want to leave this poisonous place of memories. He longed for a new home with new stories, poems, photographs, paintings, essays, and songs to center his life.

Third, Sanders wanted a community centered in a place, in a time. The countryside of Bloomington, Indiana was the location he and his wife, Ruth, chose "to work for change in the Midwest."[9] When they moved there, individualism dominated life in the United States. It was a philosophy of "Hands off...my castle; don't tread on me. I'm looking out for number one.... I'm doing my own thing. We have a Bill of Rights, which protects each of us from a bullying society, but no Bill of Responsibility, which would oblige us to answer the needs of others."[10] Sanders believed that guns and the Second Amendment supported obsessive individualism that was a public danger.[11] Groups glued together by hatred and racism, or those who "wrap up in scripture or flags," are not interested in a community that is a sensitive association of people dedicated to the "common good."[12] Unions, volunteers, homeless shelters, soup kitchens, sports teams, Scouts, 4-H, Lions, Elks, and Rotarians care about local needs. Sanders describes responding to the call of a common life this way: "For us, loving America had little to do with politicians and even less with soldiers, but very much to do with what I have been calling the common life: useful work, ordinary sights, family, neighbors, ancestors, our fellow creatures, and the rivers and woods and fields that make up our mutual home."[13] Sanders sought to restore the earth's abundance in a common life through living simply and writing contentedly.

Fourth, Sanders' faith in "fulfilling work" affected his search for a center. Whereas modern machinery and appliances save us from some types of work, "devoted work" belongs to mothers with children, to those who carry flowers to shut-ins, to fathers who change a flat tire, and to caretakers, chefs, and doctors. Sanders is convinced that work strengthens us mentally and physically. The work ethic is a belief that "creation is a sacred gift." "The chief reason for relishing work is that it allows us to practice our faith, whatever that faith may be."[14] "Faith concerns our sense of what is real, what is valuable, what is holy; work is how we act out our faith."[15] Therefore, Sanders believes that faith and work center a human being. Writing is work and living is work.

Sanders found a fifth centering force: devotion to his family, friends, and community. After living in England and Boston for many years, he and his wife came home to the Midwest and lived on a twenty-three-acre plot of rural land near Bloomington, Indiana. They found that exchanges with family and friends and neighbors needed large-scale giving and receiving. In his simple living in a common life, Sanders relished baking bread with his daughter Eva, and he hiked in the Rockies with his son Jesse to ease "knocked nerves" between the two. Sanders also finds simple pleasures in sawing wood, planting trees and flowers, and changing the oil in the car. With Ruth he shares purpose, sensual delight, and good works. What is vital to a family reverberates through the whole community. Devotion to a family helps Sanders center his life in a place and a community.

A sixth centering force for Sanders is nature—particularly nature preserves at Cedar Bluffs and Clear Creek in Indiana. There Sanders can experience a "blooming, darting, singing world," without the chaos of the civilized world.[16] However, he laments that Clear Creek has been polluted with fertilizers, pesticides, herbicides, and other chemicals within only a few years compared to the millions of years since the earth was created.[17] Hundreds of plants and animals are disappearing because of human actions such as deforestation, industrial farming, and pollution.[18] Humans are altering the intricate order and laws of nature, but with terrible consequences.[19] Sanders praises The Nature Conservancy for preserving Cedar Bluffs: "Every time I come here, I give thanks to the people who loved this place enough to salvage it from the bonfire of development...and have left it open for strangers to visit."[20]

Sanders goes to Cedar Bluffs alone. He despairs for the country which "consumes more than a quarter of the resources used up each year on the entire planet, which produces more than a quarter of the world's pollution, which has ransacked the natural wealth of a continent in two centuries, and all this for the sake of fewer than 5 percent of the world's population."[21] In reaction to such greed, he goes to his sacred sanctuary to renew his connection with the durable sanity of nature, the land, and the planet.

An optimistic Sanders in his sanctuary at Cedar Bluffs finds nature alive. Moving through the meadows, he feels the seed heads of grasses stroke his thighs and hears the scolding of birds.[22] "A speckled orange butterfly lands... on the yellow disk of an oxeye daisy."[23] "The creek pours through its channel, scooping and tossing sunlight, and birds pour song into the air."[24] He notices moss clinging to stones, dragonflies, turtles, and racoon paw prints. He realizes that "nothing we do will unsettle the universe; everything we do affects the planet."[25] When we squander nature, "we destroy ourselves and take a million species along with us," he warns.[26]

Sanders stresses, "I wish to name that within me which rises up in response to the power and beauty I meet in the world. Whether we are bound through our depths to anything eternal, I cannot say; but I am certain we are bound, through and through, to all of nature."[27] Cedar Bluffs is the sacred sanctuary where he finds "nature's nakedness" that makes him contemplate an eternal force of creation. "A true sanctuary is a sacred refuge, a holy place for worship. But there are no longer any refuges from our devices and desires. We treat nothing as holy except our pleasure and ease. We worship only ourselves."[28] When we don't revere the land, Sanders says, we lack reverence for human beings.

Through writing, Sanders centers his ideas about work, the common life, spiritual reality, the united forces of family, friends, and community, and reverence for the land, the earth, and the sacred nature of God. "Literature informs the conduct of life."[29] He realizes that a writer can be centered with certain criteria: (1) an appreciation for nature; (2) experience in a place; (3) originality, clarity, and beauty in language; (4) marriage and family stability; and (5) spiritual depth. In the end, Sanders' essays center on the following: the relationship of humans to nature; issues of social justice; the character of community, family, and friends; and the impact of science on human life.

Sanders acknowledges that many writers such as Joseph Conrad, Samuel Beckett, Ezra Pound, Ernest Hemingway, and Gertrude Stein left their homeland to write somewhere else. Other writers were rooted in a specific place: Leo Tolstoy in Russia, Robert Frost in New England, Jane Austen in England, Hugo Balzac in Paris, Cervantes in Madrid, Franz Kafka in Prague, Gunter Grass in Berlin, and Thomas Mann in Venice. Therefore, Sanders moved to Bloomington, Indiana. "I wished to make my new home ground the ground of my imagination."[30] One must feel an emotional attachment to a place as an inhabitant to contribute to its healing. In 1971, some editors and publishers asked Sanders how he could bear to live in the "backwoods" of Indiana. He replied, "Where you live is less important than how devotedly and perceptively you inhabit that place. I stay here in the Midwest out of affection for the land, the people, the accents, the foods, the look of towns and the lay of farms, for the trees and flowers and beasts. I also stay here from a sense of responsibility.... However great or small my talents, here is where they will do the most good."[31] At this time in the early 1970s, the United States was grappling with many problems, including the Vietnam War, the nuclear arms race, riots, poverty, the cult of money and power, ubiquitous advertising, mind-numbing television, and the assault on the environment. Sanders was impressed with writers who could tackle these issues and make a difference. Many of these writers had wandered the world but then settled their art in a chosen place: Thoreau, William Faulkner, Flannery O'Connor, Grace Paley, Gary Snyder, William Berry, Mary Oliver, Mark Twain. Wherever writers seek authentic writing and avoid "trails others have trampled,"[32] they can "give back to the places that fed them a more abundant life."[33]

Sanders chose to be regional and parochial in Indiana. He wanted to be away from the pressure of publishing houses in New York, London,

Paris, Boston, and San Francisco, but work systematically in a community. The Midwest was full of "gossips and boosters and Bible-thumpers who are hostile to ideas, conformist, moralistic, utilitarian, and perpetually behind the times."[34] He was cognizant of the opportunity this presented for a writer. In fact, the Midwest lately has begun to nourish a writer with a sense of purpose.[35] The rural atmosphere didn't smother or isolate a writer like Sanders. In fact, the challenge to write centered in that particular culture in Indiana: farmland, the nature of sheds and barns and silos, the shade of summer, and the acres of cultivated fields. "My deeper subject is our need to belong somewhere with a full heart, wherever our place may be, whoever our people may be."[36]

"Writing is to living as grass is to soil," writes Sanders.[37] The powers he gathered from a young age tell a story of the exigencies of his life. "The pleasure of living among words" keeps him writing stories, essays, images and characters.[38] "Stories are containers in which we carry some of those imaginings. They are the pots and bowls and baskets we use for preserving and sharing our discoveries.... Stories tell about human character and action, and the consequences of character and action; by making stories and reading them, we are testing ways of being human."[39] A loving marriage kept Sanders writing and living a centered, meaningful life. He believes that "the challenge for any writer is to be faithful at once to your vision and your place, to the truth you have laboriously found, and to the people whom this truth might serve."[40] Whereas Sanders loves words, he loves his world more. Words cannot be unhooked from the world in which we are immersed.[41]

Notes to Writing from the Center

1. Scott Russell Sanders, *Writing from the Center* (Bloomington, IN: Indiana University Press, 1995), ix.
2. Sanders, *Writing from the Center,* ix.
3. Sanders, 149-150.
4. Sanders, 17.
5. Sanders, 18.
6. Sanders, 3.
7. Sanders, 4.

8. Sanders, 6.
9. Sanders, 75.
10. Sanders, 71.
11. Sanders, 72.
12. Sanders, 74.
13. Sanders, 75.
14. Sanders, 95.
15. Sanders, 96.
16. Sanders, 55.
17. Sanders, 57.
18. Sanders, 58.
19. Sanders, 57.
20. Sanders, 55.
21. Sanders, 60.
22. Sanders, 53.
23. Sanders, 54.
24. Sanders, 56.
25. Sanders, 58.
26. Sanders, 62.
27. Sanders, 119.
28. Sanders, 61.
29. Sanders, 111.
30. Sanders, 157.
31. Sanders, 179.
32. Sanders, 149.
33. Sanders, 161.
34. Sanders, 162.
35. Sanders, 163.
36. Sanders, ix.
37. Sanders, 169.
38. Sanders, 182.
39. Sanders, 187.
40. Sanders, 186.
41. Sanders, 187.

PART 6

Thomas Jefferson and His Legacy

Thomas Jefferson at Monticello

The Virginia Colony was originally established in Jamestown in 1607 by aristocratic English entrepreneurs. As savvy businessmen, they grabbed vast areas of land and manipulated public offices to benefit the wealthy. The slave trade increased and plantations flourished as a result of the stolen labor, skills, and expertise of those held in slavery. Beginning with the election of George Washington in 1789, the presidency was controlled for the better part of fifty years by enslavers. John Adams served 1797–1801 and never held people in slavery; nor did his son, John Quincy Adams 1825–1829. In fact, at least twelve former presidents were enslavers, or more than a quarter of all those who have served in that office to date. Eighteen of thirty-one Supreme Court justices during the first fifty years of the court's history were enslavers; and pro-slavery men dominated the lower courts.[1] Virginia created a slavery empire of economic and political power for the Southern states. Into this culture Thomas Jefferson was born on April 13, 1743, on the plantation of a family that held Black people in slavery. In Jefferson's youth, an enslaved "boy" did menial tasks for him so that he could concentrate on other things such as reading, writing, and equestrian skills. "It is simply impossible to write slavery out of the life, personality, and even the very existence of Thomas Jefferson."[2] He eventually became, in the words of Wiencek, "Master of Monticello."

Some historians portray Jefferson as a "humanitarian of slavery," but in truth he supported the institution of slavery during his life, especially at Monticello. According to Annette Gordon-Reed, author of *Thomas Jefferson and Sally Hemings: An American Controversy*, new historiography has given us a clearer understanding of the effects of slavery on the United States and why Jefferson failed to emancipate most of the people he enslaved. His racist and sexist views and his relationship to the enslaved at Monticello "have been subjected to a more intense scrutiny."[3] Gordon-Reed claims that the words of formerly enslaved people such as Madison Hemings, son of Jefferson and the enslaved woman Sally Hemings, and Israel Jefferson, a formerly enslaved man at Monticello, have been taken more seriously since 1974 when a plethora of documents about Jefferson was released. Racism and sexism on Jefferson's plantation have become more significant in the twenty-first century while evaluating the life of Jefferson.

Jefferson moved into Monticello, "the mansion on the hill," in 1770 as a twenty-seven-year-old, on land he had inherited from his father. He envisioned a plantation with an ideal rural setting.[4] He had inherited forty-five enslaved people from his parents. To build Monticello, these captive workers had to shave off the mountain top with twelve-hour days of digging in clay. For a water supply, enslaved people hired by Jefferson from a nearby planter took forty-six days to excavate six feet of rock for a wall.[5] "[Jefferson] began grander plans for Monticello which he could not afford without slave labor."[6] Between 1784 and 1794 he sold 160 enslaved people to clear his debts during the construction of Monticello. On the other hand, from 1780 to 1790, 143 enslaved children were born into chattel slavery as Jefferson's property.[7] Wiencek reports that Jefferson had no moral qualms about slavery. In fact, he excused slavery as his way to introduce character, diligence, and discipline to all the enslaved. He tried to rationalize this plan to make slavery respectable for the economy and the society.[8]

Jefferson claimed to be concerned for the "happiness" of all those enslaved who labored for him.[9] But he treated them like children who could not maneuver on their own. Certainly, with "no school [available on the plantation], no marriage [permitted between slaves], [no legitimacy for children], and no ability to testify against white people, enslaved people were left to build their own inner identities in opposition to the dominant society's assault upon their humanity."[10] Granted, for humanitarian reasons,

Jefferson's grandchildren taught some of those enslaved at Monticello to read and write. "Jefferson was in favor of teaching the slaves to learn to read print and no more.... To teach them to write would enable them to forge papers [and] they could no longer be kept in subjugation."[11] Archaeologists have found writing slates and pencils all through Mulberry Row, the slave quarters at Monticello. Evidently, they wanted to become literate as "visible signs of reason and imagination,"[12] but in his *Notes to the State of Virginia,* Jefferson contended that Black people were "as incapable as children."

Jefferson's mountaintop estate at Monticello near Charlottesville, Virginia, was built on descending tiers. At the summit, Jefferson, the "Master of Monticello," created a superior view looking down the slope at the enslaved people laboring in the surrounding acres of land. The medium tier was the mansion and its occupants. Such a superior view for an enslaver was commonplace. Jefferson planned to make Monticello a model institution of slavery, and therefore, emancipation would not be necessary. Certainly, he realized that without slavery Monticello would be economically unviable and his social status in an enslaving culture would be questioned. As long as he lived, slavery was alive at Monticello.

The management of Jefferson's enslaved community at Monticello was also built on a hierarchical system. Jefferson was in the top tier at his home. "The majority [of slaves] remained farmers; above them were enslaved artisans; above them were enslaved managers; above them were the household staff. The higher you stood in the hierarchy, the better clothes and food you got; you also lived literally on a higher plane closer to the mountaintop...but differences bred resentment" among the enslaved.[13]

In 1773, three years after Jefferson moved into Monticello, he inherited 135 enslaved people at the death of John Wayles, his father-in-law, who was also the father of Sally Hemings.[14] Among the slaves who arrived at Monticello was the extended family of Elizabeth Hemings who were enslaved by Jefferson and his heirs for four generations. None of the Hemingses, male or female, was put to hard labor or became a field hand.[15] Jefferson ruled their fate at Monticello. Jon Meacham, author of *Thomas Jefferson: The Art of Power,* declares that Jefferson loved control and power. For example, he even "disliked animals [his horses] with wills of their own."[16] He whipped his horses on his daily rides through the plantation. He defined the rights for the white population of the new republic, but he overlooked the humanity of the enslaved. "Power meant much to him, but he cloaked his driven nature with the mien of intellectual curiosity and aristocratic confidence."[17]

Annette Gordon-Reed is one of the recent scholars to study the Hemingses. In her book *The Hemingses of Monticello*, published in 2008, she explains how the family maintained a coherent identity at Monticello and survived slavery. They were considered to have "superior intelligence, capacity, and fidelity to trust."[18] Julian Bond states in 1998 that "Jefferson talked about slaves as 'my family.' Obviously if some family members owned other family members, it is not family in a traditional sense.... Was Jefferson a good slave master? That's an oxymoron. There are no good slave masters."[19] Gordon-Reed believes that "family" for Jefferson meant the Hemingses in particular. Indeed, other enslaved people at Monticello were jealous of the Hemingses, who most often did inside work and received special treatment. Family identity was treasured by the enslaved. It is impossible to ignore the devastating effect on "family values" of a system, which Jefferson used, under which couples could be separated and parents and children sold away from each other, at the will of the owner.[20] Slaves Ursula Granger and Edith Fossett traveled to the White House as cooks during Jefferson's presidential years while their husbands were left at Monticello.[21]

The mansion at Monticello in which slaves labored had eleven thousand square feet of space and thirty-three rooms. Jefferson lived in "grandeur."[22] The finest side of Monticello was intentionally exposed to public view while Mulberry Row, the slave quarters, was shielded from public view.[23] Archaeologists at Monticello began excavating Mulberry Row in the 1950s. The mansion at Monticello sat over a tunnel from which the enslaved could move back and forth serving as many as forty guests. A dumbwaiter (the invention of Jefferson) descended to the basement. The abundance at Monticello was based on enslaved labor. Indeed, Jefferson mortgaged the people he held in slavery as collateral to finance building Monticello.[24] In 1819, Jefferson was in debt for $40,000, so he had to sell land, enslaved people, and his personal library of 6,847 books.[25] His economic assets in slaves rendered him deaf to the humanity of the enslaved.[26]

At Monticello Jefferson appealed to the emotions of his family and the people he held in slavery "as a way of extracting behavior he wanted, doing things to make them feel bound and grateful to him, rather than being directly coercive."[27] He believed that enslaved people could display "character" if they were content and did not have to be collared or whipped for cooperation. He believed he could create congenial people suited to perpetual slavery if he managed them properly.[28] But he found that he also had to act despotically to manage some enslaved individuals. Enslavers sometimes used values of kindness and loyalty as a "useful tool for enslavement...to teach peace to the conquered."[29] Jefferson's son-in-law, Colonel Randolph, who managed Monticello in Jefferson's absence, ultimately turned against the "sooty atmosphere" of slavery when he saw a "trust-worthy slave hanging 30 feet from the ground, in a tree, near [the Master's] door."[30] The man had been beaten into submission by an overseer. From this time forward, Colonel Randolph banned whipping at his own residence at Edgehill. According to Wiencek, "There is something about the whip he could no longer abide, it being the emblem of a species of power no one should have."[31] In cases he considered to be serious misconduct, Randolph relied on the courts and jail sentences instead of whippings and the use of chains. Furthermore, Colonel Randolph claimed that the Southern system of slavery was "a hideous monster" based on brutality and fear.[32] "It [was] the air of hell and Randolph was breathing it in Virginia."[33] Jefferson left no written, "intimate account" of the enslaved people Monticello, but he did keep careful records on them for accounting purposes.[34] He failed to acknowledge their integrity, benevolence, loyalty, or humanity.

On the Monticello plantation, Jefferson controlled "all benefits of housing, food, clothing and work assignments," so the enslaved were dependent on his favor.[35] "He determined who got fish, and how many; who got cloth and how much; and the number of blankets that were given out—the course of the lives of grown men, women, and children [were] set by this one man."[36] An enslaved person knew that the person who called himself master had the power to sell his so-called human property whenever he wished or whenever a financial crunch occurred.[37] Jefferson gave eighty-five men, women, and children as gifts to his heirs to ensure their financial security and comfort, but this "perpetuated slavery into the next generations while wrecking the Black families."[38] However, he did not want his "favored slaves" to get used to the world beyond Monticello, for when they did, like Robert and James Hemings who traveled to France, Philadelphia, Washington, D.C., and Boston, they "became restless in Jefferson's service and wanted to end their service to him."[39]

Enslaved people at Monticello were skilled artisans: carpenters, cabinet makers, masons, bricklayers, weavers, carriage makers, coopers, nail makers, spinners, tailors, seamstresses, brewers, soap makers, candle makers, midwives, maids, butlers, chefs, coachmen, watermen, and farmers. However, Jefferson even as he profited off their labor, skills, and knowledge, he complained that they were a burden. This did not lead him to emancipate them.[40] He also recognized that slavery was slowly destroying the industriousness of white people: "No man will labor for himself who can make another labor for him."[41]

Wiencek points out that Jefferson gave meager rations to the enslaved at Monticello. If they had not raised their own food as industrious farmers and gardeners, they would have starved.[42] When enslaved people became too old to work, planters cut their rations. However, archaeologists have discovered "sub-floor pits" in the used to store food for those who lived in Mulberry Row and for fugitives from slavery. They also stored stolen goods. In 1807, a British diplomat, Augustus John Foster, visited Monticello and noted that Jefferson gave a striped blanket to each enslaved person every three years. If a blanket was lost, replacements were limited.[43]

Enslaved women who found their identity, self-affirmation, and respect in their individual families were invisible to Jefferson. He had a sexist view of women. He "saw women, slaves, and children as suitably disabled under law."[44] White women and all enslaved people had no vote, no property. Jefferson believed women were under the dominion of husbands because it was "a tenet of natural law."[45] "He believed that serving was even better for women than reading."[46] Women were for the "attention of men."[47] He reproduced excerpts from poems and other literature that, according to author Gordon-Reed, "can be interpreted as hostile to women."[48] (This collection has been edited by Jonathan Gross in *Thomas Jefferson's Scrapbook*, published in 2006). Jefferson also thought white women should not work in the fields, but he would "still send [slave women] there because it suited his needs and the needs of his society."[49] Of course under the system of chattel slavery, enslaved women also supplied babies who were "economic assets" for Jefferson.

However critical Jefferson was of the industrialization of the Northern states, he established a nail factory on his agrarian property at Monticello. This lucrative business employed young, enslaved boys ages ten to sixteen, while girls became spinners and weavers.[50] Jefferson said, "I love industry and diligence. I can impose a vigor of discipline [on these boys]."[51] The nailery gave boys hard work; otherwise, Jefferson thought, they would become idle and lazy. The nailery, he imagined, would reward those who were industrious. The historian Edwin Betts, in his 1953 edition of Jefferson's *Farm Book*, deliberately deleted a letter describing how boys were whipped and lashed into work by overseers. Betts wanted a scholarly consensus about Jefferson as "a man with a lenient hand," instead of an abuser.[52] But "the Monticello machine operated on carefully calibrated brutality."[53] According to Wiencek, the nailers received twice the food ration of a field worker, but no wages. On weekends, the boys received fifty cents a day to cut wood for the nailery's fires.[54] Jefferson rationalized enslaved labor "as the power engineering American enterprise."[55] The sale of nails was very profitable; as profits increased, Jefferson's interest in emancipation decreased.[56]

Flogging and whipping as punishment was considered a potential embarrassment for the benevolent Jefferson at Monticello. However, all planters accepted some violence as necessary. In general, beating an enslaved person to death was even abhorrent to white citizens of Albemarle County where Monticello stood. Jefferson allowed his overseers and managers to discipline the enslaved, but according to Wiencek's research, Jefferson denounced these overseers as "despised brutes…, hard-handed men who got things done and had no misgivings. He hired them, issued orders to impose vigor of discipline and then spread a fog of denial over the whole business."[57] Jefferson hated conflict and violence, so he simply gave orders and removed himself from such scenes.

Some historians contend that Jefferson was bound to slavery "by convention, by society, by laws, by his family, and by debt."[58] Americans want to remember him as a benevolent man. However, Annette Gordon-Reed contends that Jefferson did not have "an internal sense of justice and fairness, depending as he did on a labor system that was constitutionally unjust and unfair. By holding upward of two hundred souls in bondage, he worked injustice and unfairness in their lives every single day."[59] Furthermore, he did not "forgive those who wounded him personally."[60] He had "a tendency toward possessiveness and controlling behavior."[61] His decisions were based more on the needs of his white family. Historians and scholars in the twenty-first century have been more probing in their analysis of Jefferson's attitudes and personality traits. He failed to see the "significant consequences for others" of his decisions.[62] He rationalized the need for slave labor in order to build the nation.

If Jefferson was mired in the Southern culture of slavery, one can understand why he made some of the decisions he made as "Master of Monticello." But he was not blind to the violence he ordered and witnessed throughout his life. He was no different than other enslavers. Henry Wiencek has recorded some of the treatment that Jefferson witnessed or sanctioned. As a boy, Jefferson saw an ad for a fugitive from slavery who had an iron collar around his neck. (An iron collar had spikes behind the ears, so turns were impossible.) Jefferson's father collared an enslaved person. An enslaved woman named Hannah, whom Jefferson knew from his family's plantation, was beaten to death by an overseer.[63] Gabriel Lilly, an overseer for Jefferson, whipped a sick boy until the boy was not able to raise his hand to his head.[64] Jefferson's system of punishment sent four people chained together to Louisiana, where three died of disease.[65] Melinda Colbert, a cook at Monticello, was freed with her children, but Jefferson cruelly sold her husband Freeman for $231.81.[66] In 1815, Jefferson sold a three-year-old girl, Sally, to an overseer for $150. However, she was allowed to stay with her mother. Indeed, the overseer was her father, so her father was buying his daughter.[67] Hubbard, a fugitive from slavery who was brought back to Monticello, was clapped in irons and flogged.[68] Jefferson sold his gardener's nine-year-old daughter at auction.[69] Incidentally, Jefferson paid spies in the enslaved community to inform on others.[70]

One family at Monticello was divided among eight buyers at auction. At Jefferson's death in 1826, 130 people were sold to the highest bidders.[71] According to Wiencek, in his will Jefferson freed a blacksmith, Joseph Fossett, but not his family of six. Two years later, the blacksmith purchased his wife, a son, and two other children, but he watched the auction of three young daughters to different buyers.[72] One daughter, Isabella, was eight years old. Jefferson made no provision to free all those he enslaved at his death. Even Sally Hemings was not emancipated, but he did free their four children when they reached the age of twenty-one.

Even if Jefferson was considered a progressive "master," his "world was crueler than we have been led to believe."[73] He was liberal, enlightened, and forward-thinking, but not on the issue of slavery. His plantation produced "inexhaustible human assets," that is, babies that grew up to be perpetually enslaved. Jefferson computed in 1792 the four percent "silent profits of slavery" when babies are born; he measured this profit against investments in manufacturing and railroads.[74] The enslaved were the second-most valuable capital asset in the United States before the Civil War.[75] Enslavers could buy and sell human beings like cattle and horses.

During his lifetime, Jefferson did not discern the cruelty of slavery as he witnessed it. He did not acknowledge that Monticello could not have been built and maintained without forced labor. He did not understand how desperately enslaved people longed for the "liberty and freedom" that he afforded to the white population. He placed control over others above compassion and moral principles.

Monticello reflected little of Jefferson's principles of liberty, freedom, education, and the pursuit of happiness. In contrast, abolitionists persistently condemned slavery as a moral catastrophe to humanity. Jefferson encountered these individuals, but they did not alter his stance because he needed enslaved labor, knowledge, and skills to maintain his opulent lifestyle. In 1770, Quakers successfully freed enslaved people in the states of Maryland and Delaware. In 1775, a Quaker in Virginia, Warren Miffin's father, freed ninety-one people but was discredited as having broken Virginia law because manumission was illegal in Virginia.[76] Among Southern planters this ignited a "war against Quakers." Jefferson explained that the Southern minority who wanted emancipation was stacked against "the greater number whose consciences were [bothered] but who needed an injection of courage to divest themselves of slaves."[77] In 1777, Vermont abolished slavery, followed by Massachusetts in 1783. George Washington freed all people held in slavery at Mt. Vernon at his wife's death in 1790. He disagreed with Jefferson's philosophy and rebuked the profiteers of his era. Washington declared that if one claims to have principles, one must abide by them.[78]

As noted in an early essay in this collection, Edward Coles, a Virginian who freed all of the people he enslaved in 1819, told Jefferson that it was wrong to maintain slavery just because their forefathers had believed in it. Coles subsequently escorted seventeen enslaved people to the free state of Illinois and gave each family 160 acres of land on which to build a new life.[79] Coles approached Jefferson, an advocate of liberty, to assist him in an emancipation program, but Jefferson excused himself due to his age.

An opportunity for Jefferson to free those he enslaved materialized in 1817 at the death of Thaddeus Kosciuszko, an old friend and hero of the Revolutionary War. Kosciuszko bequeathed Jefferson a fortune of $20,000 if Jefferson would free all people held in slavery at Monticello and purchase land and farming equipment for them to begin a life on their own. Even with debt, Jefferson refused the gift. If he had accepted the gift, half of the sum of money would have been allocated to the people he freed for land, livestock, equipment, and transportation.

Sadly, Jefferson lacked words of praise for the people he enslaved at Monticello. He was gifted with words, but he left a minimal record in letters or notes about them, and nothing about Sally Hemings in his handwriting. He knew that the people he enslaved were skilled in textiles, nail making, furniture, and carpentry, but he restricted them by making them work exclusively for him.[80] The enslaved people at Monticello did excellent woodworking; they were skilled in smithing, painting, and glazing. For example, they built his carriage. A culinary expert at Monticello was trained in France. All these capable persons, if they were free, could have thrived. Historian Richard Newman points out that in Pennsylvania in 1790, free Black communities were thriving on their own talents.[81] Black families were stable, hardworking humans who could master literacy. Jefferson continued to ignore his secretary in Paris, William Short, Edward Coles, Thaddeus Kosciuszko, and Washington in emancipation leadership because "white artisans were scarce, so costly, and often drunk."[82] "Whenever someone presented him with evidence of intelligence and achievement among Black people, he dismissed the evidence."[83] He once arrogantly said that he was waiting for "a Black aristocrat to come along, a scholar such as himself."[84]

Isaac Granger, a blacksmith, said Jefferson was "a good master."[85] As a free man in 1840, Granger recalled how Jefferson rode around his plantation in a wheelbarrow when his legs swelled too much to walk. Jefferson bowed to everyone he met, but he kept his arms folded, as a gentleman among inferiors.[86] Otherwise, politeness among equals meant he would hang his arms loosely. Granger was among the enslaved people who wanted a good match for Jefferson's white daughters, for their husbands would be their future enslavers. Cruelty came to Granger: Colonel Randolph, son-in-law of Jefferson, desperate for money, sold his nine-year-old daughter, Maria, who was taken away to Kentucky and never seen again.

The early historian Merrill Peterson contended that Jefferson managed Monticello benevolently. Jefferson encouraged diligence but was lenient. He was supposedly generous to those he enslaved. Peterson wrote that

Jefferson's "conviction of the injustices of the [slavery] institution strengthened his sense of obligation toward his victims."[87] In addition, Jefferson "hated conflict, disliked having to punish people and found ways [through his overseers] to distance himself from violence his system required."[88] Some historians praised Jefferson's intentions more than his actions.

In the five years that Jefferson was in France, the mansion at Monticello deteriorated and had to be renovated. When he returned to Monticello in December 1789, records indicate that the enslaved people there were supposedly happy to see "their oppressor." At the end of his presidency in 1808, he started building the University of Virginia. He went back to Monticello at age sixty-six and spent the final seventeen years of life in retirement there. He wanted stability, familiarity, and peace. He farmed and gardened. At Monticello he had experienced the death of his wife, Martha, at the age of thirty-four. Sally Hemings lived with Jefferson at Monticello for thirty-eight years; she died in 1835 at the age of sixty-two. "When Jefferson died, he owed creditors, in early twenty-first century terms, between $1 million and $2 million."[89] The 552 acres of Monticello were sold in 1831 for $4,500 (Boles 519).

In public life, Jefferson devoted himself to liberty, rights and responsibilities, and solutions to problems of the white population. Kareem Abdul-Jabbar states, "Certainly it was no accident that slavery was the major moral issue the signers of the Declaration of Independence failed to address when they proclaimed liberty, equality and justice for all, and [then] went home to oversee their slaves."[90] The institution of slavery was based on the powerful symbols of God, science, and profit. In 1967, Martin Luther King, Jr. stated that "no society can fully repress an ugly past when the ravages persist in the present."[91] Harold L. Dalton wrote in 1995 that slavery's enduring legacy has been imprinted in the American psyche in the twenty-first century.[92] Money, inequality, and injustice still challenge the American society.

According to Gordon-Reed, we cannot really know what human beings are like unless we understand the context in which they lived. But we know in general about mothers, fathers, families, and male-female relationships, and today we recognize the innate worth and equal humanity of all people. "In what universe could the humanity, family integrity, and honor of slave owners count for more than the humanity, family integrity, and honor of slaves?"[93] It seems especially appropriate to tell one part of the story of slavery through the Hemingses. Slavery at Monticello was embedded in the social customs of the time. Jefferson had "competing passions, flaws, sins, and virtues that [could] never be neatly smoothed out into a tidy whole."[94] He tried "to bend his philosophy" in his life's work, but the power that he possessed at Monticello would not let him bend the institution of slavery.[95]

Notes to Thomas Jefferson at Monticello

1. Garry Wills, *"Negro President": Jefferson and the Slave Power* (Boston: Houghton Mifflin, 2003), 6-7.
2. Annette Gordon-Reed, *The Hemingses of Monticello: An American Family* (New York: W. W. Norton, 2008), 283.
3. Annette Gordon-Reed, *Thomas Jefferson and Sally Hemings: An American Controversy* (Charlottesville, VA: University Press of Virginia, 1997), xiv.
4. Henry Wiencek, *Master of the Mountain: Thomas Jefferson and His Slaves* (New York: Farrar, Straus, and Giroux, 2012), 10.
5. Gordon-Reed, *The Hemingses,* 113.
6. Wiencek, *Master of the Mountain,* 89.
7. Wiencek, *Master of the Mountain,* 89.
8. Wiencek, *Master of the Mountain,* 98.
9. Wiencek, *Master of the Mountain,* 69.
10. Gordon-Reed, *The Hemingses,* 444.
11. Gordon-Reed, *Thomas Jefferson,* 18.
12. Gordon-Reed, *Thomas Jefferson,* 19.
13. Henry Wiencek, "Master of Monticello," *Smithsonian* (October 2012), 46.
14. Wiencek, *Master of the Mountain,* 33.
15. John Ferling, *Adams vs. Jefferson: The Tumultuous Election of 1800* (New York: Oxford University Press, 2004), 73.
16. Jon Meacham, *Thomas Jefferson: The Art of Power* (New York: Random House, 2012), 289.
17. Meacham, *Thomas Jefferson,* 130.
18. Gordon-Reed, *The Hemingses,* 29.
19. Quoted in Ella Mazel, ed., *"And Don't Call Me a Racist!" A Treasury of Quotes on the Past, Present and Future of the Color Line in America* (Lexington, MA: Argonaut Press, 1998), 30.
20. Gordon-Reed, *The Hemingses,* 42.

21. Gordon-Reed, *The Hemingses*, 168.
22. Gordon-Reed, *Thomas Jefferson*, 105.
23. Wiencek, "Master of Monticello," 42.
24. Wiencek, "Master of Monticello," 96.
25. Ferling, *Adams vs. Jefferson*, 214.
26. Wiencek, *Master of the Mountain*, 61.
27. Gordon-Reed, *The Hemingses*, 303.
28. Wiencek, *Master of the Mountain*, 124.
29. Wiencek, *Master of the Mountain*, 125.
30. Wiencek, *Master of the Mountain*, 125.
31. Wiencek, *Master of the Mountain*, 123.
32. Wiencek, *Master of the Mountain*, 101.
33. Wiencek, *Master of the Mountain*, 102.
34. Wiencek, *Master of the Mountain*, 37.
35. Wiencek, *Master of the Mountain*, 103.
36. Gordon-Reed, *The Hemingses*, 15.
37. Wiencek, *Master of the Mountain*, 69.
38. Wiencek, *Master of the Mountain*, 172.
39. Gordon-Reed, *The Hemingses*, 568.
40. Wiencek, *Master of the Mountain*, 157.
41. Quoted in Wiencek, *Master of the Mountain*, 46.
42. Wiencek, *Master of the Mountain*, 186.
43. Wiencek, *Master of the Mountain*, 248-249.
44. Gordon-Reed, *The Hemingses*, 642.
45. Gordon-Reed, *The Hemingses*, 301.
46. Gordon-Reed, *The Hemingses*, 237.
47. Gordon-Reed, *The Hemingses*, 119.
48. Gordon-Reed, *The Hemingses*, 93.
49. Gordon-Reed, *The Hemingses*, 119.
50. Wiencek, "Master of Monticello," 45.
51. Quoted in Wiencek, "Master of Monticello," 47.
52. Wiencek, *Master of the Mountain*, 119.
53. Wiencek, *Master of the Mountain*, 113.
54. Wiencek, "Master of Monticello," 47.
55. Wiencek, *Master of the Mountain*, 247.
56. Wiencek, "Master of Monticello," 48.
57. Wiencek, *Master of the Mountain*, 113.
58. Wiencek, *Master of the Mountain*, 271.
59. Gordon-Reed, *The Hemingses*, 582.

60. Gordon-Reed, *The Hemingses*, 491.
61. Gordon-Reed, *The Hemingses*, 502.
62. Gordon-Reed, *The Hemingses*, 631.
63. Wiencek, *Master of the Mountain*, 113-114.
64. Wiencek, *Master of the Mountain*, 122.
65. Wiencek, *Master of the Mountain*, 131.
66. Rosalind Bentley, "Exhibit Juxtaposes Slavery, Jefferson's Ideas of Liberty," *The Columbus Dispatch* (Columbus, OH), March 10, 2013.
67. Wiencek, *Master of the Mountain*, 260.
68. Wiencek, *Master of the Mountain*, 144-149.
69. Wiencek, *Master of the Mountain*, 263.
70. Wiencek, *Master of the Mountain*, 147.
71. Joseph J. Ellis, *American Sphinx: The Character of Thomas Jefferson* (New York: Vintage, 1998), 290.
72. Wiencek, "Master of Monticello," 97.
73. Wiencek, *Master of the Mountain*, 9.
74. Wiencek, *Master of the Mountain*, 9.
75. Wiencek, "Master of Monticello," 45.
76. Wiencek, *Master of the Mountain*, 81.
77. Wiencek, *Master of the Mountain*, 82.
78. Wiencek, *Master of the Mountain*, 275.
79. Wiencek, *Master of the Mountain*, 233-242.
80. Wiencek, *Master of the Mountain*, 247.
81. Wiencek, *Master of the Mountain*, 248.
82. Wiencek, *Master of the Mountain*, 248.
83. Wiencek, *Master of the Mountain*, 247.
84. Wiencek, *Master of the Mountain*, 249.
85. Wiencek, *Master of the Mountain*, 103.
86. Wiencek, *Master of the Mountain*, 106.
87. Quoted in Wiencek, "Master of Monticello," 48.
88. Wiencek, "Master of Monticello," 46.
89. Meacham, *Thomas Jefferson*, 496.
90. Quoted in Mazel, *"And Don't Call Me a Racist!"*, 27.
91. Quoted in Mazel, *"And Don't Call Me a Racist!"*, 39.
92. Mazel, *"And Don't Call Me a Racist!"*, 39.
93. Gordon-Reed, *The Hemingses*, 32.
94. Meacham, *Thomas Jefferson*, 500.
95. Meacham, *Thomas Jefferson*, 51.

Thomas Jefferson: The Patriarch

Thomas Jefferson has been lauded as a voice of American freedom and liberty. He was a governor of Virginia, president of the United States, and founder of the University of Virginia. The role of patriarch was "[Jefferson's] place in the world."[1] He once imagined himself as "the most blessed of patriarchs," and he identified with the nation he helped found.[2] At Monticello, Jefferson was also the patriarch of his family, "the white half that he loved so publicly, as well as the Black side that he claimed to love, a contradiction of extraordinary historical magnitude."[3]

Jefferson's British father, Peter Jefferson, came to America and settled in Virginia. His father bought vast acres of land through the Loyal Land Company; land and property guaranteed voting rights for men. "The Virginia of [Jefferson's] birth had been shaped by planters who controlled the government, as they feverishly acquired land, promulgated property rules that favored the landed, and developed a full-fledged slave society."[4] Men in positions of power were "socially conservative and intellectually unadventurous."[5]

In 1782, Jefferson wrote the *Notes of the State of Virginia,* a document meant to shape Virginia's future, but in it he severely denigrated slaves and the institution of slavery, which he thought put Virginia "far behind" as "a participatory democracy."[6] He wrote that "the true foundation of a republican government is the equal right of every citizen, in his person and property."[7] But Jefferson's privilege and power existed from "cradle to grave," reinforced by the Virginia culture.[8] Jefferson believed that a "natural authority" was nature's plan. Wise, intelligent men would guide the nation through progressive stages. He did not consider the "natural rights" of Virginia's enslaved people when he wrote the line "all men are created equal" in the Declaration of Independence.

Jefferson was committed to forming a "free and good government."[9] He thought that "education was a core requirement for empowering citizenship."[10] He disestablished Virginia's state-supported church and guaranteed religious freedom.[11] The Bill of Religious Freedom was passed in 1786 by James Madison. Jefferson observed that without strong checks on aristocrats, "the 'few' would always seek to dominate the 'many'—even in a republic."[12] He believed that small landowners were "the source of moral virtue."[13] He described a plan for emancipation of slaves to the House of Delegates in Virginia in 1779, but he refused to act against slavery and sacrifice his part in the white society.

Ellen Randolph Coolidge, a granddaughter of Jefferson living in Boston, claimed that the state of Virginia was provincial and backward because "the canker of slavery eats into their hearts, and diseases the whole body of this idea at the core."[14] Furthermore, she observed that Southern states could not hope to match the prosperity and improvement in the Northern states. Northerners were freer from the influence of slavery and had become sober laborers in a society with fine roads, bridges, canals, inns, horses, and "a landscape of fertile land and livable space."[15] Ellen "was passing judgment on the fate of her grandfather's early efforts and ambitions for his home state."[16]

The patriarch Jefferson could not save Virginia from slavery. Southerners had become indolent, unsteady, and "zealous for their own liberties, but tramped on those of others."[17] The authors of *"Most Blessed of the Patriarchs": Thomas Jefferson and the Empire of the Imagination*, Annette Gordon-Reed and Peter S. Onuf, state that in the late eighteenth century, "slavery turned whites into tyrants and impaired their capacity for self-control."[18] In his positions of power, Jefferson developed a will to master. He was intelligent, had personal charm, and possessed a passionate curiosity and an attractive manner. Why didn't he use his power as a Master or as Patriarch for the state of Virginia and the nation to abolish slavery? Sadly, "slavery [had] worked well for the patriarch Jefferson at all stages of his life."[19]

During his tenure as governor of Virginia from 1779 to 1781, Virginia was a prosperous commonwealth. Jefferson envisioned Virginia as a republican society where ordinary people with independence owned land, grew their own food, and made their own clothes.[20] He thought that with its growing population, fertile land, and natural resources such as coal, lead, stone, and zinc, Virginia would experience economic prosperity and political development. But the burden of slavery was not "an engine of moral progress," considering the natural rights of the enslaved.[21]

As president of the United States beginning in 1800, Jefferson would try to establish a citizen-centered society that was not based on the "planter elites." "The people" became the source of his authority. Republicanism was his dream.[22] He played his fatherly role as leader of all the states of the nation. However, slavery remained, creating "a deep and urgent moral issue."[23]

Jefferson was a professional architect for building a nation. He was the Father of "Republican Principles and Enlightenment Values" devoted to "liberty under the law."[24] As president in 1800 at the age of 50, he was at the center of his country's affairs, extolling "life, liberty, and the pursuit of happiness" for all citizens—except for the enslaved. He had helped transform the political landscape of the United States by limiting the power of the government and handing it to the people. At this time, democracy demanded a political revolution and a social one, too.[25] Jefferson and his fellow Democratic-Republicans, who valued political freedom for the common person, fought a fierce partisan battle with the Federalists, who valued a strong central government.

However, in this era, heads of households governed over wives, children, and the enslaved. These domestic hierarchies of privilege and power for men echoed Jefferson's belief in the "natural rights" of men of ability, education, and enlightenment to rule the nation. Hence, Jefferson's philosophy of human rights for every citizen was based in hypocrisy.[26] Whereas George Washington had demonstrated his greatness by resisting the temptation of power,[27] "the closest thing to a constant in [Jefferson's] life was his need for power and for control."[28]

All in all, Jefferson's presidency fathered a democratic nation, but it did not end slavery. Americans credit Jefferson for having a westward vision for the nation. He sent Lewis and Clark on expeditions in the Pacific Northwest in 1805, and his Louisiana Purchase in 1803 doubled the size of the United

States (which, of course, undermined the sovereignty of Indigenous nations). During his presidency, he moved the Capitol from New York to Washington D.C., barred voting rights for women in 1807, led white landowners to assert their political right to be heard, and nurtured enlightened, educated people to prepare for self-governance. He preserved the country's "sacred fire of liberty," independence, and national determination.[29] As he sought to achieve "an ideal America," he maintained "deep psychic connections with the needs, anxieties, and dreams of people."[30]

At Monticello, Jefferson was patriarch, master, and father of his "heavenly" mountain-top home. It was his patriarchal responsibility to provide for the well-being of his family and the enslaved people on his estate. He said, "I have my house to build, my fields to farm, and to watch for the happiness of those who labor for me."[31] Indeed, "I shall imagine myself as blessed as the most blessed of the patriarchs."[32] He had near-absolute power over hundreds of people in Monticello. According to Jon Meacham in his book *Thomas Jefferson: The Art of Power*, Jefferson spent his whole life controlling his image and touting his aristocratic status, power, and intellectual acuity.[33] At Monticello, "his commands were not challenged or questioned—ever."[34] But he had an engaging manner and a sympathetic approach that ingratiated him to people.

Monticello was a mirror of Jefferson. It was a "lofty conception of self" on a "high pedestal."[35] From this mountain home, Jefferson could look down on wild scenery and untamed woodlands, as if he were floating spiritually above worldly concerns.[36] A tall, six-foot man like him could look down at visitors; he could look down condescendingly from his horse at an enslaved person. However, the evidence of slavery scattered up and down the mountain at Monticello belied his republican political philosophy.

Jefferson included "family" as everyone in Monticello. This benevolent family harmony at Monticello appealed to visitors. "Of course, this was the powerful patriarch's vision of harmony: dissenting views were muted, and controversy, if not suppressed altogether, was certainly not encouraged."[37] But Monticello was not really a harmonious place with individual liberty. Instead, "it protected, justified, and perpetuated a regime of unequal domestic relations, including slavery."[38]

For example, the children of Sally Hemings, whom Jefferson fathered, were enslaved at the lowest rung of Monticello's social ladder, not at the top like Jefferson's children with his wife, Martha. The Hemings family, however, was treated preferentially among slaves at Monticello. They never worked in the fields; they were assigned domestic duties in the house, so equality never reigned in Jefferson's home. In another example, when Jefferson was living in Paris, he paid wages to his "servants" James and Sally Hemings who provided him services there, but when he returned to America, no law required him to pay the enslaved.[39]

The enslaved man named Isaac Jefferson recalled times when Jefferson would ride his horse throughout the Monticello plantation to observe what was being done. Thomas Jefferson had inherited the land but was not a farmer of these 5,000 acres. Instead, he was "Master," affirming "his place… at the pinnacle of this self-contained world."[40] He enslaved young boys to labor in a nail factory he created. He claimed that hard work would give young boys incentives to become skillful within the confines of slavery. His scheme was "to make slavery more humane for the enslaved."[41] Instead, the boys did repetitive work in hot, closed quarters; this would certainly have an adverse effect upon their growing bodies and their spirit.[42] Furthermore, when Jefferson was absent from Monticello, he gave other managers the power to control the enslaved. Overseer Gabriel Lilly whipped the boys. Monticello became "a gigantic machine" with moving parts that worked with "clocklike regularity."[43]

In his legal, public family Jefferson had two daughters, Martha and Maria, and fourteen grandchildren who enjoyed his love and attention. But incongruously, in his extralegal, private family, he fathered three sons (Madison, Beverly, and Eston) and a daughter (Harriet) whom he enslaved until they reached the age of twenty-one. Their mother, Sally Hemings, was an enslaved woman whom Jefferson sexually dominated. Both families cohabited Monticello, but Jefferson never sanctioned a multiracial society. "Correct family relations" were the bedrock of Jefferson's republican society in which fathers, mothers, and children were "knitted together by tender attachments."[44] But some critics and commentators in the twenty-first century "insist that it was impossible [for Jefferson] to have loved [Sally] Hemings in the early nineteenth century; even a supposed affection for Sally was worthy of ridicule."[45] Inevitably, Sally Hemings spent her entire lifetime faithful to Jefferson.[46] She was subsumed under his legal personality.

In 1809, Jefferson retired to Monticello and spent the remining years of his life with his daughter Martha and a horde of grandchildren and visitors. As a grandfather, he was playful, affectionate, and "impartial."[47] His private rooms at Monticello were not "places for casual dropping in just to chat with 'Papa,' Grand Papa."[48] Ironically, "the people who had the most contact with Jefferson's intimate space were the enslaved."[49] Sally Hemings officially was his "chamber-maid." An enslaved man named Israel Jefferson made the fires, cleaned his room, and ran errands.

When Jefferson died on July 4, 1826, at the age of eighty-three, he left his family with debts. Monticello had been his "private castle," an extravagant and expensive home to maintain for his own privacy and comfort during his declining years.[50] So, his family sold 130 enslaved people to help cover debts. In his will he freed other people, two of whom were his own sons with Sally Hemings, but he did not free her. Throughout his life, Jefferson ran Monticello completely on slavery.

One of Jefferson's greatest achievements was founding the University of Virginia; he relished that role. In 1818, he used his political, intellectual, and architectural gifts to plan the first university in Virginia. "If knowledge is power," Jefferson stated, then it was important to advance knowledge in the state of Virginia.[51] The diffusion of knowledge is a foundation for freedom, and freedom of the mind follows truth. Jefferson feared any establishment of a monarchy or dictatorship encroaching on the nation. He believed that educated people had to be the source of power in a federal system.[52]

Interestingly, in 1820 all students in the University of Virginia were male. Jefferson never sought to enlarge the public role of women, immigrants, or African Americans. "Ending slavery. . . would be the ultimate test of Virginia's [educated] republican character."[53] The young had to be educated and nursed daily to oppose tyranny.[54] Jefferson never found courage to extricate Virginia from the perniciousness of slavery, but he did disengage it from the dominance of religion. In the curriculum of the university, he abolished the Department of Divinity. He refused to include a professor of divinity on the faculty.[55] When he offered Thomas Cooper, a Unitarian, a position at the university in 1820, Jefferson was accused of being hostile to religion. In 1822, he said that "the genuine doctrine of one God is reviving, and I trust that there is not a *young man* now living in the United States who will not be a Unitarian."[56]

Finally, "Jefferson loved America most...despite fierce opposition to realize his vision: the creation, survival, and success of a popular government in America.... The father of the ideal of individual liberty..., Jefferson recognized the genius of humanity—and the genius of a new nation—lay in the possibility of progress, of discovering the undiscovered and seeking the unknown."[57] From politics on the Potomac to his complicated life at Monticello and the creation of the University of Virginia, Jefferson excelled in every endeavor except becoming the Father against slavery. Sadly, Jefferson's "Empire of Liberty" trumpeted liberty for the white population but not for the Black population.

Notes to Thomas Jefferson: The Patriarch

1. Annette Gordon-Reed and Peter S. Onuf, *"Most Blessed of the Patriarchs": Thomas Jefferson and the Empire of the Imagination* (New York: Liveright Publishing Corporation, 2016), xiv.
2. Gordon-Reed and Onuf, *"Most Blessed of the Patriarchs"*, 192.
3. Cover of Gordon-Reed and Onuf, *"Most Blessed of the Patriarchs"*.
4. Gordon-Reed and Onuf, *"Most Blessed of the Patriarchs"*, 11.
5. Joyce Appleby, *Thomas Jefferson* (New York: Henry Holt, 2003), 24.
6. Gordon-Reed and Onuf, *"Most Blessed of the Patriarchs"*, 7.
7. Quoted in Gordon-Reed and Onuf, *"Most Blessed of the Patriarchs"*, 177.
8. Gordon-Reed and Onuf, *"Most Blessed of the Patriarchs"*, 70.
9. Gordon-Reed and Onuf, 9.
10. Gordon-Reed and Onuf, 86.
11. Gordon-Reed and Onuf, 86.
12. Gordon-Reed and Onuf, 90.
13. Gordon-Reed and Onuf, 141.
14. Quoted in Gordon-Reed and Onuf, *"Most Blessed of the Patriarchs"*, 4.
15. Gordon-Reed and Onuf, *"Most Blessed of the Patriarchs"*, 9.
16. Gordon-Reed and Onuf, 8.
17. Gordon-Reed and Onuf, 4.
18. Gordon-Reed and Onuf, 4.
19. Gordon-Reed and Onuf, 70.
20. Gordon-Reed and Onuf, 81.
21. Gordon-Reed and Onuf, 176.

22. Gordon-Reed and Onuf, 40.
23. Gordon-Reed and Onuf, 8.
24. Jon Meacham, *Thomas Jefferson: The Art of Power* (New York: Random House, 2012), 254.
25. Cover of Appleby, *Thomas Jefferson.*
26. Gordon-Reed and Onuf, *"Most Blessed of the Patriarchs"*, 176.
27. Gordon-Reed and Onuf, *"Most Blessed of the Patriarchs"*, 202.
28. Meacham, *Thomas Jefferson*, 500.
29. Gordon-Reed and Onuf, *"Most Blessed of the Patriarchs"*, 138-139.
30. Appleby, *Thomas Jefferson*, xvii.
31. Quoted in Gordon-Reed and Onuf, *"Most Blessed of the Patriarchs"*, 47.
32. Quoted in Gordon-Reed and Onuf, *"Most Blessed of the Patriarchs"*, 148.
33. Meacham, *Thomas Jefferson*, 218.
34. Meacham, 290.
35. Meacham, 239.
36. Meacham, 239-240.
37. Gordon-Reed and Onuf, *"Most Blessed of the Patriarchs"*, 238.
38. Gordon-Reed and Onuf, 312.
39. Gordon-Reed and Onuf, 132.
40. Gordon-Reed and Onuf, 46.
41. Gordon-Reed and Onuf, 58.
42. Gordon-Reed and Onuf, 62.
43. Gordon-Reed and Onuf, 51.
44. Gordon-Reed and Onuf, 11.
45. Gordon-Reed and Onuf, 128.
46. Meacham, *Thomas Jefferson*, 218.
47. Gordon-Reed and Onuf, *"Most Blessed of the Patriarchs"*, 259.
48. Gordon-Reed and Onuf, 271.
49. Gordon-Reed and Onuf, 271.
50. Gordon-Reed and Onuf, 185.
51. Appleby, *Thomas Jefferson*, 149.
52. Gordon-Reed and Onuf, *"Most Blessed of the Patriarchs"*, 86.
53. Gordon-Reed and Onuf, 136.
54. Gordon-Reed and Onuf, 137.
55. Meacham, *Thomas Jefferson*, 470.
56. Quoted in Meacham, *Thomas Jefferson*, 471.
57. Cover of Meacham, *Thomas Jefferson.*

Thomas Jefferson and "Slave Power"

Thomas Jefferson is highly revered as the masterful architect of freedom, liberty and democracy; he molded the American spirit within the Declaration of Independence. He was a diplomat to France, a musician (vocal and violin), a surveyor, a lawyer, a scientist, an architect of Monticello, an inventor of the dumb waiter, an eloquent writer, a philosopher, a political thinker, and the founder of the University of Virginia. Without him, America might have become a very different nation. He is famous despite not having abolished slavery.

In the past few decades, however, scholars and historians have painted a new portrait of Jefferson. Evidence that had been overlooked, disregarded, or long suppressed is now receiving attention, revealing his mistreatment of the people he enslaved and his moral indifference to slavery. In fact, some recent scholars and authors now label Jefferson a "racist" and a "hypocrite."

The evidence we have about Jefferson includes the following: thousands of copies of Jefferson's correspondence published by Princeton University as part of the series "Papers of Thomas Jefferson"; Jefferson's *Papers* in the Library of Congress and his original writings in the U.S. Printing Office; artifacts unearthed at Monticello; documents from the Jefferson Library; Jefferson's *Farm Book;* letters written by enslaved people; DNA findings; and documents from many historical societies. Presentism, that is, judging the past by the standards of the present, can be a dangerous thing, but it is difficult for twenty-first century Americans to understand the mode of thinking that kept the system of slavery going.[1] However, writers, journalists, filmmakers, and historians continue to give us new assessments and interpretations of Jefferson's life. Jon Meacham, author of *Thomas Jefferson: The Art of Power,* believes that even "rendering moral judgments in retrospect can be hazardous. It is unfair to judge the past by the [moral] standards of the present."[2] Yet, we can render judgments on "moral actions." Jefferson tolerated slavery all around him, but abolitionists tried to stop such a system. Meacham contends that Jefferson placed political power above moral power. He was committed to Southern interests and to keeping the republic together. He claimed that the problem of slavery would be handled in due time—by others.[3] "He knew slavery was a moral wrong..., but he could not, however, bring himself to emancipation [of the enslaved]."[4] Jefferson would live in the "code of denial that defined life in the slave-owning states," and "he would live as he wished" in his mansion at Monticello.[5] He was never willing to sacrifice his aristocratic way of life by relinquishing his power he had as an enslaver. Henry Wiencek, author of *Master of the Mountain: Thomas Jefferson and His Slaves,* believes that Jefferson moved the boundaries of his moral map to make the horrific slavery system tolerable for him.[6] In keeping with the norms in the South in his time, Jefferson did not have the moral courage to oppose slavery. No politician could advance in the South if they opposed slavery. In addition, according to Wiencek, Jefferson discovered that slavery was very financially profitable. It was "a ready form of capital to keep his creditors at bay."[7]

Many Americans want to praise Jefferson for his service to his nation but ignore his shortcomings as a wealthy enslaver. But, according to Wiencek in *Master of the Mountain,* a thread of racism "weighed [him] down and eventually dragged [him] under."[8] "Jefferson wore racism like a suit of armor, knowing it would always break the sharpest swords of the idealists."[9]

Jefferson's racism and white supremacy are evident in a document he wrote in 1781, *Notes on the State of Virginia,* which was published in 1785. Jefferson was governor of Virginia for two terms from 1779 to 1781. One section of the assessment of Virginia that he wrote after his second term demeaned all Black people. In *Notes,* he proposed that Virginia gradually phase out slavery rather than abolish it. He encouraged the state legislature to pass an amendment such that, when the children of the enslaved reached adulthood, "they should be colonized to such place as the circumstances of the time should render most proper, sending them out with arms, implements of household and of the handcraft arts, seeds, pairs of the useful domestic animals, and so forth, to declare them a free and independent people...with protection, till they have acquired strength; and to send vessels at the same time to other parts of the world for an equal number of white inhabitants...."[10] Jefferson recommended that all newly emancipated people should be sent out of the state to form separate colonies. He believed that deep-rooted differences between Black and white people made it impossible for them to live together. He speculated that racial conflict in the nation "will probably never end but in the extermination of the one or the other race."[11]

Annette Gordon-Reed, author of two volumes about Thomas Jefferson and the Hemings family, asks, "How could a man who wrote such [words in *Notes*] engage in a sexual liaison with a Black person, [Sally Hemings]?... Jefferson was deeply and profoundly racist."[12] He wrote *Notes* when he was thirty-eight years old and enslaved 175 people. He knew many skilled and loyal Black people and he knew their talents as carpenters, farmers, bricklayers, metal workers, weavers, spinners, cabinet makers and carriage makers. He selfishly used the talents, labor, and knowledge of enslaved people to build and manage Monticello, his mountaintop mansion, rather than setting them free to earn a living for their families. Like other racist white people, Jefferson feared losing control of the people he oppressed and kept captive.

Jefferson accepted the stereotypes about African Americans common in his time. He thrust his racism upon enslaved people in complete disregard of the sweeping moral statements that he had penned such as "liberty for all," "all men are created equal" and "endowed by their Creator with certain unalienable Rights, that among these are Life, Liberty, and the Pursuit of Happiness." Upon this major theme, some scholars and writers contend that Jefferson was a hypocrite for the following reasons:

Known for his advocacy of citizenship, he proposed legislation to expel American-born, emancipated Black people from their own states.

He proposed expelling racially mixed children from Virginia, even though he married a woman from a racially mixed family and fathered children with his wife's racially mixed half-sister. He never wanted a multiracial society, but he created one at Monticello.

He preached "liberty," but not for those he enslaved. In his lifetime he enslaved some six hundred people, but he freed only two before his death and only five afterwards through his will. About two hundred people were auctioned off after Jefferson's death.

He believed in an educated society, but he did not provide schools for those enslaved at Monticello. He did not want them to learn to write because they might forge papers with their names to emancipate themselves. Archeologists have found writing slates and pencils in the slave quarters of Monticello, so it is evident that many people wanted to learn to read and write.

Jefferson hated conflict and avoided violence, yet he ordered his overseers at Monticello to lash and beat enslaved people.

Jefferson must be given credit for attempting to end slavery in two major statements. In a draft of the Declaration of Independence in 1776, he denounced the slave trade as "execrable commerce" and a "cruel war against human nature itself, violating its most sacred rights of life and liberties."[13] Secondly, in the Ordinance of 1784, he proposed banning slavery in any *new* territory settled in the United States, but it failed to pass. As president, Jefferson did not attack slavery, even though he may have had power to do something about the increase in slavery throughout the West. He could have proposed a gradual transition towards full emancipation, but slave states threatened to secede from the nation unless slavery was permitted. Many enslavers became rich at this time, selling human beings just like horses or oxen. Wealth seemed to be their god.

In 1820, the Missouri Compromise agitated Jefferson. He believed that Congress could not ban slavery in all states north of Missouri. He believed that states had the right to permit or ban slavery based on the vote of their legislators or their people. After the Missouri Compromise, he could see slavery as a tragedy, but he was unwilling to erase it in his nation or at Monticello. "The man who believed in the acquisition and wielding of power...chose to consider himself powerless over the economic and social fact of [slavery] in his life."[14] As long as slavery was profitable, it would not end.

In 1803 when Jefferson was president, he arranged the Louisiana Purchase and requested that senators permit slavery in Louisiana. He became "the father of slavery in Louisiana."[15] He might have changed the course of history with his political power at this point if he had valued his moral legacy.

Imagine! With political power as a diplomat in France, as secretary of state under Washington, as vice president under Adams, as the third president of the United States, and as a Founding Father of this nation, Jefferson could have expended more of his "political capital" in an effort to banish slavery in his lifetime. Had he done so, perhaps there would not have been a Civil War.

Jon Meacham contends that "Jefferson was never able to move public opinion on slavery...his powers failed him—and they failed America."[16] He was devoted to liberty and power, but he refused to give liberty to those he enslaved. For Meacham, Jefferson was a "vivid, engaging, breathing figure, brilliant and eloquent, at once monumental and human."[17] Annette Gordon-Reed believes that Jefferson made "a landmark contribution to American History."[18] However, on one occasion in 1859, Lincoln declined an invitation to celebrate Jefferson's birthday, saying, "This is a world of compensations; and he who would be no slave, must consent to have no slave. Those who deny freedom to others, deserve it not for themselves, and, under a just God, cannot long retain it."[19] Jefferson in his life did not envision "liberty" for the enslaved at Monticello. Out of six hundred people he enslaved, he freed only seven. A legacy of greatness follows Jefferson, but so do the scars of racism and hypocrisy.

Notes to Thomas Jefferson and "Slave Power"

1. Annette Gordon-Reed, *Thomas Jefferson and Sally Hemings: An American Controversy* (Charlottesville, VA: University Press of Virginia, 1997), 17.
2. Jon Meacham, *Thomas Jefferson: The Art of Power* (New York: Random House, 2012), 477.
3. Meacham, *Thomas Jefferson*, 478.
4. Meacham, 474.
5. Meacham, 455.
6. Henry Wiencek, *Master of the Mountain: Thomas Jefferson and His Slaves* (New York: Farrar, Straus, and Giroux, 2012), 210.
7. Paul Finkelman, *Slavery and the Founders: Race and Liberty in the Age of Jefferson* (London: M.E. Sharpe, 1996), 107.
8. Wiencek, *Master of the Mountain*, 261.
9. Wiencek, *Master of the Mountain*, 260.

10. Quoted in Gary Colombo, Robert Cullen, and Bonnie Lisle, eds., *Rereading America: Cultural Contexts for Critical Thinking and Writing*, 7th ed. (Boston: Bedford/St. Martin's, 2007), 487.
11. Quoted in Gary Colombo, Robert Cullen, and Bonnie Lisle, eds., *Rereading America: Cultural Contexts for Critical Thinking and Writing*, 7th ed. (Boston: Bedford/St. Martin's, 2007), 487.
12. Gordon-Reed, *Thomas Jefferson*, 134.
13. Henry Wiencek, "Master of Monticello," *Smithsonian* (October 2012), 40.
14. Meacham, *Thomas Jefferson*, 476.
15. Wiencek, *Master of the Mountain*, 256.
16. Meacham, *Thomas Jefferson*, 124.
17. Meacham, *Thomas Jefferson*, 499.
18. Annette Gordon-Reed, *The Hemingses of Monticello: An American Family* (New York: W. W. Norton, 2008), 12.
19. Quoted in Gordon-Reed, *The Hemingses*, 501.

Thomas Jefferson and the Three-Fifths Compromise

In 2004, Robert Forbes, associate director of the Yale Gilder Lehrman Center for the Study of Slavery, Resistance and Abolition, identified a clear division among historians of early America on the issue of whether slavery was central to or peripheral to U.S. history.[1] Contemporary historians such as Paul Finkelman, Leonard Richards, Don Fehrenbacher, and William Freehling have been "coming to grips with the vast octopus that was slavery" and how "the tentacles [of slavery] spread to every part of our nation and its political life."[2] For example, Paul Finkelman argues that the South found ways to interpret the Constitution to protect enslaved "property" by using "state sovereignty" or "states' rights." In addition, enslavers wanted to protect their property with the use of the militia. Southern states benefitted from the Constitution's prohibition of taxes on exports such as cotton.[3] Slavery also became embedded in the American political system through the Constitution's three-fifths compromise in Article I, Section 2 of the Constitution of the United States.

Federalist newspapers declared that Thomas Jefferson would not have been elected president in 1800 if it had not been for the three-fifths rule in the Constitution that had unjustly inflated the number of electors allocated to the South.[4] Southern "slave power" was converted into political power. Indeed, the early power struggle between the North and South involved differences over slavery and differences between industrial and agricultural interests. At the Constitutional Convention in 1787, Gouverneur Morris claimed that the proposed three-fifths clause was "an unjust support for slavery, one that gave the slave states incentive to import more slaves."[5] The three-fifths clause in the Constitution passed in 1789 added three-fifths of the enslaved population of a state to its white population for the purpose of apportioning seats in the House of Representatives.

With the three-fifths clause (also called the "Federal ratio"), power in the South derived from the legality of slavery turned into political power in the House of Representatives. "Slave power" is the power slave states wielded over free states. A misconception exists that the Founding Fathers considered Black people three-fifths of a person; the three-fifths clause did not relate to the individual worth or monetary value of a slave. Instead, the three-fifths clause established a rule to determine how many seats each state would have in the House. The more enslaved that a state had, the more seats it got. But since enslaved people could not vote, the clause significantly magnified the voice of white, male Southerners in the federal government, especially white, male Southern enslavers. Opponents of slavery bowed to this three-fifths compromise by necessity; otherwise, the slave states would not have approved the Constitution. Jefferson won the presidency in 1800 due to the Southern margin.

The three-fifths compromise was an agreement between Southern and Northern states to enumerate the enslaved population for the purposes of taxation and representation in the House of Representatives. Even though the enslaved could not vote, enslavers wanted to benefit from the actual number of persons represented in the South so that it would increase their representation in the House and in the Electoral College. In pre-Civil-War political affairs, the three-fifths ratio had a major effect upon all voters in the nation because a disproportional representation of slave states tipped the balance of power in favor of slavery. The three-fifths compromise favored Southern slave states with larger populations of enslaved people. As a result, prior to the Civil War, the South had an increased number of votes, and, therefore, dominated the presidency, the Speaker of the House, and the Supreme Court.[6]

The clause is rooted in a measure for taxation in Article XI of the 1781 Articles of Confederation that specified that "funds...shall be supplied by the several colonies in proportion to the number of inhabitants of every age, sex, and quality, except Indians not paying taxes."[7] A census was needed to determine this taxation plan, but it was impossible to conduct such a census during the Revolutionary War when the population was shifting. When the Constitutional Convention met to approve a constitution in 1787, the South objected to the taxation plan in the Articles of Confederation because the presence of a large number of non-voting enslaved people in the South would raise the South's taxes. Incidentally, the North heartily approved of this taxation plan because it had fewer enslaved people. Several questions emerged in debate. First, should only free white men with property be taxed? If so, the value of that property should include the enslaved, who were considered property along with horses, cattle, and oxen. Second, should one-half of the enslaved be counted for the purpose of allocating House seats? The South claimed that the enslaved did three-quarters of the work for the progress of the nation. However, the North claimed that they did not work at the same efficiency as freemen in the North. A third suggestion was to base taxation and representation on the value of land. A strong objection to this plan was that states would misreport land values to reduce taxation. Finally, the Deep South made it clear that it would not ratify the Constitution without a provision for including the enslaved. Thereupon, the compromise became to count three-fifths of the enslaved population for the purpose of representation in the House of Representatives.

No union of the states would have been forthcoming without the "Federal ratio."[8] The South was determined to buttress any assault on slavery. Furthermore, in 1786, the West was thought to be an extension of the South, so the Southwest was expected to become more populated. Families from slave states in the South often moved those they enslaved to the West. Whereas the Continental Congress wanted to create confidence in the Union, the Constitution with the three-fifths clause produced a regional imbalance in North-South representation in Congress. The three-fifths clause did not strengthen the Union of States. "In the long run, the South finally did not outnumber the North as expected [because of the flow of immigrants to the North], but [the South] experienced a great surge in the early years, making other regions feel a certain panic."[9] "The slave power damaged the political and commercial interests of New England," for the "Federal ratio" diminished New England's standing in the government.[10]

Garry Wills, author of *"Negro President": Jefferson and the Slave Power,* contends that the three-fifths rule had a major effect on pre-Civil War political affairs because the South had disproportional representation relative to the North. For example, in 1793 slave states would have been apportioned 33 seats in the House of Representatives based on the free population; instead, they were apportioned 47 with the three-fifths rule. In 1812, slave states had 76 seats instead of the 59 they would have had without the three-fifths rule; in 1833, the South had 98 seats instead of 73.

In his book *Adams vs. Jefferson: The Tumultuous Election of 1800,* John Ferling describes some similarities between political leaders of the late eighteenth century and the early twenty-first century. Personal ambition provoked many men to seek office. They often represented interest groups. After preaching high ideals, they traveled the low road. They smeared foes, tried to connect adversaries to scandals, and played on raw emotions. Their noble ideals masked their self-serving initiatives. As he campaigned for the presidency in 1800, Jefferson exhibited some of these qualities. Slavery in the South was not the problem for him, but it threatened his standing in the North where many active abolitionists resided. However, with the three-fifths clause in the Constitution, he would be favored in the Electoral College where he could win an election. According to William Randall, author of the biography *Thomas Jefferson: A Life,* the three-fifths compromise determined how "Jefferson and Madison were ready to lead the Republican resistance in what was perhaps the dirtiest presidential campaign in American history."[11]

What was transpiring in the nation around 1800? According to Gordon Wood, author of *Empire of Liberty,* the North was dominated by lawyers and officeholders, whereas the South and Southwest were dominated by enslavers. In the industrialized North, office seekers valued labor, whereas the white population in the South "became more and more contemptuous of work and desirous of leisure that slavery seemed to offer."[12] In his book the *American Sphinx: The Character of Thomas Jefferson,* Joseph Ellis reports that the North was strewn with representatives of the Federalist party who wanted a strong federal government controlled by the executive and judicial branches, whereas the South, with Republican influence, wanted a smaller, weaker federal government with the House of Representatives as the dominant force.[13] Wood argues that the South wanted "social hierarchy," a patriarchal system, and "a perpetuating oligarchy."[14] He also notes that the South had less paper money and fewer turnpikes, canals, banks, and corporations than the North.[15] Many men in the North and South had difficulty voting because polling centers were far from their home and required proper voter documentation. John Ferling also points out that in 1800 one in twenty-five Americans lived in cities (69,000 in Philadelphia) and one in six was enslaved (900,000 human beings). By 1800 slavery was legal except in seven free states and two free territories. Three-fourths of Northern Black people were free in 1800.[16] In so many ways, the North and South could have complemented each other, one being industrialized and the other agrarian, but they had conflicting political interests and philosophies of social order and slavery.

The three-fifths clause in the Constitution affected only the House of Representatives, not the Senate; however, the House in 1800 was the most important chamber because it controlled the caucuses that nominated candidates and the Electoral College that elected presidents. While "everyone recognized Jefferson depended on slaves for his economic existence, fewer reflected that he depended on them for his political existence. Yet the latter was the all-important guardian of the former" in Virginia.[17] Jefferson was the protector and extender of the slave system,[18] and this gave him enormous clout politically as the Southern states moved slaves westward. Unless one defended slavery, a political career was impossible in the South. With the three-fifths clause, slavery triumphed in the political career of Jefferson. He would have lost the election of 1800 without the slave count.

According to Garry Wills, the Federal ratio or three-fifths rule "was not an eternal principle meant to guide all just governing. It was a concession to an ultimatum, a necessary evil, the condition for forming a government at all."[19] The rule conflicted with the notion of equal representation and changed the political balance between the thirteen original states. The inequality of representation incentivized the South to increase the enslaved population while the Northeast gradually moved to abolish slavery entirely. In fact, Timothy Pickering in 1804 tried to separate the Northeastern states from the Union to accomplish this goal of abolishing slavery and undermining the power held by the South. Jefferson attacked Pickering as a traitor because Pickering mobilized resistance within the Union against the "slave power" of the South. Jefferson benefitted politically from the maintenance of slavery. By 1808, during Jefferson's second presidential term, "the slave power was losing."[20] Immigrants to the Northeast expanded the voting population. It is ironic that Jefferson, an aristocratic enslaver, was America's supreme spokesman for liberty, equality, and democracy.

Garry Wills points out that biographers of Jefferson have historically neglected to mention the importance of the three-fifths rule for Jefferson's election as president.[21] For example, Dumas Malone, a principal biographer of Thomas Jefferson, makes no mention of the three-fifths rule in two volumes of his work. David McCullough, who chronicles John Adams' life, mentions the rule only once. Willard Sterne Randall, author of a comprehensive biography of Thomas Jefferson in 1998, pays little attention to the three-fifths clause's role in Jefferson's election. Garry Wills believes that Americans tend to have "amnesia" over the impact of slavery on the nation. He notes that only the presidential elections in which Jefferson ran were greatly affected by the three-fifths clause. Moreover, in the nineteenth century, the dire predictions of the Southern majorities in the House of Representatives did not materialize because of the influx of immigrants in the North and the ban on the importation of enslaved people in 1808. In any case, the three-fifths clause caused all Democratic presidential nominees to be friendly to slavery for political survival.[22]

The South's power had repercussions. Southerners held most of the key positions in the Speaker's office before 1824.[23] Southern representatives had a crucial role in nominations to influential positions in the federal government. The South had a head start in management of the federal government leading up to the Civil War. In 1843, John Quincy Adams told the House of Representatives, "your country is not a democracy, it is not even a republic—it is a government of two or three thousand holders of slaves, to the utter exclusion of the remaining part."[24]

Jefferson was admired in Virginia, a solid, Southern slave state, but he faced a number of criticisms when he was a candidate for president of the United States. Jefferson's long friendship with John Adams ended over the issue of slavery. Some citizens attacked Jefferson for his unorthodox religious views, impractical scholarly interests, and extravagant cultural tastes.[25] Gossip spread regarding his affections for Maria Cosway in Paris and for the enslaved woman Sally Hemings at Monticello.

As mentioned earlier, Jefferson won the presidential election in 1800 partly because of the South's power resulting from the three-fifths clause.

He accumulated political power in the House of Representatives, in the Electoral College, in the judiciary appointments, and in foreign affairs. The ramifications of the three-fifths clause went beyond Virginia. In effect, the clause gave some legitimacy to slavery in early America. Furthermore, it stymied debate about changing the status of the enslaved. "It gave a key electoral tool for maintaining slavery against the majority of white voters."[26] Fear arose in the nation with Jefferson's election. In fact, without the three-fifths clause, slavery would have been excluded from the Missouri Compromise in 1820; Jackson's Indian Removal Act would have failed; the 1840 gag rule that suppressed free speech against slavery would not have been imposed; the Wilmot Proviso would have banned slavery in territories won from Mexico; and the Kansas-Nebraska Bill of 1854 to support the power of slave states would have failed.[27] Critical decisions on these issues for the United States were affected by the three-fifths clause.

According to Garry Wills, the size of the representation of slave states was an issue as Jefferson expanded his "empire of liberty." His initiatives in the West, the Louisiana Purchase, the attempt to add Florida and Cuba to America, and his support for slavery in Missouri demonstrate that his position on slavery evolved between 1784, when there was no three-fifths representation, and 1820, when there was. "When the chips were down, as in the Missouri crisis, [Jefferson] threw his weight behind slavery's expansion," states David Brion Davis.[28] Jefferson conserved a simple respect for his own political and economic calculus with the three-fifths clause. The Constitution rewarded him with heavy Southern support to continue slavery in new territories in the West. Wills maintains that Jefferson's "slave power" meant he had to direct his political efforts to protecting and expanding slavery wherever possible. One wonders if Jefferson, a professed Unitarian, reflected on his "slave power" in light of the Unitarian principle of "justice, equality, and compassion in human relations." Throughout Jefferson's presidency from 1800 to 1808, slavery's tentacles spread throughout the nation and its political life. According to Theodore Parker, an abolitionist, "The nation was made almost mute on the subject of slavery" during the years before the Civil War.[29]

To increase his power, Jefferson pursued the agreement with Napoleon to acquire the Louisiana Territory in 1803. Louisiana was a new state that would increase the slave count in national politics, thus benefitting Jefferson.[30] The "electoral power was shifting decisively to the South, while economic power was growing in industry and the enterprises of the Northern states."[31] Jefferson originally asked if the purchase of such a vast area of the nation was constitutional; he proposed an amendment to address this issue, but he "quickly put his scruples aside" when he realized that "it was a matter of adding slave states to the Union."[32] According to the historian and writer Annette Gordon-Wood, everyone presumed only the enslaved could work cotton fields, so limiting slavery in any way met with fierce opposition.[33]

There was controversy over governance of the new Louisiana Territory in 1803. Garry Wills writes, "The Constitution gave Congress the power to form new states," but now "Congress was being asked to turn over all the power of ruling the state of Louisiana to the executive branch," which was unprecedented.[34] Congress allowed Jefferson to rule all three branches of government in the Louisiana Territory "during its formative period."[35] He alone could appoint its governor, council, judges, and military authority. Jefferson excused his "draconian rule" over the territory by claiming that these people from many different countries (Spain, France, England) with such diverse language and cultural influences "were not capable of self-rule."[36]

But the most serious problem confronting Louisiana was slavery. Louisiana was well known for its abusive treatment of the enslaved. In 1808, Jefferson excluded foreign slave trade from Louisiana under the directions of Congress. The South supported this legislation because the price of an enslaved person decreased when there was a surplus of Black people already in the country.[37] South Carolina had already outlawed the importation of enslaved people from a foreign country, but they wanted exclusive selling rights to Louisiana.[38] Virginia was the leading seller of enslaved people and wanted to profit from selling them to fertile, new states that would raise rice, indigo, and cotton. "Louisiana looked like a bonanza to people anxious to unload their slaves at high prices—and it looked that way precisely because Jefferson excluded slave importation from abroad."[39] To obtain high prices, Jefferson sold eighty-five of the people he enslaved, a high number, since he owned 199 in 1810. He put seventy-one people up for auction—that is, into the hands of traders "unknown for their treatment of slaves."[40] Jefferson bartered human beings for the highest prices; he wrenched Black people out of their more secure communities around Monticello in Virginia. In fact, "wealthy Southerners would not move...to develop the land [of Louisiana] if they could not take their slaves. The new plantations could be worked only by slave labor."[41] Indeed, Southerners "worked with all their energy to create new states where slaves could not be self-governing."[42] Instead, it revealed "colonization as a fake humanitarian scheme."[43]

Toward the end of his life, Jefferson retired to his debt-encumbered Monticello. His farms were still worked by an enslaved population. Some thought Jefferson was a moral coward for not freeing all those he enslaved at his death.

Clearly, "in retrospect…the election of [Jefferson] in 1800 was a great tipping point in American history, signaling the demise of the Federalist domination of the government and the advent of the Republican rule."[44] However, the influence of "slave power" in the election of Jefferson in 1800 has historically been ignored. The three-fifths clause that gave a path for Jefferson to the presidency was a constitutional measure that created an unfair imbalance between the North and the South in governing the nation. Jefferson claimed that his victory was a "triumph of democracy," but, unfortunately, it was Jefferson's "ride into the Temple of Liberty on the shoulders of slaves."[45] He would have lost the election of 1800 without the Federal ratio. Instead, he spent eight years holding the reins of power in Washington, a city "where slavery would be taken for granted, where it would not need perpetual apology, excuse, or palliation, where the most honored men in the nation were not to be criticized because they practiced and defended and gave privilege to the holding of slaves."[46] Jefferson's three-fifths advantage in the 1800 election marred the country's sense of "freedom, liberty, equality, and justice for all."

After the Civil War, the Thirteenth Amendment to the Constitution abolished slavery. The Fourteenth Amendment, which was adopted in 1868, formally eliminated the three-fifths clause. Section 2 of the Fourteenth Amendment begins with this line: *Representation shall be apportioned among the several States according to their respective numbers, counting the whole number of persons in each State, excluding Indians not taxed.*

Notes to Thomas Jefferson and the Three-Fifths Compromise

1. Garry Wills, *"Negro President": Jefferson and the Slave Power* (Boston: Houghton Mifflin, 2003), xi.
2. Wills, *"Negro President"*, 13.
3. Wills, *"Negro President"*, 10-11.
4. John Ferling, *Adams vs. Jefferson: The Tumultuous Election of 1800* (New York: Oxford University Press, 2004), 208.
5. Gordon S. Wood, *Empire of Liberty: A History of the Early Republic, 1789-1815* (New York: Oxford University Press, 2009), 532.
6. Wills, *"Negro President"*, 5-6.
7. Wills, 51.
8. Wills, 57.
9. Wills, 61.
10. Wills, 105.
11. Willard Sterne Randall, *Thomas Jefferson: A Life* (New York: Henry Holt, 1993), 536.
12. Wood, *Empire of Liberty*, 530.
13. Joseph J. Ellis, *American Sphinx: The Character of Thomas Jefferson* (New York: Vintage, 1998), 198.
14. Wood, *Empire of Liberty*, 531.
15. Wood, *Empire of Liberty*, 531.
16. Ferling, *Adams vs. Jefferson*, 15.
17. Wills, *"Negro President"*, xvii.
18. Wills, *"Negro President"*, xviii.
19. Wills, *"Negro President"*, 122.
20. Wills, *"Negro President"*, 147.
21. Wills, 4.
22. Wills, 5-7.
23. Wills, 7.
24. Quoted in Wills, *"Negro President"*, 8.
25. Randall, *Thomas Jefferson*, 592.
26. Wills, *"Negro President"*, 4.
27. Wills, *"Negro President"*, 5.
28. Quoted in Wills, *"Negro President"*, 9.
29. Quoted in Wills, *"Negro President"*, 12.
30. Wills, *"Negro President"*, 115.
31. Wills, 116.
32. Wills, 116.

33. Annette Gordon-Reed, *The Hemingses of Monticello: An American Family* (New York: W.W. Norton, 2008), 529.
34. Wills, *"Negro President"*, 119.
35. Wills, 119.
36. Wills, 120.
37. Wills, 121.
38. Wills, 121.
39. Wills, 122.
40. Wills, 121.
41. Wills, 120.
42. Wills, 192.
43. Wills, 192.
44. Wills, 49.
45. Wills, 2.
46. Wills, 213.

Thomas Jefferson's Exploitive, Clandestine Affair with Sally Hemings

Historians, biographers, journalists, commentators, and writers need to truthfully analyze the mysterious secrets abounding in Thomas Jefferson's personal life. The more this life is scrutinized, the more speculation materializes about Sally Hemings, an enslaved woman who bore six children fathered by Jefferson. Historians haven't uncovered documents revealing intimate traces of Hemings and her thoughts, but there are some sources that point to the truth about the relationship between Jefferson and Hemings. "Truth," according to Jefferson, "is the proper and sufficient antagonist to error. The natural weapons of free argument and debate contradict errors and permit truth."[1] Distinguished historians of Jefferson in the early twentieth century (Dumas Malone, Henry Randall, and Merrill Peterson) denied or ignored his exploitive affair with Hemings. But in recent decades biographers and historians such as Fawn Brodie, Annette Gordon-Reed, Joseph Ellis, and Jon Meacham have looked more closely at Jefferson's personal life, pointing out his romances, racism, and sexism. Jefferson kept his personal life with Sally shrouded in secrecy, but we can see today that it contradicted some principles of his philosophy.

The relationship of Jefferson and Hemings began in 1773 when Jefferson inherited 135 enslaved people at Monticello upon the death of John Wayles, his father-in-law and the father of Sally Hemings, making her Martha Wayles Jefferson's half-sister. Among these inherited people were the members of the Hemings family, who interwove their presence at Monticello throughout Jefferson's entire life. No other enslaved family was as important for four generations as the Hemings family was at Monticello.

Elizabeth "Betty" Hemings served as the matriarch of this stable family. Jon Meacham, author of *Thomas Jefferson: The Art of Power,* traces the historical background of this family. Elizabeth was born on a slave ship bound for America to a Black African woman, Suzanne, and Captain John Hemings, "the captain of an English trading vessel." Suzanne and her daughter Elizabeth ended up enslaved in the home of John Wayles. Captain Hemings wanted to buy his daughter Elizabeth as his "own flesh." He offered "an extraordinary large price for her," but John Wales (Wayles is the American spelling) refused to sell the child. Captain Hemings plotted to "take the child by force," but his plans were thwarted when someone alerted Wayles, who then moved the mother and child inland to his plantation. In 1730, many enslaved people were imported at Williamsburg, Virginia. Elizabeth Hemings was born into slavery but with the advantage of being light skinned in a racist society. At eleven she became the "property" of John Wayles and eventually bore fourteen children during her lifetime, some of whom were fathered by Wayles. Sally (Sarah) Hemings was her youngest daughter, and Jefferson inherited her at Monticello as a Hemings family member.[2]

From the beginning, the Hemingses received preferential treatment among all enslaved people at Monticello. Although in public Jefferson opposed racial mixing and miscegenation, in private he fathered six children born to Sally Hemings. In his *Notes on the State of Virginia,* Jefferson condemned racial mixing in the strongest terms, claiming that it would enhance Black people and degrade white people. In fact, there were many people of mixed white and Black ancestry at Jefferson's Monticello plantation, and such mixing of races was common throughout the South. "Enslaved women practically and legally could not refuse consent" to a sexual encounter with a white man, particularly one who was her enslaver.[3] "It was a world of desire and denial. Sex across the color line—sex between owner and property—was pervasive yet rarely or directly addressed or alluded to. The strange intermingling of blood and affection and silence suffused the world... that Jefferson came to know."[4] Beyond his own experiences, Jefferson knew that racial mixing between enslavers and their enslaved women occurred.[5] Notably, Jefferson's wife, Martha Skelton Wayles, was a white half-sister of Sally Hemings. Despite Virginia's disdain for mixed races in the eighteenth century, the state did not outlaw sex between white men and the Black women they enslaved.[6] Thus, Jefferson could indulge in his sexual exploitation of Sally Hemings, but not without controversy.

Many historians have denied Sally Hemings' personal connection to Jefferson. In fact, "[Jefferson] never spoke publicly or wrote about Sally and her association with Monticello."[7] She was invisible in his public world. In the end, Jefferson even destroyed letters to and from his wife, Martha, that "bothered him." Likewise, he left no single letter or document about Sally; he preserved his private life from spilling over into his public life. Thereupon, although men like Jefferson transgressed cultural norms, "the fictions of white society—the bedrock upon which white supremacy rested—could continue unchallenged."[8]

In addition to opposing interracial mixing, Jefferson had some misogynistic tendencies. He had a hostile relationship with his mother.[9] He did not care much for her, so he left little written record of her.[10] "Jefferson talked of his mother, Jane Randolph Jefferson, only in reaction to his father."[11] However, she was described as "an agreeable, intelligent woman, as well educated as the other Virginia ladies of the day, of her own elevated rank in society,...and...she was a notable housekeeper."[12] Meacham continues that "she possessed a most amiable and affectionate disposition, a lovely cheerful temper, and a great fund of humor. She was fond of writing, particularly letters, and wrote readily and well."[13] When Jefferson's father Peter Jefferson died in 1757, Jefferson's mother was thirty-seven and had eight children, but she knew how to manage the Shadwell Plantation where Jefferson was born.[14] She enslaved sixty-six people and oversaw 2,700 acres of land.[15]

Jefferson inherited at least several qualities from his mother after living with her until he was twenty-seven. Like her, he was determined to have his own way.[16] He was fond of writing letters and keeping records in his *Farm Book*, like his mother enjoyed letter writing. Even if Jefferson's first encounter with women was his mother, he held her sacred in the end as a part of his home and a part of him. Her death "disoriented her son" with "emotional distress" just as he began writing the Declaration of Independence in 1776.[17]

Even though Jefferson could not disentangle himself from slavery or sexist attitudes, he was at heart a typical Southern enslaver of his time, mixing power, racism, and sexism.[18] Recent historical research has focused on the personal lives of powerful men like Jefferson, including their attitudes toward the enslaved, and to white women and children. For many American women today, Jefferson's legacy is bitter.[19] Winthrop Jordan, author of *White Over Black,* claims there were problems and instabilities in Jefferson's world of women.[20] Recent scholars shine "a bleak light" on Jefferson as an enslaver and racial theorist—and on his relationships with women of all races.[21]

According to Joyce Appleby, author of *Thomas Jefferson,* Jefferson didn't reflect on the meaning of women's existence.[22] He held the conventional belief that male dominance over women and children was "a tenet of natural law."[23] Contrary to this view, Andrew Burnstein, author of *Jefferson's Secrets: Death and Desire at Monticello,* believes that in matters of race and gender, "female delicacy was a cultural construction and not a natural distinction."[24] Jefferson thought women should be amiable, unassuming "guardians of virtue." Virginia women were to be sentimental and affectionate, and men were to have "the outward authority."[25] Furthermore, dutiful wives and nurturing mothers would help build a healthy republic.[26] Jefferson believed that women should value performing domestic duties.[27] Notably, Jefferson's daughter Martha Randolph followed her father's advice and nurtured twelve children.

Jefferson's attitudes toward women were commonplace in his time and in his culture. During his presidency, little was done to improve women's control over their own lives.[28] In 1807, those few women who had the right to vote because they were single and owned property lost that right.[29] "Yellow children" at Monticello gave a promiscuous appearance to what was going on at this plantation.[30] In Jefferson's time, "prostitution was the full-time occupation of perhaps one in twenty-five women in America's principal towns."[31]

Indeed, Jefferson "stood in the way of women's rise; he refused to link intellectual capacity to public visibility; he could not imagine female talent in the marketplace, or in government."[32] He wrote his secretary of treasury in 1807, "The appointment of a woman to office is an innovation for which the public is not prepared, nor am I."[33] He was seemingly afraid of a society in which women actively went about acquiring the tools to compete with men.[34] He feared that women would "mix promiscuously in the public meetings of men."[35] He "may have desired that women remain politically harmless, but he did not want them politically uninformed."[36] Again, during his presidency, single women who owned property could vote until 1807, when women were barred from voting at all.[37] When Jefferson opened the University of Virginia in 1825, he made no provision for the education of women. "He would liberate the human mind as long as it was male."[38]

Of enslaved women, he "never addressed the evident competence of the women around him and what implications it might have for their civil rights."[39] According to Crawford, Jefferson claimed that "slave women were of greater value than slave men: women bore children and therefore added to the work force."[40]

Unfortunately, historians have no substantial evidence of how Jefferson's wife, Martha, his daughter Martha, and Sally Hemings may have viewed Jefferson. Martha burned all but two of her husband's letters and all but one of hers to him.[41] He was away from Monticello much of the time during his active political career. His political life and his social status were imperative to him. He understood that "under the law of nature, all men are born free, every one comes into the world with a right to his own person, which includes the liberty of moving and using it at his own will."[42] The statement "all men are born free" was meant literally for white men.[43] When Jefferson wrote the affirmation of equal rights for all and the phrase "life, liberty, and the pursuit of happiness," it was a sham for the enslaved and for white women, as well.

When Sally Hemings entered Jefferson's sphere, Jefferson lived a double standard: no white woman could ever love a Black man, but a white man could love a Black woman. While Jefferson professed a standard of honor and decency toward women, in reality his repeated sexual encounters with an enslaved woman who had no practical or legal means to refuse him is evidence of his racist, sexist mindset.[44] In fact, after the Revolutionary War, he tried to revise Virginia's slave code to say that white women who had a mixed-race child would have to leave the state or else be denied legal protection. Legislators refused to act on this code.[45] He dragged his contradictions and hypocrisies through his personal as well as his political life. "Jefferson [was the] proponent of the rights of man and an opponent of the rights of women."[46]

Evidently, "there were flaws in Jefferson's judgment. He could not deny he owned human beings or that his loftiest words—'all men are created equal'—were a lie, even if by 'men' he meant only enfranchised men, white men with independent public roles.... In the pursuit of tranquil permanent felicity, a tyrant spirit was lurking."[47] "Most Americans now believe that slave-owning Thomas Jefferson was the father of biracial children, and he possibly had a warm, if not loving, relationship with one of the slaves, Sally Hemings."[48] Some, however, see him as a hypocrite to own a woman but supposedly treasure her in sexual relationship.

Sally Hemings' incredible story is an unorthodox slave narrative. She arrived at Monticello with her enslaved mother, Elizabeth, when she was two years old, and as the half-sister of Jefferson's wife, Martha Wayles Jefferson, she would be his daughters' aunt. At the age of eight, she tended to an ailing Martha with her mother. Martha died in 1782 at the age of thirty-four; Jefferson was thirty-nine. He was a lost, lonely man when his wife died. In 1785 he was assigned to serve in Paris as the United States Minister to France. He was to negotiate a peace treaty with Great Britain. His daughter Martha (Patsy) accompanied him to France, but his daughter Mary (Polly) remained in Virginia with relatives, the Eppes family. At fourteen, Hemings was considered worthy of accompanying nine-year-old Mary to France at Jefferson's request. The ocean voyage in 1787 took six weeks. Hemings was deemed intelligent, creative, capable, and mature for her age. She was light-skinned with straight, flowing hair down her back.[49]

Polly and Hemings arrived safely in Paris. Hemings resided with the family at the Hotel de Langeac where her two brothers James and Robert also resided. Hemings and her brother James "could create their own world and be their true selves within them."[50] Perhaps Hemings developed a new way of looking at herself in Paris. She was liberated from being enslaved, for slavery had been outlawed in France in 1784. While in France, Jefferson used the term "servants" rather than "slaves" and paid Hemings 24 livres per month plus a New Year's tip.[51] "Servant" seemed more socially acceptable.

Jefferson's two daughters attended school at the abbey and resided there under the care of nuns for five days of each week. Hemings became the "chambermaid to Jefferson" and the seamstress and caretaker of Patsy and Polly when they came to visit.[52] She was often alone in the apartment with Jefferson where he worked in his room; therefore, she was in close contact with him. As time went by, she shared the experience of people, places, and times with him. She undoubtedly found the pace of Paris so different from Virginia's slow-paced life.

As a teenager, Hemings had been sent to live in close quarters in a distant land with a middle-aged man. Jefferson's daughters were gone from the hotel a major part of the week. Hemings and Jefferson were not in Virginia, although it was difficult for Jefferson to free himself from that culture in which he was immersed. He attended to Hemings with care. He paid for her inoculations for smallpox; he went shopping at French boutiques for appropriate attire for her to wear in public; and he took walks with her through Paris, a city of more than 700,000 people in which they could be anonymous.[53] "Ingenious...passageways" in the hotel protected the privacy of residents.[54] Paris awakened young Hemings to the allures of dance and social life, previously unknown to her. "She had the misfortune to be born into a society where the people in power chose not to recognize that reality."[55]

Jefferson was responsible for what Hemings did in Paris and where she went. When he bought clothes for her, it "raised an intimacy level."[56] He would not have had these shopping sprees if he had been in Virginia, but in Paris no one was watching them. As Hemings approached the age of seventeen, she became even more attractive and well-developed physically and in her personality. Presidential historian Jon Meacham believes that the Jefferson-Hemings "liaison" may have begun in 1788 in Paris.[57]

Hemings had a sphere of influence much larger in France because Jefferson was not legally an enslaver there.[58] In Paris, close French associates of Jefferson—Marquis de Lafayette and Marquis de Condorcet—were abolitionists. Condorcet criticized "the character of the slave owning class."[59] The inequality of power in slavery was incomprehensible to him, whereas for Jefferson, "to own another human being, in a legal system that gave great deference to the rights of private property, meant that a master's use of a slave for work, or for sex, was really his business."[60] Even in Paris, Jefferson considered Hemings his "property." "Thomas Jefferson owned her body by positive legal right" under Virginia law in the United States.[61] Given the unequal status and power between Hemings and Jefferson, an "affair" would presumably be repeated rape instead of a loving relationship. Though slavery, race, and gender were contentious issues for Jefferson, he was a possessive person who became deeply disturbed whenever anyone in his inner circle tried to extricate himself or herself from his control.[62]

Hemings challenged Jefferson in France. She could never have done that as an enslaved sixteen-year-old in Virginia. She wanted to stay in France where she would be free from slavery. Perhaps her brother James would remain with her in France. Because she only had domestic skills, she had to consider how she could make a living and how an extended family could care for her in France if she decided to stay in Paris. Perhaps Hemings could exert her rights and make a request of Jefferson based on what was best for *her*.[63] For once, she had some control over her destiny. Jefferson was in a weak position. He was not accustomed to not having his way. He started making promises to induce a teenager to return home.[64]

If Jefferson could persuade Hemings to return to Virginia, "he could continue to own her…legally for the rest of her life."[65] Since he had promised Martha he would never marry again, Hemings was a convenient alternative to marriage. As an enslaved young woman, she was forbidden from marrying an enslaved man. She would never engage in sexual relations with another man because then she could be sold, and Jefferson would not have to keep promises he finally made to a "pregnant, enslaved, teenager."[66] Hemings hesitated in her decision to return to slavery in Virginia. However, she received promises from Jefferson that any children she would have would never be sold; that she and her family would be well-fed, sheltered and clothed; and that her children from her relationship with Jefferson would be free at age twenty-one.[67] That is, Hemings' children would not remain slaves for the rest of their lives. At this point, Jefferson was forty-seven and Hemings was seventeen. His liaison with her might hurt his daughters emotionally and change their love for him, but he made Hemings a promise. Hemings agreed to return to Virginia, but she would have no legal recourse if Jefferson broke his promise. She had to trust his intentions.

According to the 1873 memoir written by Madison Hemings, Sally Hemings' son, Sally Hemings was "duly pregnant" when she returned to Virginia. How did she feel when she stepped out of the carriage at Monticello, pregnant? One wonders if Jefferson appreciated her sacrifice to return to slavery in 1789 at the age of seventeen. Now what would the arrangement be at Monticello?

Perhaps Jefferson's sexual passions assured him that Hemings would become helpless in pregnancy, and thereupon, he would win the decision to keep her enslaved. "The extent to which Jefferson kept Sally Hemings and her children relatively anonymous in his *Farm Book* would seem to be symbolic of his entire relationship with her. It was a kind of automatic denial…that this slave woman and her children were not important to him. The denial was accepted too," even if love prevailed.[68] As long as Hemings was enslaved, and as long as there was no written record of their liaison, there was no threat to Jefferson. But if he abandoned her, she could have done social and political damage to him.[69] But he had made a promise to Hemings, and his fidelity made this promise uncompromising.

Madison Hemings wrote in his memoir in 1873 that Sally Hemings gave birth to her first child in 1790, but this was not recorded in Jefferson's *Farm Book*. Furthermore, the child died. In the Monticello household, Hemings became the chambermaid and seamstress, with a room of her own within the house. One wonders if she viewed Jefferson differently in Paris than she did in the conservative, slavery-infused Virginia. The children resulting from their relationship bore the names of Jefferson or his friends who were important to him. Evidently, naming those children was "the work of a woman who wanted to please…a man or of a man who felt his children should bear his mark,"[70] even in secrecy.

Jefferson's conservative, sexist attitude was normal for his time. There could not be a truly respectful, equal relationship between an enslaved woman and her enslaver.? She was fixed in Jefferson's "orbit." He would not let her make a decision to leave him; if she did leave him, she would be pursued and sold. "To demure [as Madison Hemings recorded in his memoir] was to refuse, and Jefferson was unaccustomed to encountering resistance to his absolute will at all, much less from a slave…. His whole life was about controlling."[71]

When Jefferson sought the presidency in 1800, his relationship with Hemings might have become a source of public trouble for him. He kept silent about his personal life, even with the gossip floating relentlessly through the political arena and the plantation. Hemings had been exposed by the *Richmond Recorder* newspaper, but Jefferson denied the story. That Hemings should be sent away must have been unthinkable to him. However, enslavers always made decisions on the basis of the needs of their white families, and Jefferson must have needed Hemings, for she conceived a child each time he was in the proximity of Monticello.

When Jefferson became the third president of the United States in 1801, he could not bring Hemings to Washington, D.C. without all sorts of complications, "not the least of them cute babies running around who looked like [Jefferson]."[72] As speculation arose about Jefferson's relationship with

Hemings, "Sally may have been the most well-known enslaved person in America."[73] Instead of revealing his four children by Hemings, Jefferson told a friend, John Page, that the death of his daughter Maria was a loss of half of all he had. His other daughter, Martha, was the other half. He did not reveal any other person whose loss would devastate him. In 1806, Hemings was thirty-five and Jefferson was sixty-five. Hemings' four children were considered "white" by Virginia law standards, so why would Jefferson allow "whites" to be enslaved at Monticello? The prevalence of white enslaved people at Monticello would need explanation. Jefferson did not free slaves, so when two of Hemings' children arrived at the age of twenty-one, he recorded that they "ran away," not that they were freed. Miscegenation would have created a scandal if the mother of these children had been discovered. Jefferson was cowardly for not freeing his own children at their birth, but his behavior was consistent with the culture of secrecy at the time.

In the 1800s, a "gentleman" could carry on a "liaison" with an enslaved woman and not be stigmatized as an "abusive individual."[74] White society did not consider it to be exploitation. A girl fourteen or fifteen was eligible for male companionship in order to maintain order in this society. Could Hemings have refused Jefferson's advances? It is hard to believe that she could have influenced him in any significant way. She was an impressionable youth, and vulnerable in Paris. She wanted to survive. Perhaps she tried to refuse the long-running drama of the sexual domination of enslaved women by their white enslavers. She had extraordinary privilege in France, and she seemed mature enough at seventeen to make a decision about her life. But Jefferson ensured that she returned to Virginia without emancipation from slavery.

At Monticello, Hemings was entrusted "with the care and tending of Jefferson's private rooms and his wardrobe.... [Jefferson] trusted her with the things he valued most."[75] He listed her as "house servant" and "seamstress" in his *Farm Book*. James A. Bear, resident director of Monticello, claims that there was "no secret stairway" for any affair.[76] According to Alan Pell Crawford in his book *Twilight at Monticello: The Final Years of Thomas Jefferson*, Hemings was kept in close contact with Jefferson. Monticello was "a three-story farmhouse designed to look like a one-floor villa, a masterpiece of architectural deceptions beginning with the way Jefferson concealed its workrooms, slave quarters, and other dependencies beneath the terrace and main house."[77] One room opened into another, nothing hidden. Most rooms on the first floor had expansive entrances. Jefferson's bedroom was on the south side, along with two guest rooms. The family slept upstairs, far away from Jefferson's bedroom. But his bedroom was equipped with two entrances: a front door off the entrance hall and a back passage from the library and study. The back passage allowed anyone to slip unnoticed through the library and study to the bedroom. According to Crawford, a new entrance was added during Hemings' childbearing years. "The first was a set of what he called 'porticoes,' or louvered verandas that shielded the interior of his study and library from a passerby on the terrace outside. There were two such porticoes, and both adjoined exterior stairways to slave quarters below the house."[78] At this time Hemings was moved from a log cabin to a servant's room underneath those porticoes. "These porticoes may not have been built specifically to facilitate Sally's nocturnal visits, but they certainly would have concealed them," states genealogist Helen F. Leary in the *National Geographic Society Quarterly*.[79] Jefferson also added another access to his bedroom: "This was a circular staircase that led directly into Jefferson's library from the slave quarters under the terrace where Sally's 'servant's room' was located. Sally Hemings could easily have entered Jefferson's private chambers at any time of day or night, without being seen or heard."[80] She was the chambermaid.

According to historian Fawn Brodie, "The peace and serenity of Monticello was enforced by Jefferson's remarkable will, by his capacity of ordering a general happiness, by his denial of suffering, the humiliation, and the ugliness [of slavery]."[81] "Loving Sally brought no solution to secrecy, denial, humiliation, guilt, and loss."[82] In essence, Hemings and all of the people Jefferson enslaved were denied many rights, which also denied them of their dignity and the ability to develop their talents.[83] Miscegenation became Jefferson's legacy in his personal life with Hemings. She was dedicated to him for thirty-eight years. He was a man of "appetite, sensuality, and passion."[84] To Jefferson, "Sex was the strongest of the human passions.... He was not a man to deny himself of what he wanted."[85]

In retrospect, historians question why Jefferson destroyed letters to and from his wife, Martha, and perhaps some from Sally Hemings, as well. Evidently, any documents from Martha, and particularly Hemings, troubled Jefferson since he was sensitive about history's judgment of him. No letters to Hemings or Jefferson's daughters after 1788 have been discovered.[86] All the letters Robert Hemings, a literate enslaved man, wrote to Jefferson are no longer available.[87] Though Sally Hemings and James Hemings were literate, there are no traces of a letter sent from Paris to their mother. There are no letters from Jefferson's daughters, Patsy or Polly, that mention Hemings.[88] No letters or diaries remain to know the thoughts of Jefferson's wife, Martha, or of Sally Hemings. However, Jefferson wrote over 40,000 letters in his lifetime.[89] Perhaps private papers were destroyed by fire, flood, or carelessness.[90] "This raises the question whether or not someone at some time went through Jefferson's papers, systematically eliminating every possible reference to Sally Hemings."[91] Historians need documented sources to further illuminate the "illicit relationship" between Hemings and Jefferson.

Historians are "lured by [Jefferson's] mysteries, baffled by [his] ambivalence, and captured by his special genius."[92] Nathan Schachner, a Jefferson biographer, finds Jefferson "a delight and despair" for biographers.[93] He was one of the least self-revealing men. The biographer Merrill Peterson claims that Jefferson was an "impenetrable man."[94] Henry Adams declares that Jefferson continually needed to have secrecy in his private life.[95] Love letters between Jefferson and Maria Cosway, a married woman in France, were kept hidden by the family until 1944. So, it would not be surprising if Jefferson wanted to conceal his feelings for Hemings. Of course, at the time, to reveal his affair with her would have been political suicide, but word about her revealed after his death and in papers released in 1974 did tarnish his legacy.[96]

In 1998, DNA findings about presumed descendants of Jefferson were published in the British science journal *Nature*. Subsequent reevaluation of the results established the high likelihood of Jefferson's sexual relationship with Sally Hemings—a liaison long denied by mainstream historians up until that point—which gave energy to the image of Jefferson as a hypocrite.[97] "For Jefferson, the code of silence on the issue of sex across the color line appears to have been total."[98] DNA established that a male member of Jefferson's family fathered the last of Sally Hemings' children.[99] "The person most likely to have fathered Eston Hemings was Thomas Jefferson himself."[100] In 2000, DNA research eliminated the possibility that one of Jefferson's nephews, Peter or Sam Carr, was the father of one of Hemings' children.[101] Also, in 2000, statisticians at the Thomas Jefferson Memorial Foundation analyzed DNA data and reported that Jefferson was the father of Eston, Hemings' youngest son.[102] The "Report of the Research Commission on Thomas Jefferson and Sally Hemings," published in 2000, concludes that, based on careful DNA tests and other evidence, there is a high probability that Thomas Jefferson fathered Hemings' last child, and there is a significant likelihood that Jefferson was the father of all of Hemings' children.[103]

The author Annette Gordon-Reed reports that, as of 1974, none of the mainstream white historians who wrote biographies of Jefferson accepted that there was an illicit relationship between him and Sally Hemings.[104] We cannot know Jefferson in full if we portray him as a defender of liberty and equality but ignore that he was an advocate of slavery and inequality at Monticello.[105] The character of major leaders in American history can be reexamined through documents, but if key documents have been destroyed by the people close to them, posterity can only make incomplete or inaccurate judgements based on supposition or speculation. In the end, human attributes can only be revealed by those intimately connected to an individual. Fortunately, the words of enslaved Black people such as Madison Hemings and Israel Jefferson now carry as much evidentiary weight concerning Jefferson as the past written accounts of upper-class white people.

Jefferson's white grandson, Thomas Jefferson Randolph, claimed that Jefferson could not have fathered children at Monticello. However, Fawn Brodie cites evidence that Peter and Samuel Carr, Jefferson's nephews, were not at Monticello when Hemings conceived.[106] Also, Peter and Samuel never publicly defended Jefferson's innocence, and Jefferson never blamed his nephews for Hemings' pregnancies.[107] Jefferson's granddaughter, Ellen Randolph Coolidge, wrote a letter to her husband on October 24, 1858 in which she claimed that Jefferson's honor would not have permitted him to engage in any immoralities. She asserted that the Carr nephews fathered Hemings' children. But Annette Gordon-Reed reminds us that what Jefferson and his white family members "wrote, and did not choose to write, does not define the total reality of either their lives or the lives of those whom they enslaved."[108] Madison Hemings, son of Sally Hemings and Jefferson, published a memoir in 1873 that tells a different story about their relationship than that given by Jefferson's white descendants.[109]

Historic records have gaps that cannot be fully resolved, but Black historians have long accepted the story of the Hemings–Jefferson relationship as accurate.[110] Historian and law scholar Annette Gordon-Reed, author of *Thomas Jefferson and Sally Hemings: An American Controversy*, provides considerable evidence of the relationship:

- Madison Hemings' memoirs are believable.
- Enslaved man Israel Jefferson corroborated Madison Hemings' words in his memoir.
- Jefferson did actually free Hemings' children when they turned twenty-one, so he kept his promise; however, he did not emancipate any other enslaved people when they reached that age.
- James Callender published an account of the Jefferson-Hemings relationship in the *Richmond Recorder* newspaper on September 1, 1802. He reported that Jefferson kept an "African Venus" as his "concubine." He identified Sally Hemings.[111] Jefferson never directly responded to the charge in an 1805 letter.
- John Cocke, a member of the Board of Trustees at the University of Virginia, wrote in 1853 and in 1859 that Jefferson had a "mistress."
- Sally Hemings conceived her seven children only when Jefferson was in the proximity.
- Hemings' children did not have to labor in the nailing factory and received special treatment.
- Hemings was assigned a private babysitter so she could work in the house.
- Thomas Jefferson Randolph, grandson of Jefferson, stated that Hemings' children had a marked resemblance to Jefferson.
- Hemings and Jefferson named their children after the Jefferson-Randolph family or close friends of Jefferson.
- All three sons of the Hemings–Jefferson relationship were talented on the violin, just like Jefferson.
- No documents, statements, or DNA evidence support the claim that the Carr brothers were responsible for Sally's pregnancies.

Gordon-Reed also details some arguments by those who refute the claim that there was a relationship between Hemings and Jefferson:

- No letters or notes "between Sally Hemings and Thomas Jefferson have as yet found their way into the public record; one explanation could be that there never were any."[112]
- "Leading authorities" regard Jefferson's affair as myth.[113]

- As a public figure, Jefferson professed a standard of morality, honor, and decency. Shame and guilt would have followed him if he had had an affair with a slave. Miscegenation revolted his whole being.
- Jefferson did not plead guilty to having an affair with Sally Hemings. Jefferson would not lie.
- There is no proof that Jefferson was the cause of Sally's pregnancy in Paris.
- Jefferson carefully cultivated his public image and so would not risk a public scandal of having a "mistress" or having children by a "mistress," especially an enslaved woman who was his property.
- Callender was a slanderous, corrupt, malignant individual; his reporting is unreliable.

Many historians did not believe that Jefferson's personal life with Hemings would compromise his great legacy in American history. In fact, despite the rumblings of an affair, Jefferson was re-elected president for a second term in 1804. Generations of Americans refused to believe that he had an affair. It would have been out of character for him to have had sexual relations with an enslaved woman; that would have gone against "a southern gentleman's unbreakable code of honor."[114] In Jefferson's account record, Sally Hemings was listed only by her first name, and her value was set at $50 after giving Jefferson service for thirty-eight years. She did not appear in his will. Indeed, Hemings was one of the most vilified women of her time.

When historians ignore Sally Hemings, they protect the image of Jefferson. In contrast, Fawn Brodie and Annette Gordon-Reed have searched for the truth about the Hemings–Jefferson relationship. According to Gordon-Reed, to say they could never love one another is false. In the same way, we cannot assume that there was no jealousy, hatred, greed, sympathy, mirth, or possessiveness in their relationship.[115] Jefferson promised his wife, Martha, that he would never marry again after her death, so an enslaved "mistress" may have been a convenient substitute. The historian Fawn Brodie claims that Jefferson never fell in love again after his happy marriage to Martha.[116] Do we assume that if Jefferson did not love Sally, he was using his power merely for sexual gratification? Perhaps the relationship was "a treaty" because both had made promises that they needed to abide by morally and spiritually.[117]

The historian Noble Cunningham states that "there [is] no valid, historical evidence," supporting the claim that Jefferson had a sexual relationship with Sally Hemings,[118] writing, "[t]he evidence indicates that any romance between Jefferson and Sally belongs to a work of fiction, not of history."[119] More plausibly, Jefferson maintained a "dignified silence" about Hemings.[120] Still, she actually lived in history, but only in Jefferson's private sphere from 1789 to 1826.

Dumas Malone and Merrill Peterson, both from an earlier generation of Virginia historians, regarded Madison Hemings' memoir published in 1873 as unreliable. They claimed that the testimony of Israel Jefferson, also a formerly enslaved man at Monticello who affirmed Madison's recollections, was equally unreliable. Malone and Peterson seemed to abhor the idea of Hemings' children being fathered by Jefferson, so they avoided it in their volumes.

According to the 1873 memoir written by Sally Hemings' son Madison Hemings, Sally Hemings had become "Mr. Jefferson's concubine" and was pregnant when Jefferson was preparing to return to the United States from France. According to Madison Hemings, "[Jefferson] desired to bring my mother back to Virginia with him but she demurred.... She was beginning to understand the French language well, and in France she was free, while if she returned to Virginia she would be re-enslaved. So, she refused to return with him.... To induce her to do so he promised her extraordinary privileges, and made a solemn pledge that her children should be freed at the age of twenty-one years.... In consequence of his promise, on which she implicitly relied, she returned with him to Virginia.... Soon after their arrival, she gave birth to a child, of whom Thomas Jefferson was the father. It lived but a short time. She gave birth to four others, and Jefferson was the father of all of them.... We all became free agreeably to the treaty entered into by our parents before we were born."[121] This return trip from France to Virginia was made in 1789, but Hemings' first baby is recorded in Jefferson's *Farm Book* in 1798. The entry lists only "Sally," whereas all other births of slaves were recorded with the father's name. Scholars speculate that Madison received the contents of his memoir from conversations with his mother, Sally Hemings.

John C. Miller of Stanford University, an opponent of the liaison story, contended that Jefferson had honor and humanity that would have prevented him from becoming a "seducer of a young, innocent, attractive, Colored girl, hardly out of puberty."[122] Further, the author Henry Wiencek states that if this were true, Jefferson "deserves to be regarded as one of the most profligate and consummate hypocrites ever to occupy the presidency."[123] In his biography of Thomas Jefferson, Merrill Peterson stated that Jefferson strongly opposed miscegenation, so he "never would have indulged in a sexual affair with a slave girl."[124] Fawn M. Brodie, an historian and biographer, began writing *Thomas Jefferson: An Intimate History* in 1970 and professed by 1974 in her article "Blinking Historians" that historians and biographers of Thomas Jefferson applied a "deaf pen" to Jefferson's personal life story. The biographer Henry S. Randall circulated the story of Peter Carr as the father of Sally Hemings' children; it was debunked by DNA blood samples. Biographers Dumas Malone and Merrill Peterson denied the evidence of a liaison because they claimed it wasn't supported "by the country's most distinguished Jefferson biographers."[125] Both Malone and Peterson considered themselves as "liberal-minded, but socially conservative Virginia gentlemen." According to C. M. Halliday, author of *Understanding Thomas Jefferson,* their rejection of the recollections of Sally's son, Madison Hemings, in his memoir reflects a contemptuous, white-supremacist view.[126] To counter the accounts of a liaison between Jefferson and Hemings, the Jefferson-Randolph clan kept Jefferson on a "godlike pedestal" to protect his legacy from DNA conclusions.[127] Defenders of Jefferson assailed "speculation" about his personal life in biographies.

Jefferson evidently remained true to Hemings. He did not desert her. She chose to come home to Virginia, where she would be enslaved, so she must have trusted that he would keep his promise. She had to believe that he understood and valued what she would sacrifice in returning to Virginia.[128] He had a moral debt to her. He never sent her away from Monticello. He protected her from hard labor by keeping her in the house. "Hemings was a visible presence" to Jefferson,[129] but she was invisible to the public. He either loved her or controlled her. For thirty years of their lives together, "he would never openly challenge society's expectation of him as a white man."[130] Hemings remained at Monticello for many years after Jefferson's death.

Sally Hemings was literate, but her thoughts were never written in any account of her life with Jefferson. There are questions that historians would like to pose to her. When you made the decision in France to return to Virginia, was it due to love for Jefferson or because of the power he had over you?[131] Did you ever confront him about his views on slavery in *Notes for the State of Virginia* and how your image is slandered therein?[132] How did you have the strength to endure during the thirty-eight years you devoted to him?[133] Do Jefferson's actions exonerate him? When you knew the contents of Jefferson's derogatory statements about the Black race in *Notes,* in which he feared a slave uprising, what did you think? How did you feel when the Randolph family inherited the Monticello estate, not your children? How did the secret relationship affect your life? Was Jefferson a loving man? Since he never sent you away from Monticello, did you ever long for Paris? What did you do at Monticello with your time and talents? Did Jefferson turn to you often for solace? Did you grieve when he died? Did you expect to be included in his will? In what ways did you influence him?

Hemings was born into slavery in 1773 and died enslaved in 1835 at the age of sixty-two. Jefferson never freed her, but after his death, his daughter Martha Randolph allowed Hemings to retire with her two sons in Charlottesville, Virginia. How tragic that Jefferson never freed Hemings and that he never admitted his relationship socially. Also, he kept his own children enslaved at Monticello until they were twenty-one years old. "He could not educate his own children. In essence, he must banish [Sally's and his] children."[134]

History is incomplete when Sally Hemings is left out of the picture. The historian Fawn Brodie summarizes Jefferson's life and legacy in this way: "His ambivalences, instead of corroding his principles, corrupting his essential decency, and incapacitating him for work, were in the most extraordinary fashion harnessed to creative endeavor—to the perfect constitution, the non-despotic state, the ideal home and garden, the enlightened university. Only his conflict over the just treatment of the Black people in his life, whose voices, certainly articulated at the time but silent in the documents that have come down to us, remained unresolved, troubling, and corrosive. The Jefferson legacy, then, may be looked at as a fountain of dazzling complexity, its beauty compounded by the sunlight of his rare intelligence, but its sources of power—including the rewarding but intermittently tragic secret loves—hidden and deep in the earth."[135]

Twenty-first century scholars of Thomas Jefferson are still trying to gain a fuller understanding of Jefferson's liaison with Sally Hemings. The historian E. M. Halliday, who wrote *Understanding Thomas Jefferson,* speculated that Hemings "may have been much in love with her master."[136] Writers Fawn Brodie and Barbara Chase-Riboud also believe in this possibility. It is possible to believe "that their love affair went far beyond passion but involved devotion. Perhaps believers would contend that it was of a genuinely conjugal relationship despite 'the quasi-secrecy' that surrounded it."[137] However, "it has been a puzzle to many people how a man, made world-famous by his passion for human freedom, could have adapted to a prominent role in a system of involuntary servitude that he frequently denounced as evil."[138] "Jefferson had a deep-rooted racial bias...and [was] an implacable segregationist."[139] All his life, Jefferson clung to the idea that miscegenation was a "contamination" of white people.[140] So, how then could he carry on the "liaison" with Sally Hemings? "Not enough attention has usually been given to a mixture of guilt and fear about slavery that existed at some level in Jefferson's mind for much of his life."[141] Perhaps in private Jefferson tempered some of his racist attitudes. But Hemings lived in Monticello under a secret mask, for racial compromise seemed impossible to Jefferson.[142] He turned out to be "the most timid of abolitionists."[143] "He had done nothing during his years of retirement to advance the cause [of the emancipation of slaves]."[144]

In the South, law and society protected white men who sexually exploited enslaved women. We cannot know how Jefferson pursued intimacy with Hemings or if she truly consented to it in France where she had some degree of agency over her life (in Virginia consent was, of course, a moot issue since she was enslaved). He evidently did not plan to educate Sally except to give her experience in France. He never improved her social position. He did not free her in his will. According to the writer Winthrop Jordan, perhaps through Hemings he resolved his inner conflicts over slavery, women, and miscegenation.[145] "Jefferson would end his days without risking his way of life or alienating himself from the mass of his fellow Virginians by publicly planning an antislavery standard on his Albemarle mountaintop."[146] Today Jefferson has a mixed legacy as an intellectual, politician, enslaver, father, and founding father. "That Jefferson carries the odium of slavery for his generation is a wry tribute to his status as the voice of America's best self," writes Joyce Appleby.[147]

The humanity of Jefferson should have been enshrined at Monticello on July 4, 1926, the one hundred and fiftieth anniversary of the Declaration of Independence. His demands for the colonies' freedom from the British clashed with his "habits of benevolent despotism, his affection for power tempered by his extraordinary guilt over its abuse, his normal need for sexual fulfillment coupled with his attraction for the forbidden, his hunger for affection and esteem assuaged...by friendship [and] several loves, but also by his fanatical obedience to his larger fantasies of what constituted his duty to the state."[148]

Notes to Thomas Jefferson's Exploitive, Clandestine Affair with Sally Hemings

1. Quoted in Forrest Church, *The Cathedral of the World: The Universalist Theology* (Boston: Beacon Press, 2009), 67.
2. Jon Meacham, *Thomas Jefferson: The Art of Power* (New York: Random House, 2012), 54-55.
3. Annette Gordon-Reed, *The Hemingses of Monticello: An American Family* (New York: W. W. Norton, 2008), 106.
4. Meacham, *Thomas Jefferson*, 55.
5. Gordon-Reed, *The Hemingses*, 99.
6. Gordon-Reed, *The Hemingses*, 88.
7. Gordon-Reed, *The Hemingses*, 384.
8. Gordon-Reed, *The Hemingses*, 385.
9. Fawn Brodie, *Thomas Jefferson: An Intimate History* (New York: W. W. Norton, 1974), 26.
10. Gordon-Reed, *The Hemingses*, 93.
11. Meacham, *Thomas Jefferson*, 12.
12. Meacham, 11-12.
13. Meacham, 12.
14. Meacham, 11.
15. Meacham, 11.
16. Meacham, 11.
17. Meacham, 98.
18. Annette Gordon-Reed, *Thomas Jefferson and Sally Hemings: An American Controversy* (Charlottesville, VA: University Press of Virginia, 1997), 148.
19. Joyce Appleby, *Thomas Jefferson* (New York: Henry Holt, 2003), 132.

20. Winthrop D. Jordan, *White over Black: American Attitudes Toward the Negro, 1550-1812* (Chapel Hill, NC: The University of North Carolina Press, 1968), 462.
21. R. B. Bernstein, *Thomas Jefferson: The Revolution of Ideas* (Oxford: Oxford University Press, 2003), 194.
22. Appleby, *Thomas Jefferson,* 143.
23. Gordon-Reed, *The Hemingses,* 301.
24. Andrew Burnstein, *Jefferson's Secrets: Death and Desire at Monticello* (New York: Basic Books, 2005), 91.
25. Burnstein, *Jefferson's Secrets,* 91.
26. Burnstein, *Jefferson's Secrets,* 88.
27. Gordon-Reed, *The Hemingses,* 279.
28. Appleby, *Thomas Jefferson,* 87.
29. Appleby, *Thomas Jefferson,* 43.
30. Alan Pell Crawford, *Twilight at Monticello: The Final Years of Thomas Jefferson* (New York: Random House, 2008), 139.
31. Burnstein, *Jefferson's Secrets,* 151.
32. Appleby, *Thomas Jefferson,* 87.
33. Quoted in Appleby, *Thomas Jefferson,* 88.
34. Appleby, *Thomas Jefferson,* 88.
35. Crawford, *Twilight at Monticello,* 138.
36. Burnstein, *Jefferson's Secrets,* 98.
37. Appleby, *Thomas Jefferson,* 43.
38. Brodie, *Thomas Jefferson,* 448.
39. Appleby, *Thomas Jefferson,* 43.
40. Crawford, *Twilight at Monticello,* xviii.
41. Brodie, *Thomas Jefferson,* 107.
42. Quoted in Brodie, *Thomas Jefferson,* 92.
43. Brodie, *Thomas Jefferson,* 92.
44. Gordon-Reed, *Thomas Jefferson,* 106.
45. Henry Wiencek, *Master of the Mountain: Thomas Jefferson and His Slaves* (New York: Farrar, Straus, and Giroux, 2012), 57.
46. Gordon-Reed, *Thomas Jefferson,* 105.
47. Burnstein, *Jefferson's Secrets,* 10.
48. Burnstein, *Jefferson's Secrets,* 114.
49. Gordon-Reed, *Thomas Jefferson,* 165.
50. Gordon-Reed, *The Hemingses,* 226.
51. Gordon-Reed, *The Hemingses,* 236.
52. Gordon-Reed, *The Hemingses,* 238.

53. Gordon-Reed, *The Hemingses,* 231.
54. Gordon-Reed, *The Hemingses,* 273.
55. Gordon-Reed, *The Hemingses,* 263.
56. Gordon-Reed, *The Hemingses,* 299.
57. Meacham, *Thomas Jefferson,* 216.
58. Gordon-Reed, *The Hemingses,* 354.
59. Gordon-Reed, *The Hemingses,* 301.
60. Gordon-Reed, *The Hemingses,* 320.
61. Gordon-Reed, *The Hemingses,* 313.
62. Gordon-Reed, *The Hemingses,* 339.
63. Gordon-Reed, *The Hemingses,* 342.
64. Meacham, *Thomas Jefferson,* 218.
65. Gordon-Reed, *The Hemingses,* 345.
66. Meacham, *Thomas Jefferson,* 218.
67. E. M. Halliday, *Understanding Thomas Jefferson* (New York: HarperCollins Publishers, 2001), 23.
68. Meacham, *Thomas Jefferson,* 293.
69. Meacham, *Thomas Jefferson,* 294.
70. Gordon-Reed, *The Hemingses,* 518.
71. Meacham, *Thomas Jefferson,* 218.
72. Gordon-Reed, *The Hemingses,* 563.
73. Gordon-Reed, *The Hemingses,* 575.
74. Gordon-Reed, *Thomas Jefferson,* 108.
75. Meacham, *Thomas Jefferson,* 234.
76. Virginius Dabney, *The Jefferson Scandals: A Rebuttal* (New York: Dodd, Mead & Co., 1981), 26.
77. Crawford, *Twilight at Monticello,* 142-143.
78. Crawford, *Twilight at Monticello,* 144-145.
79. Quoted in Crawford, *Twilight at Monticello,* 145.
80. Crawford, *Twilight at Monticello,* 145.
81. Brodie, *Thomas Jefferson,* 441.
82. Brodie, *Thomas Jefferson,* 441.
83. Brodie, *Thomas Jefferson,* 432.
84. Cover of Meacham, *Thomas Jefferson.*
85. Meacham, *Thomas Jefferson,* 217.
86. Gordon-Reed, *The Hemingses,* 316.
87. Gordon-Reed, *The Hemingses,* 501.
88. Gordon-Reed, *The Hemingses,* 243.

89. Gary Kowalski, *Revolutionary Spirits: The Enlightened Faith of American Founding Fathers* (New York: Blueridge, 2008), 131.
90. Gordon-Reed, *The Hemingses*, 402.
91. Brodie, *Thomas Jefferson*, 234.
92. Brodie, 23.
93. Brodie, 23.
94. Brodie, 24.
95. Brodie, 24-25.
96. Brodie, 32.
97. Meacham, *Thomas Jefferson*, 507.
98. Meacham, 380.
99. Meacham, 523.
100. Bernstein, *Thomas Jefferson*, 196.
101. Meacham, *Thomas Jefferson*, 522n.
102. Bernstein, *Thomas Jefferson*, 196.
103. Halliday, *Understanding Thomas Jefferson*, xi-xii.
104. Brodie, *Thomas Jefferson*, xvi.
105. Bernstein, *Thomas Jefferson*, 191.
106. Brodie, *Thomas Jefferson*, 495-497.
107. Brodie, *Thomas Jefferson*, 501.
108. Gordon-Reed, *The Hemingses*, 435.
109. Gordon-Reed, *The Hemingses*, 126.
110. Brodie, *Thomas Jefferson*, 31.
111. Appleby, *Thomas Jefferson*, 74.
112. Dabney, *The Jefferson Scandals*, 58.
113. Dabney, *The Jefferson Scandals*, 66.
114. Gordon-Reed, *Thomas Jefferson*, 230.
115. Gordon-Reed, *The Hemingses*, 368.
116. Brodie, *Thomas Jefferson*, 28.
117. Gordon-Reed, *The Hemingses*, 358.
118. Noble E. Cunningham, *The Pursuit of Reason: The Life of Thomas Jefferson* (Baton Rouge, LA: Louisiana State University Press, 1987), 115.
119. Cunningham, *The Pursuit of Reason*, 116.
120. Crawford, *Twilight at Monticello*, 142.
121. Quoted in Meacham, *Thomas Jefferson*, 218.
122. Halliday, *Understanding Thomas Jefferson*, 98.
123. Henry Wiencek, *Master of the Mountain: Thomas Jefferson and His Slaves* (New York: Farrar, Straus, and Giroux, 2012), 269.

124. Merrill E. Peterson, ed., *Thomas Jefferson: A Profile* (New York: Hill & Wang, 1967), 176.
125. Halliday, *Understanding Thomas Jefferson*, 162.
126. Halliday, *Understanding Thomas Jefferson*, 168.
127. Burnstein, *Jefferson's Secrets*, 179.
128. Gordon-Reed, *The Hemingses*, 339.
129. Gordon-Reed, *The Hemingses*, 342.
130. Gordon-Reed, *The Hemingses*, 371.
131. Meacham, *Thomas Jefferson*, xxv.
132. Meacham, 216.
133. Meacham, 217.
134. Brodie, *Thomas Jefferson*, 467.
135. Brodie, *Thomas Jefferson*, 470.
136. Halliday, *Understanding Thomas Jefferson*, 112.
137. Halliday, 158.
138. Halliday, 143.
139. Halliday, 150.
140. Halliday, 153.
141. Halliday, 154.
142. Burnstein, *Jefferson's Secrets*, 131.
143. Burnstein, *Jefferson's Secrets*, 136.
144. Cunningham, *The Pursuit of Reason*, 347.
145. Jordan, *White over Black*, 467.
146. Cunningham, *The Pursuit of Reason*, 348.
147. Appleby, *Thomas Jefferson*, 139.
148. Brodie, *Thomas Jefferson*, 470.

Sally Hemings in 2018

Belatedly in history, Sally Hemings gained recognition in 2018 in *The New York Times.* Editorial board member Brent Staples notes that a new room has been added to Thomas Jefferson's estate at Monticello, and a new narrative explains that Sally Hemings lived in this place during the time she bore and raised children fathered by Thomas Jefferson.[1] No one in Jefferson's white family admitted that there was a long-term relationship between Jefferson and Hemings, but the enslaved people at Monticello knew what was going on, and the family could not miss the truth. Historians of the past avoided recognizing the unequal interracial relationship until DNA reports surfaced in the 1990s, and then substantial scholarship in the twentieth and twenty-first centuries unveiled the historic truth. A long-running deception to the public is now unveiled in exhibits at Monticello which explain the centrality of slavery at the estate of Thomas Jefferson. In an entire lifetime, Jefferson freed only seven enslaved people: two before his death, and through his will he freed five more.

Hemings' intriguing story began in 1787 when she accompanied Jefferson's young daughter Polly to Paris, France. Jefferson's wife, Martha, had died in 1782 and he held a diplomatic position in France. The family and Hemings lived at the Hotel de Langeac. In 1788 or early in 1789, Jefferson at forty-six began a sexual relationship with sixteen-year-old Hemings. Hemings became pregnant with Jefferson's child. Slavery had been outlawed in France by this time, and it certainly was not appropriate to show affection to a servant. But in the South in the United States, enslaved Black women who were exploited in sexual servitude often gave birth to mixed-race children resembling the white men of the household.

Even though Jefferson was a prolific writer, the only things we know about Hemings come from the observations and letters of others. Jefferson burned all but one of the letters he and his wife exchanged with each other, and he wrote nothing about Hemings. A letter in 1847 from an enslaved man named Isaac Jefferson reveals one important quality of Hemings: "She was mighty near white." Other records indicate that she was pretty, that is, "beautiful"; she had long, straight black hair that cascaded down her back. In appearance, in the tone of her voice, and in her mannerisms, Hemings reminded Jefferson of his wife, Martha, for in reality, Sally and Martha were half-sisters. Jefferson had promised Martha that he would never marry again after her death, and in a sexual capacity at the least, Hemings played the role of a wife.

In France, Hemings had some limited power over Jefferson. She could remain in France with her brother James where she would be a free woman, or she could return to Virginia and be an enslaved woman. However, with only one brother and no friends or other family in France, she would be isolated. By 1789, Hemings had "considerable insight into Jefferson's mind and some sense of what he could be obligated to do."[2] With training as a chamber maid, with her lightly colored skin, and with her education in French and her diction that probably matched Jefferson's, the social distance between them was narrowed. "Sally Hemings would have been keenly aware of this."[3] So Hemings advanced an offer to Jefferson: If she returned to the United States, all children of their relationship would be emancipated from slavery at the age of twenty-one. Jefferson conceded and kept his promise.

When the Jefferson family and Hemings returned home to Virginia, USA, Hemings lived with her relatives in a stone house along Mulberry Row in slave quarters at Monticello. Then she moved into one of the three slave rooms built underneath the estate which directly connected to the main part of Monticello. There Hemings could easily move along the underground corridor and up the steps of the private stairway, directly to Jefferson's quarters. She became the "chamber maid" assigned to Jefferson. Through this convenience, she bore six children: Harriet, Beverly, Madison, Eston, and two who died young. She was never freed in the thirty-six years she served Jefferson. In Jefferson's will, she was not freed because the "public image" and credibility of Jefferson's legacy had to be preserved. Sally Hemings died in 1835 at the age of 63 in Charlottesville, Virginia, where she lived with her two sons, Madison and Eston.

In 2018, Monticello added a separate room under a portico near Jefferson's quarters as a symbolic reminder of Sally Hemings' presence. The exhibit displays a typical chamber maid's dress on a mannequin, a fireplace, and a chair in a sparsely furnished room. "This places Sally Hemings at the center of plantation life, where she clearly belongs. It also shows that Jefferson's baronial mountaintop estate was just like any other plantation when it came to matters of sexual conduct."[4] "The exhibit underscores the fact that the Jefferson estate was an epicenter of racial mixing in early Virginia, making it impossible to draw clear lines between Black and white. It reminds contemporary Americans that slave owners like the Jeffersons often held their own Black [sons and daughters], aunts, uncles and cousins in [slavery]. And it illustrates how enslaved near-white relations used proximity to privilege to demystify whiteness while taking critical measure of the relatives who owned them."[5]

Notes to Sally Hemings in 2018

1. Brent Staples, "The Legacy of Monticello's Black First Family," *New York Times*, July 5, 2018.
2. Staples, "The Legacy."
3. Staples, "The Legacy."
4. Staples, "The Legacy."
5. Staples, "The Legacy."

Thomas Jefferson and His Son Tom

In his 2001 book, *A President in the Family,* Byron W. Woodson, sixth-generation descendant of Thomas Jefferson, tells of his struggles to correct what he believes is an omission in previous biographies of Jefferson. Through meticulous research, Woodson establishes that Jefferson was the father of Sally Hemings' first-born child, Tom. The story of Tom sheds new light on a missing family member in the Sally Hemings/Thomas Jefferson saga.

It is important to establish the historic truth about Tom, as he has been ignored by many past historians and Jeffersonians. That search for the truth flows from the Unitarian Universalist belief in "the inherent worth and dignity of every person." We seek "justice and equality" in human relations and stress "acceptance of one another" and "respect for the interdependent web of all existence." It should be noted that the connection between Tom and Thomas Jefferson is rooted in the oral history of Tom's descendants, but many scholars and historians today do not believe there is convincing evidence that Tom was a son of Jefferson. To date, DNA tests have not supported the claims of Tom's descendants.

"After the death of slavery, the idea of race lived on."[1] In the nineteenth century, the radical Populist Party conspired "to keep poor whites and Blacks locked into a subordinate political and economic position."[2] But Tom resisted subordination.

Journalist James Callender published an article in the *Richmond Examiner* on September 1, 1802 that set in motion 200 years of scandal and controversy about Thomas Jefferson. According to the newspaper, "Jefferson kept a concubine, one of his slaves. Her name is Sally. The name of her eldest son is Tom."[3] At this time, Tom was twelve years old.

Sally Hemings returned to the state of Virginia pregnant in 1789 after her liaison with Jefferson in Paris, France. The following year, 1790, she bore a son, Tom, whose name Jefferson recorded in his own handwriting in his *Farm Book.* Jefferson did not record the name of a father. "The presence of [Tom's] name, also written in...Jefferson's own hand in Jefferson's *Memorandum Books,* was never disclosed by Jeffersonians."[4] The entry of Tom in both cases was erased by someone, so the evidence of who was the father has been destroyed. There was gossip that Tom had drowned or died, but apparently he had become enslaved at Monticello. Jefferson, who was president of the nation in 1801, denied that Tom was his son; however, Tom bore a striking resemblance to the president.[5] Sally's children were lighter skinned than other enslaved people at Monticello.

Records show that a servant named Thomas received a gift of $2.00 in December 1800 and in February 1801. Tom was then ten years old. After a quarrel with his father in which Tom was "indignant toward the idea that he did anything wrong,"[6] Tom was banished from Monticello and sent to the farm of John Woodson, where he formalized his name as Thomas Woodson. By all accounts, Thomas never returned to Monticello, but he visited his mother at Jefferson's Poplar Forest Plantation in Virginia.

Indeed, the truth is that Thomas Woodson was a real, living, breathing human being. The name Thomas Woodson was recorded in the 1820 U.S. census, and he was listed as a "free Colored head of a household" in Greenbriar County, Virginia.[7] However, Thomas was listed in the county tax records in 1820 as a white man.[8]

When Jefferson became president in 1801, Thomas was living in Greenbriar County, Virginia, just west of the Allegheny Mountains, approximately 150 miles from Monticello. Thomas, apparently an enslaved man on the Woodson farm, eventually married Jemima, an enslaved woman also on the Woodson farm. In 1821, they "packed their children and household wares into...wagons and headed westward to Ohio on the Midland Trail, then a dependable, obstacle-free road."[9] Ohio had outlawed slavery. At first, they rented a farm, but later they bought land under the government Land Act of 1820 and settled in Chillicothe, Ohio along the Scioto River. The Woodsons attended a Methodist Church in their community. Unfortunately, in 1821, the Methodist Church separated congregations of African Americans and white people. According to Rev. McAdow, the Woodson family was saddened to have to worship separately from white Methodists. African Americans had to occupy the north gallery of the church, and at meetings "the white members commenced first and the Colored members last."[10] Black people didn't enjoy equal rights and privileges with their white brethren even though they helped pay for church expenses. Thereupon, twelve couples formed a new church, and records include the names of "Thomas Woodson and his wife."[11] This separate church became the first African Methodist Episcopal (A.M.E) Church organized west of the Allegheny Mountains.

Thomas and his family of eleven lived in Chillicothe, Ohio for nine years. "The Woodsons made quite an impression on neighbors, as they were well remembered."[12] The whole family was considered mixed-race farmers. "They were very genteel and industrious people, the Old man and his sons always going well dressed and riding fine horses.... They were rather exclusive and did not associate with the town darkies."[13] The slur in this final clause reveals the racism at the heart of this ostensible praise for the Woodsons, who were active in the "web of life" community; they assumed duties as teachers, organizers, businessmen, ministers, and civic activists.

Thomas bought 160 acres of land in Jackson County, Ohio, thirty-five miles southwest of Chillicothe, under the Land Act of 1820.[14] This section of land was later named Berlin Crossroads, stretching from Cincinnati to Dayton. Southeastern Ohio was a prosperous area in the Miami River Valley. Tax records state that Thomas owned five horses and a head of livestock. A year later he bought fifty more acres. When coal was discovered on his land, he sold land to the Coal and Iron Company. The Woodson family prospered. The Black population in Ohio rose from 9,568 in 1830 to 36,673 in 1860.[15]

Though equality for African Americans was not truly practiced in Ohio, freedom to live free from slavery seemed secure for Thomas and his family. He formed the Bethel A.M.E. Church in Chillicothe, and that led to engaging in the communal struggle of all African Americans. As "the Underground Railroad began to take shape, the Woodsons were among the early instigators."[16] A.M.E. churches expanded across the country. "For the next twenty years, the A.M.E. Church consolidated and strengthened its organization and significantly expanded the number of churches in the North."[17] In reality, "in many communities, the church was the only place where African Americans could publicly speak against slavery."[18] The A.M.E. Church clandestinely supported the Underground Railroad. They also raised money to buy the freedom of fugitives from slavery who were caught in the North. They encouraged the purchase of "goods free from slave labor" and distributed newspapers aimed at African American audiences.[19] Three sons of Thomas Woodson became ministers in the A.M.E. Church. Ohio began to fund education for white people in 1829; by 1847, funds were available for Black children to be educated in private schools.[20]

As Thomas managed more acreage in Jackson County—and perhaps because he was considered white—he "secured a favorable financial standing" in the community.[21] Freed Black people and transients worked portions of his property. His unusual family history was kept a secret in Ohio. "Anonymity was a family practice."[22] However, in 1842, the *Philanthropist,* an Ohio Slavery Society publication, reported that a settlement of Black farmers in Jackson County was a success story. The publication noted that Farmer Thomas owned this settlement of 2,055 acres of fine land. The settlement contained 161 persons formerly enslaved in Virginia. Indeed, "One Thomas Hordron [Thomas Woodson disguised] was said to own 150 hogs and 400 head of cattle and to have grown 1,500 to 3,000 bushels of corn as well as a large quantity of hay. Four of [Thomas'] sons are schoolteachers. The people are putting up a good house for a permanent school."[23] A white neighbor declared that "the Negroes are all that care anything about education around here...still they are treated with great injustice by whites;...they are making steady progress in moral and intellectual improvement."[24]

Thomas Woodson died at the age of 89; Jemima died at the age of 85. They were married for 63 years. Jemima Woodson witnessed extraordinary change in Ohio. The Industrial Age was benefiting all Americans. "She was amazed at the steamboats that came to master the rivers, then amazed at the railroads that raced across the land. She saw her youngest daughter, Sarah Jane, graduate from Oberlin College and become the first African American to teach at a college; Jemima witnessed the Civil War and Emancipation."[25] "Jemima Woodson spent a lifetime with one husband, raising a huge family [eleven children] and an industrious family."[26] The Woodsons' descendants have been educators, ministers of the A.M.E. Church, construction trade contractors, soldiers, activists in the Voting Rights struggle, and businessmen. Lewis Woodson, a son, was the founder of Wilberforce University.

Thomas, the Woodson patriarch, was "tall, handsome, self-assured."[27] He looked white so he could choose to be free and white.[28] "Earlier in life, he told his children they were the grandchildren of Sally Hemings and Thomas Jefferson."[29] In his last years, he told his grandchildren of his biological origin and his departure from Monticello. He handed down "a legacy of self-reliance, strong family traditions, and a defiance of injustice."[30]

According to the author Byron S. Woodson, "Thomas Woodson's life is largely unimaginable. In a word, it was triumphant, but any single word ignores its complexities, its contradictions, and its entanglement in [one of] America's greatest dilemmas."[31] Byron Woodson asks, "How did life marred by family separation at a tender age become filled with love of so many wonderful children, in-laws, and neighbors?"[32]

There is some documentation to support the oral history of six generations of the Woodson family, descendants of the Sally Hemings/Thomas Jefferson lineage.[33] Minnie and John Woodson authored the *Woodson Source Book* in 1977, researching Thomas Woodson's life. "No longer can a tainted history be force-fed to Americans," asserts Byron Woodson.[34] The Woodson family is a visible example of Black success. They conducted themselves in a moral, dignified fashion that elicits enormous respect.

Notes to Thomas Jefferson and His Son Tom

1. Byron W. Woodson, Sr., *A President in the Family: Thomas Jefferson, Sally Hemings, and Thomas Woodson* (Westport, CT: Praeger, 2001), 26.
2. Woodson, *A President in the Family*, 33.
3. Woodson, 49.
4. Woodson, 250.
5. Woodson, 4, 49.
6. Woodson, 61.
7. Woodson, 82.
8. Woodson, 82.
9. Woodson, 87.

10. Woodson, 89.
11. Woodson, 90.
12. Woodson, 91.
13. Woodson, 91.
14. Woodson, 101.
15. Woodson, 124.
16. Woodson, 103.
17. Woodson, 104.
18. Woodson, 104.
19. Woodson, 104.
20. Woodson, 95.
21. Woodson, 107.
22. Woodson, 119.
23. Woodson, 119.
24. Woodson, 119.
25. Woodson, 126.
26. Woodson, 126.
27. Woodson, 66.
28. Woodson, 67.
29. Woodson, 128.
30. Woodson, 128.
31. Woodson, 139.
32. Woodson, 139.
33. Cover of Woodson, *A President in the Family.*
34. Woodson, *A President in the Family,* 250.

Thomas Jefferson and His Legacy of Religious Philosophy

Thomas Jefferson had a fervent religious philosophy and wrote often about moral integrity. Edwin S. Gaustad, in his book *Sworn on the Altar of God: A Religious Biography of Thomas Jefferson,* notes that Jefferson was the most self-consciously theological of all presidents. He dedicated himself deeply and deliberately to the reform of religion in the nation. He delivered the roots of religious freedom to Virginia by law in 1786 and to the nation in the Declaration of Independence. Finally, he was responsible for the wall of separation between church and state in the First Amendment to the Constitution signed in 1789. However, one cannot box Jefferson into any ecclesiastical institution. In fact, no single doctrine outlines Jefferson's religious ideas because at any given period in his life, slight variations of philosophy kept surfacing.[1]

In the early system of Virginia state government, wealthy elites practiced a form of nobility in their powerful position. According to Jonathan Martin and Michael D. Shear in a January 23, 2014 article in *The New York Times,* these Virginia leaders were obligated morally to act with honor, kindness, and generosity. Therefore, Jefferson followed this philosophy in a spirit of moral introspection, but the moral inconsistencies in his philosophy tainted "his conduct [when it] clashed with his expressed beliefs."[2]

Jefferson's philosophy was shaped by early American history. The first settlement in Virginia was in Jamestown in 1607 with English colonists, two-thirds of whom were unskilled laborers or farmers and a third of whom were artisans.[3] The migration of Royalist immigrants from the south and west of England set the South's cultural history in Virginia and in America. The "oppressed Royalist elite" of England, a third of whom had lived in London, became Virginia's ruling class in 1655. The Royalists were a society of aristocratic families from Kent, Devon, and Warwickshire. This South and West triangle of territory in England by the Middle Ages had slavery in Mercia, Wessex, and Sussex. The land was "dominated by the great estates of the gentry."[4] Many links connect the area of southern England with southern Virginia: inequalities, agriculture, rural settlements, oligarchy, and the Anglican faith.[5]

Among these Royalists were merchants, businessmen, traders, and lawyers from England. By 1660, every seat in the Virginia Royal Council was filled with five connected English family members; in 1724, twelve members were family related.[6] Since the distribution of land in Virginia was assigned by the governor's cabinet, legislature, and the Supreme Court, large estates were owned by "people of fortune" who dominated Virginia's society for more than a century.[7] Aristocratic families in Virginia professed allegiance to the Anglican Church of England. The Chesapeake Colony was highly stratified, socially and economically, and males ruled supreme. The Jefferson family was considered one of the gentry families in England and then in Virginia.[8]

In his early life, Jefferson was innovative and resourceful. He was a "reaper of ideas" about religion, selecting what he wanted to believe out of traditional religion and ignoring the rest.[9] The Anglican Church followed the settlers into Virginia and dominated their religious life for nearly a century. In fact, the Church influenced the early part of Jefferson's life. "The clergy sought to protect Anglicanism in Virginia by maintaining, in as far as possible, a monopoly on all religious services in the colony."[10] Indeed, the tentacles of the Anglican Church penetrated the social life and the government of the early colony. By legislation, people in Jamestown in 1610 had to attend morning and evening prayer sessions. Those who were absent were punished according to the law; they would "lose a day's provisions for the first offense, be whipped the second, and for the third,...the oceangoing galleys for six months."[11] In 1642, the Governor of Virginia added laws that required non-Anglicans to leave the colony. In 1661, a law was passed to punish Anglicans who extended…"love to Quakers."[12]

The Anglican hierarchy meted out punishment according to social rank. For example, when a convicted felon read from the Bible at his trial, he escaped hanging. Leniency was handed to masters. The poor and illiterate went to the gallows.[13] The Anglican creed, the Common Book of Devotions, and the seventeen canon laws were highly enforced by government decree in 1724. Laws by 1776 in Virginia mandated regular church attendance and made it a criminal offense to maintain any other religious opinion than Anglicanism. The Church of England prescribed ceremonies, liturgy, rituals, and forms of worship. In addition, the denial of the Trinity was punishable by imprisonment; heresy was a capital offense; Roman Catholics could not hold civil office in Virginia; freethinkers might have their children taken from them; and taxes were levied for the salaries of the clergy. In 1705, very few religious dissenters were found in the Anglican Church.[14] However, by 1820, no religious denomination was prominent in Virginia, so in 1822 Episcopalians, Presbyterians, Methodists and Baptists could meet freely.

In his youth, Jefferson was faithful to the Anglican Church, perhaps because his father, Peter Jefferson, was a vestryman in the parish of St. Anne's Church in Charlottesville, Virginia, which Jefferson attended. He read the prayer book and was baptized into that church. Later, Anglican clergymen performed his marriage to Martha Wayles in 1772. His children were baptized in the Anglican Church, to which he gave money. Clergyman Frederick Hatch officiated at Jefferson's funeral in 1826. In essence, Jefferson began and ended his life in the Anglican Church, but Anglican doctrine did not intrude into his philosophy. He steered away from his family, culture, and friends, to liberate all individuals of the nation from government interference in matters of religion.[15] He sought to eliminate laws that required conformity to beliefs of the Anglican Church in Virginia. In the Declaration of Independence, "he stripped his own Church of England of any lingering power in the name of religion to afflict the bodies and minds of his fellow citizens."[16] This document "stands among other things as an enduring witness to Jefferson's religious, moral, and political views."[17]

Jefferson objected to the use of public funds to promote an individual church. For example, he believed that Quakers, Baptists, and Methodists should not have to pay the salaries of pastors of a dominant church or be taxed to support the established Anglican Church.[18] He distrusted clergymen, priests, and ministers.[19] In essence, he believed that priests crimp the minds of humankind.[20] He admired the Quakers who could live without priests and who could follow their own consciences.[21] According to Jefferson, "priest-ridden" societies lacked political freedom.[22] He believed that people could make moral decisions without authoritative sources.[23] In addition, he thought "creeds, formulas, and dogmas have been the bane...of the Christian Church" because these were fatal inventions of leaders.[24]

The Anglican hegemony in early Virginia encased England's aristocratic fervor in politics, the social structure, the economy, and the culture. Jefferson was eminently shaped by this fervor. Whereas he was sincerely and profoundly religious, his freethinking, liberal view of religion led Federalists in the presidential election of 1800 to call him an atheist without personal morality. In the *Syllabus of an Estimate of the Doctrines of Jesus*, Jefferson wrote, "I am a good Christian, a man who reveres Jesus, though I cannot accept his godhood. Still, I accept his moral system as being better than either that of the ancient philosophers (Plato and Socrates) or that of the ancient Jews. The moral system of Jesus...if filled up in the style and spirit of the rich fragments he left us, would be the most perfect and sublime that has ever been taught by man."[25] Despite this religious clarity, Jefferson lacked compassion by his human debasement of the enslaved whom he relegated as inferior without rights in a society or a nation.

When Jefferson was a student at William and Mary College, he was influenced by William Small, chair of the Philosophy Department. Small "enlarged [Jefferson's] liberal mind" and introduced him to the Enlightenment Movement.[26] Jefferson was intrigued by the logic of Francis Bacon, the science and mathematics of Isaac Newton, the politics, philosophy, and religion of John Locke, and the law instruction of George Wythe. In harmony with Jefferson's philosophy, Bacon thought that experience and reason should not be separated from each other, that "the empirical and the rational" pointed us to the truth. Further, since truth is not born in humans, "it had to be learned and earned and won through experiment and experience."[27]

As an assumed deist, Jefferson "rarely invoked a personal God who would interfere in human affairs—except when he talked about God's judgment of slavery. He knew he lived and benefited from a [slavery] system drenched in sin."[28] Still, denying this system a few years before he died, he advised a namesake on how to live a virtuous life: "Adore God. Reverence and cherish your parents. Love your neighbor as yourself and your country more than yourself. Be just. Be true. Murmur not at the ways of Providence. So shall the life which you have entered be the portal of one of eternal and ineffable bliss."[29]

Isaac Newton influenced Jefferson's philosophy of nature and the natural laws. "Newton taught Jefferson that God's world was orderly, dependable, regular, and predictable"; for example, planets don't just "wander," but they move by specific laws. All motion and matter proceed by design.[30] "God speaks through nature," maintained Jefferson.[31] He believed that the design of the universe compels one to believe in a Creator: heavenly bodies; land, water, atmosphere; animal and vegetable life; the human mind; insects; atoms; matter and motion.[32] Such a design has infinite power in every atom of the earth's composition.[33]

Federalists in the presidential election of 1800 accused Jefferson of being an atheist, a deist, a theist, a Unitarian, and an anti-clericalist, which presented him with identity problems in his campaign. He could not have been an atheist because he used "Creator" in the Declaration of Independence and in the Bill of Rights. But did he believe that the Creator endowed all men with certain unalienable rights? In his book *White over Black*, Winthrop Jordan contends that the Creator would not have created two species "equipped with more than one set of rights."[34] In Jefferson's philosophy, "nature is orderly, harmonious, and benevolent."[35] According to Forrest Church in his essay "America's Founding Faiths," "Life, liberty, and the pursuit of happiness" is from nature and nature's God is grounded in rights.[36]

Perhaps Jefferson wasn't inspired by snowflakes or flowers, but he observed nature as a scientist. He declared that those facts in the Bible which contradict the laws of nature must be examined with more care.[37] For example, Joshua commanded the sun to stand still, an impossibility in the operation under nature's laws. Furthermore, Jefferson thought that if God created human beings with a sense of right and wrong, then morality is a natural part of human nature; just seeing, hearing, and feeling is the true foundation of morality.[38] Therefore, Jefferson believed that every human being has a moral sense, a compass, embedded in a conscience that guides him or her in life. In fact, one's conscience and reason could even question the existence of God. He reasoned, "I am alert to a sense of right and wrong because my conscience is my guide."[39] But, unfortunately, he could anesthetize his conscience "whenever he felt discomfort" about "the tragedy of slavery."[40]

In his *Notes to the State of Virginia*, published in 1787, Jefferson postulated that Black people did not have the same natural endowments as white people.[41] The "real distinction nature has made" is their "color."[42] In addition, he viewed Black people as unimaginative and inferior in intellect. Since he thought that reason and experience were the greatest marks of intellect, one wonders, as a scientist, how he could observe Black people all his life, and especially at Monticello, and not arrive at the truth in the natural laws.

Important elements of Jefferson's philosophy were individual freedom in religion and freedom of conscience. The conscience has a moral sense that enables human beings to perceive and choose good; for example, the consciences of men such as Abraham Lincoln, Samuel Chase, and Charles Sumner were troubled by the contrast between the faith they professed and the practice of slavery.[43] Lincoln stood firm for the emancipation of the enslaved; Chase became chief justice of the Supreme Court and energetically worked against the South's dominance in the government; and Sumner became a leader of the antislavery forces in Massachusetts. Jefferson practiced slavery in accordance with his moral sense. Likewise, he believed that each individual needs to follow his or her own conscience. To be self-reliant in one's own reasoning is to exercise freedom of the mind. When religious conformity was tolerated, minds were constricted and constrained. He proclaimed, "I have sworn on the altar of God eternal hostility against every form of tyranny over the mind of men."[44] However, his defense of the tyranny over the minds and consciences of the enslaved as justifiable was one of his notable paradoxes.

Tyranny over the mind and conscience of fellow citizens, according to Jefferson, dismisses human reason and experience in religious thought. Further, God has planted reason in the mind as a light for guidance.[45] Reason and common sense remain the tests by which to judge all things.[46] The mind (reason) operates upon data and sifts through the senses (compassion, experience) to arrive at truth.[47] According to the writer Andrew Burnstein in his book *Jefferson's Secrets: Death and Desire at Monticello*, Jefferson often detached his mind from experience with slavery. He failed to connect his reasoning with understanding.[48] He preferred quiet surroundings in which he could read and think. He was not a gifted orator, but he was a brilliant writer. Although he was polite, amiable, and dignified, compassion was not his strong suit.

In many ways, Jefferson's ideals of morality, integrity, reason, freedom, and conscience constituted his highest moral standards. But slavery prevented him from reconciling his ideals with reality. In 1784 he did make an attempt as a public leader to abolish slavery—he drafted an Ordinance for the Continental Congress that would have prevented slavery in all the new Western territories after 1800. The slavery prohibition in the Ordinance was narrowly rejected by legislators. When he returned to Virginia from France in 1789, he was not able to transcend his economic interests and articulate his professed ideals of freedom.[49] He failed this moral test all his life by failing to emancipate the enslaved. Furthermore, he never encouraged other countrymen to free those they enslaved.

Jefferson could have done much more to fight against slavery. He was a powerful politician in his era. He was a wealthy elite who owned 10,000 acres and more than 200 enslaved people.[50] Some of his intellectual, political, and cultural peers such as Benjamin Franklin of Philadelphia, John Jay of New York, and confidantes Ben Rush and George Wythe of Virginia were abolition-minded citizens.[51] Jefferson did not exercise courageous moral leadership on slavery during his entire life and especially during his presidency. Idealism was secondary to reality in his culture with his social status. Garry Wills writes in *Jefferson and the Slave Power* that "Jefferson felt he had no choice but to defend the evil [of slavery]" even though it fostered tyranny in the minds and consciences of the enslaved.[52]

Though Jefferson had unconventional Christian beliefs, he "appreciated the power of spiritual appeals."[53] *The Jefferson Bible* reveals Jefferson's moral values wrapped in a Christian cloak about Jesus. Early in life, he began to examine the texts of the Bible for their precepts, especially in the doctrines of Matthew, Mark, Luke, and John in the New Testament. He concluded that the authentic, original words of Jesus in these texts are simple, comprehensible, and morally sound. Jesus came the nearest to a religion of liberty, science, and free expansion of the mind.[54] In fact, Jefferson believed that Jesus had a "genuine doctrine" and was "the most venerated reformer of human error."[55] All in all, Jesus was poor, benevolent, patient, firm, and sublimely eloquent—a model for humankind, according to Jefferson.[56] In fact, Jefferson believed that the teachings of Jesus were "the purest system of morals ever before preached to man."[57]

During his presidential years (1801-1809), Jefferson wrote a forty-six-page work, *The Philosophy of Jesus of Nazareth,* which he extracted from the New Testament texts of Matthew, Mark, Luke, and John. In retirement he returned to his writing and this time it was *The Life and Morals of Jesus of Nazareth.* These two papers evolved into *The Jefferson Bible,* completed in 1819 at Monticello, which contains only the passages of the spoken words of Jesus. Jefferson removed all references to the supernatural, original sin, the Virgin Birth, the miracles, demonic possessions, the Resurrection, and the Crucifixion. He believed that "the New Testament was not dictated by Jesus but by 'fallible men' and 'not best educated men.'"[58] He wanted to "distinguish the moral philosophy of [Jesus] from the religion that was later created around Christ."[59]

Was Jefferson a Unitarian? Though he never officially declared his affiliation with a Unitarian congregation, his religious philosophy coincides with many of the beliefs and principles of Unitarianism. Jack Mendelsohn summarizes these basic beliefs in *Why I Am a Unitarian.* First, God is one unit. Second, freedom of religious belief is the principle of the free mind. Third, the free mind depends on reason and responsibility; that is, freedom requires individual responsibility and reason. Fourth, a fundamental principle of Unitarianism is a tolerance of differing views and practices; unity with diversity instead of conformity awakens a deeper spiritual tolerance.

Jefferson was Unitarian-leaning in his belief that religion is a matter that lies solely between an individual and God.[60] Individual freedom of thought protects the freedom of conscience.[61] True happiness can arise only in a life free from the shackles of tyranny.[62] Like Unitarians, Jefferson did not believe in the divinity of Jesus. Jesus did not claim divinity, the Bible did not proclaim it, and reason could not honor it.[63] Jefferson tried to remove "the divine" wherever possible. For instance, he did not allow a "divinity school" or Christian curriculum at the University of Virginia in 1825.[64] Instead, he substituted math, science, and language courses. He recognized that the God who gave us life, gave us liberty at the same time.[65] For the nation, Jefferson was convinced that religion had a cultural role.[66] But he was adamant that church and state affairs must be separated. The symbol of Americanism became a church-state separation, one of his greatest accomplishments. This wall of separation was legislated for Virginia in 1786 with the Statute for Establishing Religious Freedom, and for the nation in the First Amendment to the Constitution. Jefferson insisted that the government should not "make [any] law respecting an establishment of religion, or prohibiting the free exercise thereof."

In 1820 the Unitarian movement was strong. Jefferson wrote Thomas Cooper, a Unitarian, that he believed Unitarianism would become the majority religion in the nation.[67] Jefferson wrote Unitarian Jared Sparks that "thinking men of all nations rallied...to the doctrine of one...God, and embraced it with the pure morals which Jesus inculcated."[68] He advised Unitarians not to lose the faith of Jesus.[69] Jesus may not be the "Son of God," but he must have been inspired by God.[70] In retirement, Jefferson associated with Unitarians more frequently. He counseled them to apply reason to every opinion, for religion requires "careful thought, not reflexive acceptance."[71] He felt his country was blessed because it had not "surrendered its creed and conscience" to kings or priests.[72] Based on the letter he wrote to John Adams at the death of Abigail Adams, Jefferson had a "detailed version of the after-life, seeking comfort from the present pain of the loss of loved ones in the expectation that they would meet again beyond time and space."[73]

Many biographers and scholars extol the greatness of Jefferson and minimize his flaws. Jefferson is "carved in marble" and celebrated in larger-than-life statues. Americans accept Jefferson as "the moral standard of the Founder's era."[74] On the issue of slavery, Jefferson attempted to find an intellectual middle ground between what he knew to be wrong and what he could not do without.[75] He must have known that Jesus never believed in holding humans in bondage. Perhaps this brought some disharmony in his life. In essence, Jefferson stood for high standards of morality, but he was quite willing to rely on expediency and existing law when it served his purposes. For example, in reality, the "life, liberty, and the pursuit of happiness" phrase in the Declaration of Independence proposes liberty for property-owning men, but it denied liberty to everyone else—white women and children, the slaves, criminals.[76] According to the author Garry Wills in *Jefferson and the Slave Power*, Jefferson was "a moral coward."[77] Historian Paul Finkelman points out that he was "devoid of any moral or ethical concerns about slavery."[78]

The greatest flaw in Jefferson's religious philosophy lay in the contradiction between his early promotion of emancipation for the enslaved and his acceptance of racism. Henry Wiencek points out that there were "violent contradictions" in Jefferson's personal notebooks—"a turmoil of doubts, loathings, self-recriminations, all vying with the imperative to create a productive plantation."[79] Jefferson was the "architect and planter, struggling against the moralist [inside]...to absorb this foul, repugnant system [of slavery]."[80] However, after 1784, he capitulated to slavery out of self-interest and because he thought it could not be eliminated without destroying the republic; no longer would he advance any legal attempt to end slavery in the nation.[81] Thereafter, he "virtually ceased" his effort to emancipate the enslaved.[82] He freed only seven enslaved people in his lifetime. He took the attitude that "justice is on one scale, and self-preservation on the other."[83]

Jefferson was untrue to his principles on matters of slavery and color. When he published his *Notes on the State of Virginia,* he viewed Black people as inferior. He condemned them to "permanent inequality."[84] His "negrophobia," noted by the writer Garry Wills, was profoundly integrated into a racist pseudoscience without evidence. According to Paul Finkelman in *Slavery and the Founders: Race and Liberty in the Age of Jefferson,* Americans have little to admire about Jefferson as a symbol of Americanism when it comes to the issue of slavery.[85]

Americans credit Jefferson with identifying universal freedom for people and faith in individual inquiry.[86] But there were many inconsistencies between his words and deeds. He believed that an educated populous promotes democracy. He outlined an elaborate system of elementary and secondary schools for white children in Virginia. He wrote, "To be literate is a visible sign of reason and imagination."[87] However, he denied education to the enslaved of all ages at Monticello because he believed Black people were not capable of learning science, math, poetry, and music. Furthermore, he did not teach Black people any of the uses of his telescope, microscope, thermometer, and surveying equipment. In addition, when he established the University of Virginia in 1825, it admitted only young, white men.

Jefferson "tended to bury [anger deep] inside himself and regard the disjunction between his ideals and worldly imperfections as the world's problem rather than his own."[88] When Thomas Callender exposed his liaison with Sally Hemings in the newspaper *The Richmond Recorder,* he refused to answer the accusation. Jefferson had a great talent to envision what should be, what could be, what ought to be, rather than being a leader to enact that vision. The willingness to lead others toward what is morally right is a test of greatness.

Although searching his conscience to do good and what is morally right, Jefferson often put his personal self-interest first.[89] Accustomed to a politically powerful, wealthy, well-connected, aristocratic life, in Paris he rented a fashionable three-story dwelling in Hotel de Langeac that had salons, separate bedroom suites, a handsome dining area, a stable, gardens, servants, maids, cooks, a coachman, and a gardener.[90] It cost more than his annual salary, so he went into debt and borrowed money. When he returned to Virginia in 1789, he brought back 160 crates containing 63 oil paintings, 48 Windsor chairs, 14 sculptures, 4 full-length mirrors with gilded frames, 4 marble-topped tables, and other luxury items that he had bought in France.[91] To pay off his debt for these items, he sold eighty-five enslaved individuals in 1790. His lifestyle was more important to him than his moral philosophy.

In *Master of the Mountain*, the author Henry Wiencek claims that Jefferson could be deaf to humanity, ignoring his own philosophy of fairness, justice, freedom, liberty, and compassion if it suited him.[92] Enslaved people were a valuable asset to him. According to Finkelman, his debt of $100,000 at his death was a terrible burden for his heirs, who sold off nearly 200 enslaved people.[93] Jefferson even refused the sum of $20,000 entrusted to him in the will of Thaddeus Kosciuszko because he would have to free Kosciuszko's enslaved people and give half of the money to them. Jefferson failed to transcend his economic interests and show the moral courage to implement his ideals.[94]

In his book *Thomas Jefferson*, R. B. Bernstein summarizes the contradictions between Jefferson's philosophy and his deeds (see table, next page).

In 1912, Woodrow Wilson honored Thomas Jefferson with the following statement:

"Jefferson's principles are sources of light because they are not made up of pure reason, but spring out of aspiration, impulse, vision, sympathy. They burn with the fervor of the heart."[95] Truly, honor belongs to Jefferson for sustaining the principles of democracy in a new nation. History will endear many Americans to Jefferson for his search for moral completeness, his fervor for the freedom of the white population, his vision of church-state separation, and his dedication to theological wisdom; but Americans of all races still face the consequences today of his failure to tackle slavery with all his will.

BELIEFS	DEEDS
Believed he could build a "palace" at Monticello in luxurious European taste	Indebtedness forever; mortgaged enslaved people
Articulated freedom, self-expression, liberty	Never applied these virtues to the enslaved, nor to white women or children
Wanted out of politics	Loved power; "His philosophy was a tool of control over others and himself"[96]
Envisioned human equality	Racial inequality prevailed in his mind
Valued slaves	"He never expressed regret for the treatment of slaves"[97]
Believed in an agrarian life	Envied the North and its roads, canals, and railroads
Deplored manumission theory	Freed seven enslaved people in his life
Feared amalgamation of the races	Accommodated his own sexual passion for an enslaved woman
Proposed a more humane criminal code	Advocated harsh, almost barbaric, criminal punishment for enslaved and free Black people[98]
Expanded the views of citizenship	Proposed legislation that made emancipated slaves "outlaws" in Virginia. No vote for Black men or women of any race. As president, wrote a law excluding Black people from carrying U.S. mail.[99]
Opposed miscegenation	Proposed expelling children of a white woman and a Black man from Virginia[100]

Notes to Thomas Jefferson and His Legacy of Religious Philosophy

1. Merrill E. Peterson, ed., *Thomas Jefferson: A Profile* (New York: Hill & Wang, 1967), 246.
2. R. B. Bernstein, *Thomas Jefferson: The Revolution of Ideas* (Oxford: Oxford University Press, 2003), xiv.
3. David Hackett Fischer, *Albion's Seed: Four British Folkways in American History* (New York: Oxford University Press, 1989), 228.
4. Fischer, *Albion's Seed*, 245.
5. Fischer, 246.
6. Fischer, 222.
7. Fischer, 225.
8. Fischer, 216.
9. Edwin Gaustad, *Sworn on the Altar of God: The Religious Biography of Thomas Jefferson* (Grand Rapids, MI: William B. Eerdmans Publishing Co., 1996), 25.
10. Gaustad, *Sworn on the Altar*, 4.
11. Gaustad, 2-3.
12. Fischer, *Albion's Seed*, 234.
13. Fischer, 399.
14. Fischer, 333.
15. Jon Meacham, *Thomas Jefferson: The Art of Power* (New York: Random House, 2012), 31.
16. Gaustad, *Sworn on the Altar*, 15.
17. Gaustad, 47.
18. Meacham, *Thomas Jefferson*, 123.
19. Fawn Brodie, *Thomas Jefferson: An Intimate History* (New York: W. W. Norton, 1974), 55.
20. Gaustad, *Sworn on the Altar*, 93.
21. Meacham, *Thomas Jefferson*, 473.
22. Alf J. Mapp, Jr., *The Faiths of Our Fathers: What America's Founders Really Believed* (New York: Fall River Press, 2003), 15.
23. E. M. Halliday, *Understanding Thomas Jefferson* (New York: HarperCollins Publishers, 2001), 200.
24. Peterson, *Thomas Jefferson*, 253.
25. Quoted in Brodie, *Thomas Jefferson*, 370-373.
26. Gaustad, *Sworn on the Altar*, 17.
27. Gaustad, 20.

28. Joyce Appleby, *Thomas Jefferson* (New York: Times Books, 2003), 40.
29. Quoted in Meacham, *Thomas Jefferson*, 486.
30. Gaustad, *Sworn on the Altar*, 21.
31. Andrew Burnstein, *Jefferson's Secrets: Death and Desire at Monticello* (New York: Basic Books, 2005), 252.
32. Peterson, *Thomas Jefferson*, 255.
33. Burnstein, *Jefferson's Secrets*, 262.
34. Winthrop D. Jordan, *White over Black: American Attitudes Toward the Negro, 1550-1812* (Chapel Hill, NC: The University of North Carolina Press, 1968), 458.
35. Alan Pell Crawford, *Twilight at Monticello: The Final Years of Thomas Jefferson* (New York: Random House, 2008), 79.
36. Forrest Church, "America's Founding Faiths," *UU World* XXI, no. 4 (Winter 2007), 29-30.
37. Gaustad, *Sworn on the Altar*, 33.
38. Gaustad, 32.
39. Quoted in Burnstein, *Jefferson's Secrets*, 53.
40. Forrest Church, *The Cathedral of the World: The Universalist Theology* (Boston: Beacon Press, 2009), 42.
41. Gaustad, *Sworn on the Altar*, 75.
42. Quoted in Gaustad, *Sworn on the Altar*, 76.
43. Jack Mendelsohn, *Being Liberal in an Illiberal Age: Why I Am a Unitarian*, 2nd ed. (Boston: Skinner House Books, 2006), 75.
44. Quoted in Gaustad, *Sworn on the Altar*, 181.
45. Gaustad, *Sworn on the Altar*, 29.
46. Gaustad, 35.
47. Gaustad, 7.
48. Burnstein, *Jefferson's Secrets*, 238.
49. Paul Finkelman, *Slavery and the Founders: Race and Liberty in the Age of Jefferson* (London: M.E. Sharpe, 1996), 105.
50. Finkelman, *Slavery and the Founders*, 110.
51. Finkelman, *Slavery and the Founders*, 10.
52. Garry Wills, *"Negro President": Jefferson and the Slave Power* (Boston: Houghton Mifflin, 2003), xviii.
53. Meacham, *Thomas Jefferson*, 71-72.
54. Gaustad, *Sworn on the Altar*, 120.
55. Quoted in Gaustad, *Sworn on the Altar*, 472.
56. Brodie, *Thomas Jefferson*, 273.

57. Quoted in Dumas Malone, *Jefferson the Virginian* (Boston: Little, Brown & Co., 1948), 109.
58. Mapp, *The Faiths of Our Fathers*, 16.
59. Cover of Thomas Jefferson, *The Jefferson Bible* (New York: Penguin, 1940).
60. Church, "America's Founding Faiths," 31.
61. Church, "America's Founding Faiths," 26.
62. Church, "America's Founding Faiths," 31.
63. Gaustad, *Sworn on the Altar*, 112.
64. Brodie, *Thomas Jefferson*, 55.
65. Church, "America's Founding Faiths," 31.
66. Meacham, *Thomas Jefferson*, 471.
67. Peterson, *Thomas Jefferson*, 253.
68. Quoted in Meacham, *Thomas Jefferson*, 471.
69. Peterson, *Thomas Jefferson*, 254.
70. Peterson, *Thomas Jefferson*, 254.
71. Meacham, *Thomas Jefferson*, 169.
72. Quoted in Meacham, *Thomas Jefferson*, 470-471.
73. Meacham, *Thomas Jefferson*, 372.
74. Henry Wiencek, *Master of the Mountain: Thomas Jefferson and His Slaves* (New York: Farrar, Straus, and Giroux, 2012), 275.
75. Joseph J. Ellis, *American Sphinx: The Character of Thomas Jefferson* (New York: Vintage, 1998), 171.
76. Fischer, *Albion's Seed*, 412.
77. Wills, *"Negro President"*, 199.
78. Finkelman, *Slavery and the Founders*, 124.
79. Wiencek, *Master of the Mountain*, 22.
80. Wiencek, *Master of the Mountain*, 22.
81. Christopher Hitchens, *Thomas Jefferson: Author of America* (New York: Harper Perennial, 2005), 188.
82. Henry Wiencek, "Master of Monticello" *Smithsonian* (October 2012), 40.
83. Hitchens, *Thomas Jefferson*, 184.
84. Finkelman, *Slavery and the Founders*, 108.
85. Finkelman, *Slavery and the Founders*, 138.
86. Appleby, *Thomas Jefferson*, 150.
87. Quoted in Wiencek, *Master of the Mountain*, 19.
88. Ellis, *American Sphinx*, 41.
89. Hitchens, *Thomas Jefferson*, 188.

90. Jack McLaughlin, *Jefferson and Monticello: The Biography of a Builder* (New York: Henry Holt, 1988), 212.
91. Finkelman, *Slavery and the Founders,* 150.
92. Wiencek, *Master of the Mountain,* 61.
93. Wiencek, *Master of the Mountain,* 105.
94. Wiencek, *Master of the Mountain,* 105.
95. Quoted in Meacham, *Thomas Jefferson,* 497.
96. Wiencek, *Master of the Mountain,* 61.
97. Finkelman, *Slavery and the Founders,* 136.
98. Finkelman, *Slavery and the Founders,* 106.
99. Finkelman, *Slavery and the Founders,* 127.
100. Finkelman, *Slavery and the Founders,* 106.

PART 7

Religion

Why I Am a Unitarian

After a long search, I found that I am a Unitarian at heart. My choice of Unitarianism is a personal one, made consciously after experiencing religious alternatives, namely the Church of the Brethren and Methodism. Unitarianism gives me freedom to use my conscience as my guide. It encourages honest thought, freedom to question, and boldness to develop my own personal spirituality. It is founded on the right of every person to follow the dictates of reason, conscience, and experience as one's guide. This religion makes sense to me. Let me explain.

I was born in North Manchester, Indiana in 1930. My grandfather had been a minister in the Church of the Brethren; my father was a teacher and a devout Brethren; and my brother would graduate from Bethany Theological Seminary, a Brethren enclave. As a child, I wanted to please my father whom I dearly loved, so I acquiesced to his ardent faith. He never demanded compliance from me in religion, but I followed him because I felt secure in his faith. I earned gold seals for ten years of faithful attendance at church. My family always prayed before meals. I was baptized at the age of ten in the "Dunkard" way, which was three immersions of my head in water for the "Father, Son, and Holy Ghost." I was terrified of baptism because I had never learned to swim, and I imagined I would need to know how to breathe under water.

In college I began to dissent from the Church of the Brethren. For financial reasons, attending Manchester College, which was a Brethren liberal arts college in my hometown, was my only option. I refused to take a year of "Survey of the Bible," a prerequisite to biblical credit required to graduate. I substituted other courses. Furthermore, I didn't particularly like "self-righteous" students. "Prayer cells" repulsed me; in them, I never found solace in prayer or spiritual contact with God. Chapel attendance was required once a week. Dancing was not permitted during my four years in college, but in my senior year I helped sponsor a chaperoned dance off campus, for which the president of the college verbally chided me. Also, I was invited to discuss some of my essays from class with my philosophy professor, but I didn't. I had a different view, and I wanted acceptance of it, not criticism.

Briefly, the tenets of the Brethren religion as I remember them from my experience were the following: (1) Like the Quakers, Brethren were a church without a creed but with a set of "rules" for the Brethren disciple; (2) Like the Quakers, they took a pacifist stance of nonresistance; (3) Brethren found it important to live a simple life; a minority wore clothes resembling those of Mennonites and Quakers; (4) Dancing was associated with "sensuous living"; (5) Divorce was shunned as a solution for relationships gone awry; (6) The Brethren rite of baptism involved immersing the body three times in water; (7) The "love feast" was a communion service with a meal of bread dipped in meat broth and the washing of feet; (8) Brethren dedicated their world-wide service to people in need of food, clothing, shelter, and relief in times of disaster; (9) Brethren believed that the Bible alone was a sufficient guide for living. Four of these tenets began to bother me: the simple life, the love feast, baptism, and the Bible as the total source of guidance. However, I have been deeply influenced by my Brethren heritage; I still believe in the commitment to pacifism and the obligation to serve other people in need.

Why did I object to much of the Brethren philosophy? First, I did not totally accept the simple life because I cared about wearing lipstick, having pretty clothes and an attractive home, being romantic, and dancing. Second, I didn't believe that baptism washed away sins, let alone that at the age of ten, when I was baptized, that I was sinful or could make judgments about God, Jesus, and the Bible. Third, the "love feast" included washing the feet of your neighbor sitting by you at the table. It was to humble oneself. Humbleness does not come by washing feet; it is a human attribute that is molded in an already good person. Finally, I did not believe that salvation rested on "repentance from sins," "obeying the commands of Christ," conforming to "the image of God's Son," or being "kept by the power of God." To be "commanded" by some powerful being did not rest well with me. Instead,

I wanted to say, "I am saved by love, faith, trust and devotion to a spiritual world that includes God."

I attended the Wesley Foundation in graduate school and therefore, when my husband and I moved to Delaware, Ohio, we thought Methodism was the religion for which we were looking. But our tenure in the Methodist Church was short-lived. By 1968, we felt such discontent with the evangelical scope of the church we were attending that we withdrew our family of four children from *any* church for nearly fifteen years. Instead, our family spent Sundays enjoying parks, playgrounds, and our football field-sized backyard.

At this point in my life, religion plunged me into a depression, so I escaped from it by listening to the reasoning of my inner self. I must confess that these memories of religion from my past were painful when I began an emotional religious conversion. I blamed the religion of my past for the pain. In truth, I was emotionally upset with guilt when I changed my religious philosophy, separating from my family and my religious past. I even felt a tinge of emotional pain when I looked at a minister of a church, when I walked into a church, or when I thought about religion. I wanted to be free from the constraints that bound me. I conquered this turmoil inside by listening to my conscience, the voice within me. I drew on my own strength, overcame guilt for not attending to religion, and found a redemptive spirit within me. In her novel *Christy*, the author Catherine Marshall wrote, "...those who've never rebelled against God or at some point in their lives shaken their fists in the face of heaven, have never encountered God at all."[1] From this experience facing religion, I declared that my children must have a religion they develop, not copy from me. During this time away from traditional religion, I reaped inspiration from the presence and actions of my children, for they seemed to be the light of the sun in the daytime and the light of the stars at night. I was awakened through reading, listening to music, and contemplating love.

The "Enlightened Religion" of Unitarianism dawned upon me in the 1980s; it was the greatest revelation—a force for freedom. I found solace in it during the insular years away from organized religion; I found it by reading Jack Mendelsohn's book, *Why I Am a Unitari*an; I found it in like-minded friends, meeting together for discussions and fellowship; I found it in peaceful freedom within myself. "Unitarian religion's gift to me has been the opportunity to unfold: the special joy of breaking out of a cocoon, of finding a greater freedom in the exercise of my intelligence and in the growth of my experience of love, beauty, and justice."[2] "...the inner life, shaped by the power of high and sane ideals, brings to [my] soul the finest, most enduring satisfactions...."[3]

I searched for what Unitarians believed. Historically, the early Christian scholar Origen of Alexandria rejected anything that was unreconcilable with reason. The theologian Pelagius "preached a Christian faith blessed by God with freedom of moral choice."[4] The Renaissance humanist Michael Servetus attacked the errors of the Trinity. In the nineteenth century, Joseph Priestly from England brought a liberal breeze to the Unitarian movement, calling for a greater use of reason in the interpretation of scripture, questioning the doctrine of predestination, considering the exercise of free moral will, and believing in the unity of God, not a God divided into three parts. Unitarian ministers William Ellery Channing and Theodore Parker championed the view that human nature bestows a moral sense of goodness to perceive and choose good over evil. Parker declared that "the permanent truths of the spiritual life are confirmed by experience and practice."[5] Ralph Waldo Emerson did not lull us to sleep with assurances: "Nothing is secure but life, transition, the energizing spirit. No love can be bound by oath or covenant to secure it against a higher love. No truth so sublime but it may be trivial tomorrow in the light of new thoughts. People wish to be settled; only in so far as they are unsettled is there any hope."[6]

I found other beliefs within Unitarianism that confirmed my inner beliefs. First, it is repugnant to think that individuals are punished *by* their sins, not *for* them. Second, an upright character in unselfish service is to be admired above all. Thus, Unitarian service and related social justice issues are prominent. Third, whereas most religions consider their doctrines, creeds, dogmas, and catechisms as "closed articles of faith," Unitarians believe that religious inspiration can come from many sources, even Socrates, Gandhi, T. S. Eliot, Emerson, or Barack Obama. Unitarians travel with a library of books, not just the Bible; their religious beliefs are based on individual reason and not dependent on outside authorities or a literal translation of the Bible. Fourth, freedom of reason brings responsibility for one's actions. Fifth, a fundamental principle is tolerance of differing views and practices. Differing views are healthy and natural. Sixth, all persons are encouraged to seek truth as experience unfolds. Seventh, for Unitarians, salvation is rooted in ethical striving, respect for personalities and convictions of others, faith in human dignity and potentiality, aversion to sanctimony and bigotry, hearty enjoyment of life and people, confidence in the true harmony of science and religion, faith in the ability to love, and a quest for broad, deep religious expression. Eighth, most Unitarians reject the belief in the divinity of Jesus, the Trinity, and Christ as Savior. Finally, communion with bread and wine is not required and baptism is not the major entrance into Unitarianism.

The freshness of the Unitarian outlook offered me a spiritual niche. Individualism was honored; trust in human nature was praised. I was not encumbered by what I *should* be; rather, I felt nurtured by what I *want* to be. For many Unitarians, discovery of self is indeed the beginning of a discovery of God. Based on self-examination, I asked, "How shall I live while I live."

In what ways has Unitarianism contributed to my courage to live?

- I have found courage to live with myself and live in service to others. I find strength and peace by being useful.
- I am content to live a simple life, not an exalted one.
- My inner determination has helped me "break out" of past restraints.
- Unitarianism inspires me to be creative with my limited talents in music and speaking.
- So far in my life, I have been able to rebound after tragic occurrences.
- I keep my moral sense in balance when I rely on my conscience.
- I trust that there are fresh, new potentials for all of us in our spiritual life. Each person is encouraged to make the best contribution to enrich and strengthen others in a congregation.
- I celebrate human reason that guides my moral and ethical decisions. I understand that self-giving is having a self to give. We are not little centers of selfishness and sin.
- As a creative religion, Unitarianism has attuned me to modern ideas.
- I am proud of the moral leaders in our Unitarian heritage, including John Adams, Nathaniel Hawthorne, Ralph Waldo Emerson, Louisa Mae Alcott, Florence Nightingale, Susan B. Anthony, Margaret Fuller, Horace Mann, Dorothy Dix, Henry Bellows, Frank Lloyd Wright, Robert Burns, Albert Schweitzer, Charles Darwin, Isaac Newton, Bela Bartok, and Arthur M. Schlesinger.

Unitarians take a liberal stance. Within Unitarianism, I do not have to have unconditional proof of the mysteries of life. Eternal beauty has been placed in nature. I recognize that humans and nature are interdependent. I do not believe in an afterlife or resurrection from life lived on Earth; however, what I cannot explain, I will accept.

The struggle for self must deeply weave life to purpose. The Delaware Unitarian Universalist Fellowship has been my lasting connection to Unitarianism since 1971. I have made deep friendships that have secured my faith. I have been able to use my talents with like-minded people. So far in my life, I have found strength in Unitarianism during trying times. Therefore, though I do not know what mountains I will need to climb in the future, I affirm the principles of Unitarianism.

Notes to Why I Am a Unitarian

1. Quoted in Jack Mendelsohn, *Why I Am a Unitarian* (New York: Thomas Nelson & Sons, 1960).
2. Mendelsohn, *Why I Am a Unitarian,* 13.
3. Mendelsohn, 31.
4. Mendelsohn, 53.
5. Mendelsohn, 65.
6. Quoted in Mendelsohn, *Why I Am a Unitarian,* 15.

The Enlightenment Era in American Religious Life

Three chapters in Garry Wills' book *Head and Heart* concern Unitarians, Quakers, and deists during the Enlightenment era of American religious life. The Enlightenment was an eighteenth-century philosophy stressing the power of human reason and innovations in political, religious, and educational doctrine. In this era, "The overthrow of Calvinism by the Unitarians" was a "breakthrough toward liberal thought."[1] The theme of Garry Wills' *Head and Heart* is that "our minds (reason) must conspire with our heart (emotions)" to think logically; otherwise, being too intellectual or too emotional in decision-making will promote polarization. The author traces American Christianity through the time of the Puritans, the Great Awakening of Calvinism and the backlash to it in Enlightened Religion, the Romantic Era (Transcendentalism and a Second Awakening in 1800-1830 of evangelical Methodists), the rise of Evangelicals of the Christian Right, and the Karl Rove era in the 2000s. The Calvinist "Great Awakening" seemed radical, if not mad, to many who viewed the era's Pied-Piper preachers as "raw, illiterate, weak, conceited young men or lads." willing to undermine church stability by preaching with "fire and brimstone" rhetoric.[2] The reaction to radicalism always seems to be a swing back to reasonableness. This pattern keeps repeating itself. An aggressive surge of religious activity inevitably goes too far for the general population of a country. When religious zealots hang, burn, behead, or torture other human beings who hold different ideas, their actions come to be seen as inhumane, unreasonable, and repulsive.

John Locke was an enthusiast of the Enlightenment view that there is a reasonable guide to religion. He was against the philosophy of the Trinity and said that "the existence of more than one God is contrary to reason."[3] His text "An Essay Concerning Human Understanding" was published anonymously. Critics classified it as atheist in intent. Between the years of 1548 to 1612, denial of the Trinity was cause for an individual's execution, and it was still condemned in 1689 in the Act of Tolerance.[4] Leading intellectuals such as John Milton, Isaac Newton, and John Locke often did not publish their writings about religion during the seventeenth century. But by denying the Trinity, these brave, reasonable men, according to Wills, laid the foundation for much of later American religion.

In the cause of reasonableness, Locke explained that we do not know what transactions occurred between God and Jesus; therefore, we cannot know God's wisdom or providence in this agreement.[5] Likewise, we cannot know what exact words Christ uttered in his preaching and teachings with his apostles because the books of the New Testament were composed many years after his death. So God had to supplement teachings through revelations in the scripture, but all revelations in the Bible must be assessed with reason.

Wills claims that a "religious revolution occurred in the eighteenth century...that saw the emergence of an Enlightened religious culture whose hallmarks were tolerance for other faiths and a belief that religion was a matter best divorced from political institutions—the proverbial 'separation of church and state.'"[6] He credits James Madison and Thomas Jefferson for this separation of religion from government in the Constitution. I contend that Jefferson, Madison, and John Adams were Unitarian-thinking individuals whose Enlightenment-inspired reasoning helped transform the American religious landscape. The framers were deists in practice, and they exercised strong moral leadership in early America.

To enlighten is to give intellectual or spiritual light, instruct, impart knowledge, illumine, edify, or inform. The story of American Enlightenment may have begun when the Puritans hanged Quakers and exiled Dissenters, silenced heretics, and burned their books. Mary Dyer was a Quaker woman in her forties, the mother of six children, and wife of a respected colonial official in Rhode Island. On June 1, 1660, she was hanged from an elm tree. Her husband had unsuccessfully petitioned to save her from hanging for the crime of not submitting to the authority of the rulers of a Puritan community. She was "a disturber of the temporal peace." As she ascended the ladder to the elm branch, she said defiantly, "Nay, I come to keep blood guiltiness from you, desiring you to repent the unrighteous and unjust law of banishment upon pain of death made against the innocent servants of the Lord."[7] Quakers were a problem to Puritans. "Even to bring a Quaker book into the community was forbidden."[8] A ship captain was fined for bringing Quakers into the Massachusetts Colony. Others were fined for bringing in books or pamphlets espousing non-Puritan interpretations of the Bible. Quakers believed in an "inner light" above the Gospels. Mary Dyer's punishment, and that of Quakers, Presbyterians, and Baptists in general, would eventually become too severe for the public to tolerate.

Shifts in public opinion after the cruelty inflicted upon Mary Dyer helped usher in the American Enlightenment in the eighteenth century. Supernatural miracles gave way to natural, scientific explanations. The understanding of human nature changed when the doctrine of original sin diminished in importance. Samuel Sewall, a judge in the Salem witch trials, later apologized for his error of judgment. He began arguing that slavery "instills cruelty in its perpetrators."[9] He fought against slavery using scripture and arguments from humane natural reason. Keep the Golden Rule in mind, he wrote in 1700: "All things whatsoever ye would that men should do to you, do ye even so to them." "Slavery inflicted as a punishment cannot be considered just except for some grave crime...since liberty, by common agreement, is the nearest thing to life itself."[10]

Roger Williams is another precursor of the American Enlightenment. He was a prophet of the First Amendment. He believed in the separation of church and state. However, John Winthrop drove him out of the Massachusetts Colony because he was "incendiary" and a "total relativist." Perry Miller states that Williams believed that "no man could say for certain what is ultimate truth."[11]

Key issues in the Awakening period of Calvinist religious life in early America were conversion, the power to punish, and the Trinity. "The Awakening, like all radical renewal movements, created a liberal backlash among those whom it had judged spiritually cold...."[12] "Unitarianism is the most common form of Enlightened religion."[13] The overthrow of Calvinism by the Unitarians arrived with the belief that God was not vengeful. "Besides, as the early Unitarians emphasized, the doctrine of the Trinity is explicit only in the early creeds and councils of the church, not in the New Testament."[14]

Throughout the American Revolution, it was hard to have a common theology of Unitarianism because various factions were divided in their belief about the war. Enlightened religion took shape in America as a reaction to the Awakening movement. A number of individuals became sources for Enlightenment. Jonathan Mayhew was considered "a modern infidel" because he ridiculed old Calvinist doctrines.[15] Charles Chauncy, a Universalist, quietly kept his book *On the Benevolence of God* out of circulation because it concluded that God would not create human beings to be consigned to eternal torture and damnation. Chauncy believed that all would finally be saved, perhaps after a period of purgation.[16] He doubted that a benevolent, powerful God would assign millions to misery forever for his own glory.[17] John Adams adopted a similar view of God's benevolence. Ebenezer Gay, William Hazlitt, and Joseph Priestley's son, William, helped bring British Enlightenment to America in 1759. "Hazlett persuaded some to omit the Trinitarian doxology from church prayers."[18]

Enlightened religion became firmly anchored in the Middle Colonies in New England at King's College in New York in 1754. Then, upon becoming president of the College of New Jersey (later renamed Princeton University) in 1768, John Witherspoon, a Scottish Presbyterian minister, made the college a center of Enlightenment education in America. Witherspoon trained many of the founding generation, which made him the most influential educator in American history. Among the graduates of the College of New Jersey were twelve in the Continental Congress, also five delegates, President Madison, forty-nine U.S. representatives, twenty-eight senators, three Supreme Court justices, twenty-six state judges, one secretary of state, and two foreign ministers. "Witherspoon was fortunate. He flourished at a time when Americans were receptive to the Enlightenment."[19]

Enlightenment philosophy would flourish under Unitarianism, emphasizing "a belief in the 'laws of nature and of nature's God'..., [and holding] that reason is the tool for understanding those laws, and that humane conduct is what those laws teach."[20] It stressed science and reason, tolerance, and compromise. Whereas Jefferson had predicted that the future belonged to more liberal Unitarians, he turned out to be wrong. In the first part of the nineteenth century, Methodists, Baptists, and Presbyterians experienced an evangelical revival—today known as the Second Great Awakening. By 1860, according to Wills, Evangelicals made up 85 percent of the American church population.[21] But Enlightenment philosophy had already done its work. "It had founded the nation in 1776, drafted the Constitution with the separation of church and state, and passed the First Amendment, and in the labors of the Quakers, it had begun the long struggle to end slavery in America."[22]

Garry Wills argues that the Karl Rove Era, which began in 2000, pushed American society towards the Christian Right movement. The era was "highly religious..., highly Christian—highly biblical."[23] Implementing its policy of "compassionate conservatism," the George W. Bush administration allowed faith-based organizations to receive government funds to provide social services. Placing born-again Christians in major positions in his administration, Bush gave Evangelicals "faith-based war, faith-based law enforcement, faith-based education, faith-based medicine, and faith-based science."[24] Evangelical organizations were given the right to draft bills and install their implementers. Karl Rove had cultivated the extensive network of "Republican Rights" agencies.[25] Thereupon, anti-gay policies, abstinence programs, and creationist ideas flourished throughout the government bureaucracy under Evangelical influence. "The president himself called for an amendment to the Constitution outlawing abortion."[26] Bush also "joined the effort to ban gay marriage by a constitutional amendment."[27] Karl Rove, Bush's key political strategist, implemented strategies to inject religion into politics and cement the Christian Right's alignment with the Republican Party.[28]

But this commingling of religion and politics created a public backlash. A post-Rove movement opened the American electorate to think beyond "absolutes that knotted American discourse in future acrimony the first years of this [twenty-first] century. There is a bigger world out there."[29] The Constitution separates religion and politics. One's own religious conviction cannot be enacted into law. If legislators impose a religious point of view and oppose another, they create social discord. In a truly democratic country, the state simply cannot require a particular religious belief as a *political* duty. In the face of the "Evangelical hypertropism" orchestrated by Karl Rove, many Americans were disgusted by the intrusion of preachers and politicians into family decisions. "The anti-rational attack on Darwin and doctors and scientific research [of the Enlightenment period] culminates a growing anti-intellectualism in the Evangelical camps."[30] Wills believes that the Enlightened and the Evangelical faiths represent two temperaments; the creative tension between them is disruptive and often "wildly out of balance."[31]

In his book *Why I Am a Unitarian,* Jack Mendelsohn states that Unitarianism is an ethical doctrine with freedom of reason.[32] It has strengthened each member in "making human life more splendid, more precious, more secure."[33] It nurtures "the highest forms of life that experience and imagination can devise."[34] "For many Unitarians, discovery of self is indeed... the beginning of a discovery of God."[35]

Notes to The Enlightenment Era in American Religious Life

1. Garry Wills, *Head and Heart: American Christianities* (New York: Penguin Press, 2007), 123.
2. Wills, *Head and Heart,* 103.
3. Wills, 125.
4. Wills, 125.
5. Wills, 127.
6. Cover of Wills, *Head and Heart.*
7. Quoted in Wills, *Head and Heart,* 17.
8. Wills, *Head and Heart,* 19.
9. Quoted in Wills, *Head and Heart,* 89.
10. Quoted in Wills, *Head and Heart,* 91-92.
11. Quoted in Wills, *Head and Heart,* 93.
12. Wills, *Head and Heart,* 123.
13. Wills, 126.
14. Wills, 113.
15. Wills, 129.
16. Wills, 129.
17. Wills, 129.
18. Wills, 130.
19. Wills, 133.
20. Wills, 3.
21. Wills, 288.
22. Wills, 134.

23. Wills, 497.
24. Wills, 498.
25. Wills, 498.
26. Wills, 500.
27. Wills, 501.
28. Wills, 530.
29. Wills, 546.
30. Wills, 550.
31. Wills, 552.
32. Jack Mendelsohn, *Why I Am a Unitarian* (New York: Thomas Nelson & Sons, 1960), 37.
33. Mendelsohn, *Why I Am a Unitarian*, 39.
34. Mendelsohn, 40.
35. Mendelsohn, 99.

The Failing Faith

Unitarianism has never failed me. In 1970 when I read Jack Mendelsohn's book *Why I Am a Unitarian,* I could say, "That's a perfect fit for my general philosophy. It's a religious faith that harmonizes with my personality." I had been searching for the right fit for twenty years. Unitarian principles have nourished me. Over the years my Unitarian beliefs have been tested through joys, doubts, disappointments, insecurities, happiness, sickness, and the death of relatives. Unitarianism has been a vital part of my being.

In the decade of the 2000s, I grew curious to know what arguments people of other faiths in the United States might give to challenge my personal religious beliefs. I initially read five books on the matter: Peter Singer's *The President of Good and Evil* (2004), Richard Dawkins' *The God Delusion* (2006), Christopher Hitchens' *God Is Not Great* (2007), Gary Wills' *Head and Heart* (2007), and Scott Russell Sanders' *A Personal History of Awe* (2008). In the end, I learned about some other ways to look at religious faith.

I ran across a letter to the editor in *The New York Times* on December 8, 2006, from a contented, non-combative atheist in Pittsburgh named Katherine Carlitz. She wrote, "Raised without religion, I've never felt a need for it, and I love truth, beauty and a gorgeous sunset as much as anyone. I feel no need to persuade others. I don't disdain religion; I just don't feel drawn to it."[1] By 2009 I noticed some articles being written about the declining number of American adults who had an affiliation with a major church denomination. Why was this happening? Was it an ominous sign of a failing faith, especially in Christianity? I took solace in the words of Albert Einstein:

"To sense that behind everything that can be experienced there is a something that our mind cannot grasp and whose beauty and sublimity reaches us only indirectly and as a feeble reflection, this is religiousness. In this sense I am religious."[2]

Robert Wright, a journalist and author of *The Evolution of God*, chronicles the history of religion. He thinks that new atheists emerged after the 9/11 attacks. The rise of fundamentalism in Islam and Christianity highlighted the dark side of religion, causing more people to renounce religion altogether.[3] Furthermore, Wright contends that Richard Dawkins and Christopher Hitchens have a naïve view of religions and ignore their obvious benefits. Religion has the capacity for good when people see themselves as having something to gain from peaceful interactions with other people.

According to the 2008 American Religious Survey, 27 percent of Americans do not want a religious funeral and 30 percent of married couples do not have religious wedding ceremonies, indicating that organized religion is declining in significance in daily lives.[4] Based on the 2008 survey, an estimated 15 percent of Americans (34 million people) do not have a religious identity.[5] The percentage of Mainline Protestants (Methodists, Lutherans, Presbyterians, Episcopalians, and members of the United Church of Christ) in the U.S. population fell from 17 percent in 1990 to 12.9 percent in 2008, while in the same period the percentage of Pentecostals and Catholics remained nearly the same.[6]

According to a survey published in 2009 by the Pew Forum on Religion and Public Life, 28 percent of American adults "have changed the religious affiliation from that in which they were raised.[7] Taking into account those adults who have abandoned religion, changed their affiliation within their religious tradition, or switched to another religious tradition, 44 percent of adults are no longer affiliated with the religion in which they were raised.[8]

What about Unitarian Universalists in the United States? When Unitarians and Universalists merged in 1961, their combined membership was 151,557. Membership declined in the 1970s, rose in the 1990s and 2000s, and began falling again after 2009. By 2020, there were 152,921 members of churches in the Unitarian Universalist Association (UUA)—about the same number as in 1961.[9] However, surveys indicate that over 600,000 Americans describe themselves as Unitarian Universalists, even if they aren't a dues-paying member of a UU congregation. Unitarian congregations have an increasing number of 20- to 30-year-olds with little or no prior religious affiliation.

From my probing of trends in religious faith, I have found some of the reasons for the flight from religious affiliation:

- Individuals sometimes abandon religion or switch from one faith or denomination to another because they marry someone of that new faith, because their old faith wasn't meeting their spiritual needs, or because they simply enjoy the music, service, and style of worship in a new place.
- Some nonbelievers want transcendence from everyday life, not dogma or doctrine. Some of them find solace in literature, philosophy, and the beauty of the natural world. This is spiritual to them.
- There is a backlash against the fundamentalist, evangelical movement in the United States, which increasingly rejects science and reason. Moderates do not want to be associated with extreme beliefs.
- People are *not* generally against God or truth, but against others claiming exclusive rights to God and truth.
- Older generations are sticking with Christianity, but the young are moving away from it. Many youths are turned off by being forced to listen to drivel in churches and by being discouraged from questioning what seem like lies.

Why aren't there more Unitarian Universalists? There are at least several reasons:

- While most people turn to religion for comfort, Unitarian Universalists keep challenging people to find answers. Some people find the UU emphasis on questioning to be disconcerting.
- Most religions in the United States are authoritative, and many people want their religion to provide the answers to life's mysteries. In contrast, Unitarian Universalism stresses reason and the individual's freedom of belief.
- Most Americans do not realize that Unitarian Universalism even exists as a religion or that it has a deep history in the United States.

- Unitarian Universalists are averse to proselytizing, and only one American in every 1,300 is a UU. Therefore, new members tend to be those who "stumble" upon our religion.

Rev. Dr. Laurel Hallman, a candidate for UUA president in 2009, described the need for UU congregations to do more to retain new members of the faith: "The problem we have is not when people come in the door, but a year or two later when they are yearning to go deeper in our faith and don't find enough to sustain them. They drift away and that's what causes us problems. We need to look at how we are religious and what we can do to help people examine meaning and purpose in their lives. It's *how* we are religious that we need to work on."[10]

Many religious people find it hard to imagine how, without religion, one can be good. What would the ordinary conscience be without heavenly guidance? In Fyodor Dostoyevsky's novel *Brothers Karamazov*, the character Smerdyakov states, "If there is no God there is no morality." However, in *The God Delusion*, atheist Richard Dawkins states that the Ten Commandments are a compass for the nonreligious as well as the religious; most people learn these principles. He believes that human conduct sets a standard for human goodness. He suggests that love and thought have everlasting value, even if you take God away. Moreover, he asserts, "You can be an atheist who is happy, balanced, moral, and intellectually fulfilled."[11]

Christopher Hitchens points out that Socrates was not an atheist, but he advocated free thought and unrestricted inquiry. He said that conscience is the innate quality to guide human beings. Hitchens contends that "human decency is not derived from religion. It precedes it." Albert Einstein wrote, "I do not believe in a personal God.... If something is in me which can be called religious, then it is unbounded admiration for the structure of the world as far as our science can reveal it."[12] Hitchens contends that the United States needs a new Enlightenment in religion that values tolerance, intellectual openness, and pluralism.

Literature and poetry address eternal ethical questions and can help an individual develop religious belief. I have found the fullest accounts of ethical and moral conduct in the characters I have read about in literature. Where can one find better lessons about jealousy and deception than in Shakespeare's *Othello*? Isn't Tim O'Brien's *The Things They Carried* one of the most powerful condemnations of war? Who dissects individual foibles better than Chaucer in *The Canterbury Tales*? Who portrays the triumph of the spirit better than Sidney Poitier in his autobiography *The Measure of a Man*? And where can one find as much courage, optimism, and love—even in the face of a debilitating illness—than in the words of Morrie Schwartz in Mitch Albom's *Tuesdays with Morrie*? Literature can be a Bible. In literature I can find human behavior to probe for life's lessons and a faith to live by.

Notes to The Failing Faith

1. Katherine Carlitz, "It's O.K. Not to Believe," letter to the editor, *New York Times*, December 8, 2006.
2. Quoted in Richard Dawkins, *The God Delusion* (Boston: Houghton Mifflin, 2006), 40.
3. Robert Wright, *The Evolution of God* (New York: Little, Brown and Company, 2009).
4. Barry A. Kosmin and Ariela Keysar, *American Religious Survey Report (ARIS 2008): Summary Report* (Trinity College, Program on Public Values, March 2009), 10. https://www.washingtonpost.com/wp-srv/metro/documents/aris030609.pdf.
5. Kosmin and Keysar, *American Religious Survey*, 3.
6. Kosmin and Keysar, *American Religious Survey*, 5.
7. Pew Forum on Religion and Public Life, "Faith in Flux: Changes in Religious Affiliation in the U.S" (Pew Forum on Religion and Public Life, April 2009), 2. https://www.pewresearch.org/wp-content/uploads/sites/7/2009/04/fullreport.pdf.
8. Pew Forum, "Faith in Flux," 2-3.
9. "UUA Membership Statistics, 1961-2020," Unitarian Universalist Association, accessed April 15, 2021. https://www.uua.org/data/demographics/uua-statistics.
10. Donald E. Skinner, "Membership Growth in UUA Slows Down," *UU World*, May 11, 2009. https://www.uuworld.org/articles/membership-growth-in-uua-slows-down.
11. Dawkins, *The God Delusion*, 23.
12. Quoted in Christopher Hitchens, *God Is Not Great: How Religion Poisons Everything* (New York: Twelve, 2007).

God Helps Those Who Help Themselves?

In her book *The Mighty and the Almighty*, former U.S. Secretary of State Madeline Albright writes one of my favorite stories about Abraham Lincoln:

"One day, when he was still a young lawyer riding from courthouse to courthouse in search of clients, he came across a pig struggling in vain to free itself from a bog. Lincoln paused for a moment, torn between sympathy for the pig and concern about what the mud might do to his new suit. He rode on. After about two miles, he turned back, unable to stop thinking about the animal and its plight. Arriving at the scene, he laid out some wood planks on which he descended into the bog, reaching the pig and hauling it out at great cost to his clothing. When asked why he had done all that for a pig, Lincoln replied, in essence, 'I didn't do it for the pig; I did it for me—to take a pain out of my mind.'"[1]

In rescuing a pig at the cost of his suit, Lincoln didn't cogitate about an Islamic or Christian or Buddhist principle "to do good," nor was he driven by self-interest or vanity. Rather, he felt a moral duty to help a living creature escape from a desperate circumstance. He had an inner impulse to apply an ethical principle of goodness so that a desperate pig could stay alive. Throughout his life, the pain of others awakened his conscience. His good works came intuitively and naturally, the evidence of an inner grace. Furthermore, his personal theology led him to make decisions on the basis of their likely consequences. By demonstrating a civic duty to a broad community of animals and people, he became a model of public good.

Lincoln had a Unitarian Universalist inclination. In his book *Abraham Lincoln's Philosophy of Common Sense,* psychiatrist Edward J. Kempf writes that Lincoln "believed neither in the divinity of Christ nor God as a personal being, although he did believe in God as a universal, impersonal creative Intelligence," a Providence, Maker, or God in contact with human beings through the soul.[2] Furthermore, states Kempf, Lincoln believed "that the Bible was unnatural and false in many claims and violated reason, that Jesus was not the son of God any more than any other [human being], that the Bible did not contain the full record of all divine revelations of God to [humans]. We know that later Lincoln expressed belief that [human beings] today receive revelations from God through a conscience, and he himself relied on the dictates of his conscience when he had to make difficult decisions between right and wrong for the public welfare."

In an article entitled "The Christian Paradox" appearing in the August 2005 edition of *Harper's Magazine,* environmentalist Bill McKibben writes, "America is simultaneously the most professedly Christian of the developed nations but the least Christian in its behavior."[3] He points out that three quarters of Americans believe the Bible teaches that "God helps those who help themselves," even though this statement was uttered by Benjamin Franklin and never appears in holy scriptures. Franklin's maxim has been construed to favor individualism, whereas it should summon us to be concerned primarily with the consequences of our actions. Without individual initiative and determination, individuals flounder, but when individualism becomes the belief that each of us is a distinct entity and ought to assert independence from others, we forfeit the willingness to offer our service for the common good.

McKibben further states that Christ was pretty specific in his teachings about what he wanted his followers to do: give aid to the poorest, feed the hungry, slake the thirsty, clothe the naked, welcome the stranger, and visit the prisoner. But let's look at several examples of the consequences of our conduct in the United States:

- Americans have the lowest life expectancy at birth of any major industrialized nation.[4]
- 25 percent of American children live in poverty,[5] indicating that we don't care for the least among us.
- In 2007, 30 percent of Americans between the ages of 19 and 24 had no health insurance.[6]

- In 2015, five million persons of color lived within 1.8 miles of a hazardous waste facility.[7]
- In 2014, the top 10 of income earners in the United States owned 81 percent of all stocks.[8]

Even in the face of these dismal statistics, the Christian Right proposes that we declare Christianity as the official national religion of the United States. In contrast, people in countries like Norway and Sweden, where religion is not heavily accentuated, are dramatically cutting back on carbon emissions, living in smaller homes, taking public transit, giving significant aid to the poor, and making sure everyone has healthcare.

Self-righteous individuals become hypocrites when they disconnect belief from action. Lincoln did not. He rescued a pig not for notoriety, fame, or vanity, but out of compassion for a struggling animal. Caring for a pig was more important to him than an untidy, muddy suit. He ignored the conventional message that "God helps those who help themselves," preferring instead to focus on the common good rather than serve his individual needs. Furthermore, consider the many books and sermons that give "how-to" advice to individuals: how to discipline your children; how to reach your professional goals; how to invest your money; how to repair your broken marriage; how to reduce your financial debt; how to get God to serve your needs. All of these publications have sensible advice for individuals, but they ignore the needs of others. Indeed, the fixation on individualism—the hallmark of American culture—leads us to emphasize self-improvement, self-esteem, self-confidence, and self-help. We have ended up creating a culture of unrelenting self-obsession. While individualism can give a person freedom and independence, McKibben believes that "when [individuals] hunger for selfless love and are fed only love of self, they will remain hungry."[9]

"Love your neighbor as yourself" is a rather radical notion when one thinks about it. The neighbor we are supposed to love is a poor person, a sick person, a naked person, or a hungry person, according to the Gospels. By and large, many churchgoers have done a pretty good job of loving the neighbor in the next pew. But what about loving neighbors farther away in war-ravaged communities, those who lack security, those who are maimed, abused, depressed, or hungry, in places such as Darfur, New Orleans, Iraq, or Syria? Because ordinary citizens cannot reach them physically, they might donate money to worthy organizations that can assist the desperate. But the connection between an individual and that broader community usually doesn't involve a personal sacrifice. In this realm, loving one's neighbor has been hijacked by those who have applied the theory that "God helps those who help themselves." In essence, I take care of myself, so you take care of yourself. Pick up, walk on, survive on your own and God will reward you.

Consider taxation as a means to helping others. Supreme Court Justice Oliver Wendell Holmes once declared, "Taxes are the price we pay for civilization."[10] No taxes, no government. But today a hard-working individual is likely to hear, "Your income is your money. The government has no right to take it from you." In his 2004 book *The President of Good and Evil,* Peter Singer grants that it is *your* money, but he also contends that the government can take some of it to meet the needs and priorities of citizens who may jointly benefit from it.[11] An individualist claim to the right of property doesn't trump civic duty. For example, if I decide to go into a national forest and pick 20 baskets of berries, are these *my* berries or do I need to share them with others in a village nearby because I picked them on public land? I would say: I can gather and keep the berries for myself, provided there are still enough berries on public land for others to pick.

An individual achieves success because others in society have provided the opportunity for that individual to succeed. Each individual draws on social capital--technology, organizations, government, and collective trust. A corporation that manufactures cars needs the labor of individual workers and a stable economic system. An Amish farmer cannot manage a farm singlehandedly; others regularly pitch in. Teachers depend on people in the community for their success. It is a total fallacy to say that we arrive at success completely on our own. We are the individuals we are because *many others* gave us opportunities. Thus, the truth is, "God helps those who help others."

In the case of Lincoln, he assuaged his guilt and improved himself by helping a pig in distress. He found self-esteem through his deed; he made the right decision, according to his conscience. His individual intuition led him to a moral result. Empathy for a lowly pig consequently governed his duty to society because the pig was either a pet for someone, a product for sale, or a victual for dinner.

I see several Unitarian Universalist principles in the simple story of Abraham Lincoln and the pig:

- Each individual develops his or her own personal theology without fear of censure. (How foolish Lincoln must have looked, wallowing in the mud for the sake of a pig.)
- Individual reason and conscience are the ultimate arbiters in religion, not a church or document or an official.
- The revelations which appear to the human spirit are infinitely numerous, eternally fruitful, and wondrously exciting.
- The main governing principles in human relationships are love and concern for the welfare of other living creatures.

Notes to God Helps Those Who Help Themselves?

1. Madeline Albright, *The Mighty and the Almighty: Reflections on America, God, and World Affairs* (New York: Penguin Group, 2004), 51-52.
2. Edward J. Kempf, *Abraham Lincoln's Philosophy of Common Sense: An Analytical Biography of a Great Mind (Part 1)* (New York: The New York Academy of Sciences, 1965).
3. Bill McKibben, "The Christian Paradox: How a Faithful Nation Gets Jesus Wrong," *Harper's Magazine*, August 2005.
4. Peter Singer, *The President of Good and Evil: The Ethics of George W. Bush* (New York: Penguin Group, 2004), 23.
5. Singer, *The President*, 23.
6. Stephen M. Caliendo, *Inequality in America: Race, Poverty, and Fulfilling America's Promise* (Boulder, CO: Westview Press, 2015), 125.
7. Caliendo, *Inequality in America*, 130.
8. Timothy Noah, *The Great Divergence: America's Growing Inequality Crisis and What We Can Do about It* (New York: Bloomsbury Press, 2012), 177.
9. McKibben, "The Christian Paradox," 675.
10. Quoted in Singer, *The President*, 17.
11. Singer, *The President*, 14.

Norman Mailer's Concept of God

Until 2014, I had never read a single book written by Norman Mailer, but one Sunday I walked into the small Beehive Bookstore in Delaware, Ohio, and I saw a copy of *On God* by Mailer on the bargain counter. Months later I read it and found it original and unpredictable, but with a unique vision of the world in which "God needs us as much as we need God."[1] This idea gave me a fresh way to think about God as a divine presence.

On God documents a conversation between Norman Mailer, the writer, and Michael Lennon, an English professor who was Mailer's authorized biographer and the author of *Norman Mailer: A Double Life*. The dialogue between these two authors occurred from July 17, 2003 until June 14, 2006 in Lennon's home on the Bay of Provincetown Harbor in Massachusetts. Mailer dedicated his book *On God* "to my wife, my sister, my children, and to my grandchildren" in 2007, the year he died. Over his eighty-four years of life, he wrote at least thirty works that touch upon themes of war, sex, culture, and politics. The following account capitalizes on Mailer's part of the conversation in *On God*.

Mailer establishes his own belief system, one that rejects both organized religion and atheism. He believes in the tripartite division of power in our solar system among God, the Devil, and humanity. That is, "Our God created the world we live in and is in constant conflict with the Devil."[2] Mailer reflects, "I offer nothing but my own ideas.... I have spent thirty-odd years of my life as an atheist and the last fifty years trying to contemplate the nature of God. It took many years to recognize that I did believe in God—that is, believed there is a divine presence in existence."[3] "I'm not trying to found a religion," he assures us,[4] but he believes that "having a view of the universe that makes sense to oneself is [a] prescription for mental health."[5] One must find his or her own vision of God.

Basically, Mailer employs existentialism, which is a philosophical attitude that stresses the individual's unique position as a self-determining agent responsible for his or her choices. Because humans have choices, his vision proposes that God and the Devil are forces in constant war with each other for the souls of humans. Indeed, humans have been given freedom to choose a responsible path; they are rewarded or punished in reincarnation based on the complex mix of good and evil actions that they took in their life.

As a novelist, Mailer became convinced that he had a right to believe in the God that he, not theologians, could visualize—"an imperfect, existential God doing the best He [or She] could manage against all the odds of an existence that not even [God], our Creator, entirely controlled."[6] He perceives God as an "Artist," not an all-powerful lawgiver who assumes a moral stance in a celestial war.[7] God, the Creator and the greatest artist, enshrines human beings and animals as His or Her most developed artworks. Perhaps on occasion the Devil tampered with evolution. Successes for an artist may be marred by some failures, like the hideous eyes of fish. God must have greeted dinosaurs with immense excitement, but they proved to be too big—badly designed. God may be limited in power to change a volcano, for God may not be a perfect engineer. In that case, God is not punishing humans with a volcano, but passing a shiver through our religiosity. "God does not understand us completely any more than we understand our children. We can know them well in terms of their habits, some of their virtues, and some of their faults, but we certainly don't understand them altogether. So God wants to know more about His Creation, whereas the Devil is attempting to muck up precisely that clarity."[8]

Some good came out of the Enlightenment era because humans had marvelous freedom of thought, especially in science, but it also gave rise to "the subtle, insidious abuses of technology."[9] "Evil is the consequence of God permitting humans to have free will. Human cruelty is the price of freedom.... [God does not] interfere. Without the possibility to choose to do good or evil, humanity would be robots."[10] The notion of the Devil shapes Mailer's understanding of human motives. When we act with great energy, it is God and the Devil collaborating on the same outcome. Often God and the Devil may not know which side we are on at any given moment, or whether we are independent of both entities with a humanitarian sense, but we have freedom of choice.

Of the Christian study of death, judgment, heaven, and hell, Mailer states, "I believe that our childhood notion of Heaven has to be relinquished.... I don't believe in Hell anymore [either],"[11] and certainly it is not eternal punishment. "I see Heaven, Purgatory, and Hell as wasteful institutions."[12] On earth, in life, "we do experience Heaven as the extraordinarily perfect moments; we know what Heaven is in the luminous joy it gives us."[13] "We certainly know what Hell is. Hell can be as simple as having a case of gout or a streamer of a drug trip or a nerve gone crazy in a tooth."[14] Or hell can be a towering depression.[15] Hell is more available to humans. "My notion remains that the only Heaven and Hell we ever receive—the only judgment that comes to us—is by way of reincarnation. To wit, as a reward we can be given a better possibility in our next life. Or we can be born with a worse one, if that is what we deserve."[16] "One function of reincarnation may be to give God further insights into us.... God does not understand us completely."[17]

As far as the rich and the poor are concerned, Mailer says, "People who were born in rich and favorable circumstances in one life and grew spoiled... and disappointing...might be reborn as poor people. Others who were poor but never turned bitter or felt that they were deprived might be rewarded [with wealth]."[18] Our conscience is vital in our choice of good or evil. It gives us a clue to what is likely in our future. "If I am to be reborn, I want to be able to do more in my next incarnation than with this [present] one."[19] God controls the process of reincarnation, perhaps with a number of monitoring angels. Reincarnation—our placement in the next life—is the only divine judgment we receive. "If you have no desire to live again, God's decision may be, 'No, no need to be reborn.' True death. End of existence."[20]

God must be an artist, Mailer insists. "Let's think of the size of the Creation. Even if God is not All-Powerful, we have only to contemplate the vast extent of flora and fauna, the painterly touches...revealed in the chromatic scales of a butterfly's wings."[21] Mailer maintains that God as an artist is portraying His or Her conception of the metamorphosis in each character's destiny. "There's nothing more irritating to most of us than the feeling that we are not completely under our own power, that other forces are pushing us...that are stronger than we are."[22] "I would assume technology is indeed the Devil's force."[23] Also, plastic is a "perfect weapon in the Devil's armory, for it desensitizes human beings."[24]

In the past hundred years, "the measure of our human development as ethical, spiritual, responsible, and creative human beings may be worse."[25] In 1900, the average American lived to be forty-six. Six percent of Americans graduated from high school. Only 14 percent of homes had a bathtub. The flush toilet was a rarity. A vast majority of homes had hardly any books. Though life is easier today, it is filled with a general anxiety. "Life is certainly more comfortable than it used to be, and there are more opportunities for most than there were [in the 1900s]."[26] However, "I think we are weaker and more confused."[27] Our uneasiness manifests itself in ways that we don't even realize. "You can ask yourself. Is this society better when it has every creature comfort that's been developed up to now?"[28] "It may be that people are finally much less interesting today than they were one hundred or two hundred years ago, when they didn't have flush toilets, but did live with interesting windows and doors" opening to the outside world.[29]

Humans are a part of an enormous spiritual laboratory.[30] They assume God, like us, "is doing the best that can be done under the circumstances. God is our Creator. God put us here. We are God's artistic vision."[31] Like a good parent, God doesn't always look for control. God gives us "lightning and thunder and extraordinary sunsets" for us to appreciate God's sense of beauty; however, the horrors of modern history demonstrate that God isn't all-powerful. "We are all engaged in a vast cosmic war and God needs us.... [We] live in the depths of confusion...with the belief, the hope, the faith...that there is a purpose to it all."[32] "There are no answers. There are only questions."[33] We learn from God and God learns from us.[34] "There are periods where we may get more from God—when we're young, for example. When we're old, we may be obliged to give back more, not necessarily to God, but to the way we influence other people, the way we amplify His or Her vision or worsen it. Indeed, there are some things God can learn only from contemplating our direct experience."[35] For the last five decades, America has ravaged the environment. "We've ruined the freshness of the air, the cleanliness of the rivers, the integrity of the earth.... America is not a country whose spiritual goodness is guaranteed to hold up under examination."[36]

Mailer confesses that he was a fierce atheist at one time in his life, but now it seems incomprehensible that there isn't a Creator. Otherwise, how can we be here and insist that there's nothing behind our existence?[37] If it all ends badly for humans, we are responsible, but if one believes in an all-powerful God, we aren't responsible. Fundamentalists follow all the rules so that they don't have to take responsibility. But the Devil's strongest tool is to stop people from thinking. "So long as people are incapable of pursuing a thought to where it leads, they can't begin to carry out God's notions...they become desensitized to the sensitivities of divine will.... They wall themselves out."[38]

"I'd like to keep huge respect for the fact that we were created by something or someone marvelous, who is not wholly unlike ourselves. Therefore, we can identify with that God, identify with God's drama as well as our own and thereby feel larger.... The reason I've never found Islam the least bit attractive is...the prayer ritual. Kneel down; bend your head to the ground; recognize that you are weak before the wrath of God? If this is what religion consists of, the recognition of being totally weak and that God will take care of us, provided we never cross any one of a thousand carefully laid-out lines of behavior, then I have to believe that existence is knotted up."[39] "But God hates to give up on interesting artistic possibilities in a human."[40] In fact, God even sees wonderful potential in awful people.[41]

Mailer believes that there is a mixture of God and the Devil in each of us.[42] We have the right to explore anything and everything at our spiritual peril. "He gave us free will. Or She gave us free will...then the Book is the first obstacle to [free will]."[43] The Commandment "Do Not Kill" has been ignored in war. People in bad marriages commit adultery as a sort of escape. The Ten Commandments are messages to the conscience, like guides, but Mailer doesn't believe we should abide by them slavishly.

"Compassion is probably the finest emotion humans can have. When tears come to our eyes for the sorrow of someone else, that may be as close as we get to reaching the best element in ourselves."[44] "Sometimes people die whom you thought you didn't care about, and you discover you have lost something or someone valuable to you. There is a constant element of discovering yourself."[45] "The degree one is brave, one finds more love than when one is cowardly."[46] Love is a reward. When one feels compassion and love, a goodness is present that is useful to another person. However, when a person acts out ugliness, this injures terribly one's personal freedom of choice.

Perhaps "God's needs are greater than ours. God's woes are more profound than our own when God sees [human] failures in fulfilling a vision." Our threats of nuclear warfare, our ethnic wars, our terrorism, and our spread of pollution may disappoint God's vision for humans on earth.[47]

"The Catholic Church is a study not only in immense human wisdom but of applied skill at maneuvering our thoughts around the most non-navigable corners."[48] Mailer claims that he felt strongly attuned to the revelations of Judaism and Christianity, but he was less familiar with Islam, Hinduism, Buddhism, and Gnosticism, so he felt less negative about those religions. However, he ventures that he would find the Koran as difficult to live with as the Old and New Testaments.[49]

Mailer admits, "I feel no attachment whatsoever to organized religion."[50] He sees the New Testament as too attached to the concept of Jesus as the son of God. He claims that "to accept the Bible as the absolute map of our spiritual universe is comparable to using the kind of charts Christopher Columbus had to look at, before he set out for the West.[51]

"We can't pretend more pleasure comes to us from technology. It tends to cramp our senses and reduce us to people who are able to live in a closed environment."[52] Mailer derides mass media and digital communication, encouraging us to express our own creativeness and use our own spirit. He sees mental powers reduced with technology.[53] The great leaders of the past thought independently, without the mediation of electronic machines.[54] A profound difference lies between early and later technology. In the past, the search for information was a vital part of intellectual development. Now, "we are being buried under lava flows of data."[55] Technology that replaces God would be an absolute disaster to the conscience.

Prayer, Mailer claims, is "an immensely abused communication system… in human affairs."[56] "Prayers are not usually answered."[57] He assumes that "God can pick up human messages without the need for prayer."[58] However, he grants that prayer intensifies a sense of focus in the mind and that a friend's prayer for you can give you warmth. He sees prayer as cleansing for many; it is a concentration of one's greatest need at that moment; it renders hope. Prayer encourages modesty and humbleness; it inspires courage in some people. "Prayer can also enable one to come closer to what is most awful in oneself."[59] Prayer offers solace amid overwhelming grief; in case of confusion, it offers theological comfort. "I can see exceptional cases where prayer is so beautiful and comes out of such depth in a human and has such inner resonance that divine attention is paid."[60] Such a prayer is like a fine artist who comes from the depths of experience and "shows a hard-earned balance of perception and passion of forgiveness and true human need."[61] When a parent prays for an ill child, whether it is heard or not, it is an honorable focus on love.

Mailer contemplates what kind of political system God would want. "I would argue that unless we have some real understanding of the needs of the poor, and the rights of the poor, plus the passion of the poor to become more," our democracy could end badly.[62] He supposes that "if a socialist society should ever come into being with a belief in an existential God,... we might begin to find some more developed stirrings of human equity."[63] Corporations cannot be trusted with political power; small businesses and the notion of community serve democracy best.

In summary, Mailer believes in an "existential God who does not demand my unwavering faith but prefers instead that we look to find, despite God's flaws and ours, a core of mutual respect as we set out together to attempt to create a viable vision that can lead us into the unforeseeable future out there with its galaxies, its light-years, its enigmas, and ultimately, let us hope, its availability."[64]

Speaking to his audience, Norman Mailer humbly professes, "Let me conclude, however, by thanking you for the order and stimulation you brought to this theologically ignorant mind."[65]

Notes to Norman Mailer's Concept of God

1. Cover of Norman Mailer, *On God: An Uncommon Conversation* (New York: Random House, 2007).
2. Mailer, *On God*, 4.
3. Mailer, xvi.
4. Mailer, 20.
5. Mailer, 26.
6. Mailer, xvi.
7. Mailer, xvi-xvii.
8. Mailer, 111.
9. Mailer, 9.
10. Mailer, 177.
11. Mailer, 20.
12. Mailer, 105.
13. Mailer, 105.
14. Mailer, 106.
15. Mailer, 20.
16. Mailer, 20-21.
17. Mailer, 111.
18. Mailer, 111.
19. Mailer, 22.
20. Mailer, 99.
21. Mailer, 42.
22. Mailer, 43.
23. Mailer, 48.
24. Mailer, 48.
25. Mailer, 7.
26. Mailer, 52.
27. Mailer, 52.
28. Mailer, 53.
29. Mailer, 62.
30. Mailer, 60.
31. Mailer, 73.
32. Mailer, 77.
33. Mailer, 75.
34. Mailer, 61.
35. Mailer, 61.
36. Mailer, 136.

37. Mailer, 54.
38. Mailer, 54.
39. Mailer, 57.
40. Mailer, 59.
41. Mailer, 59.
42. Mailer, 63.
43. Mailer, 64.
44. Mailer, 70.
45. Mailer, 78.
46. Mailer, 29.
47. Mailer, 86.
48. Mailer, 104.
49. Mailer, 55.
50. Mailer, 5.
51. Mailer, 114.
52. Mailer, 116.
53. Mailer, 116.
54. Mailer, 117.
55. Mailer, 138.
56. Mailer, 201.
57. Mailer, 198.
58. Mailer, 202.
59. Mailer, 209.
60. Mailer, 206.
61. Mailer, 206-207.
62. Mailer, 213.
63. Mailer, 213.
64. Mailer, 183.
65. Mailer, 196.

The Politics of God

In Antiquity, religion and the state were intertwined. Creon, King of Thebes in Sophocles' drama *Antigone,* decreed that the body of Polyneices, the brother of Antigone, must be left unburied. "No one shall bury him, no one mourn for him,/ But his body must lie in the fields, a sweet treasure/ For carrion birds to find as they search for food."[1] Antigone argued that Polyneices must have a proper burial. "It was not God's proclamation. That final Justice/ That rules the world below makes no such laws...The immortal unrecorded laws of God./ They are not merely now: they were, and shall be,/ Operative forever, beyond man utterly."[2]

Creon replied, "...I say to you...that I have nothing but contempt for the kind of Governor who is afraid, for whatever reason, to follow the course that he knows is best for the State; and as for the [woman] who sets private friendship above the public welfare,—I have no use for [her], either. I call God to witness that if I saw my country headed for ruin, I should not be afraid to speak out plainly.... These are my principles."[3]

Thomas Hobbes (1588–1679), an English philosopher, believed that human beings at their core are selfish, competitive creatures who need "collective security" from a government. Hobbes was suspicious of religious leaders claiming to speak in God's name on issues of politics. He didn't want humans to abandon their natural condition to pursue their own personal religious beliefs. He was against the separation of government powers between state and church.[4]

In contrast to Hobbes, John Locke (1632–1704), another English philosopher, adopted the idea that political power should be limited, divided, and widely shared among individuals. He made a strong argument for the separation of church and state. He wanted the state to protect the civil interest of society: "life, liberty, health, and indolency of the body."[5] The state (or government) cannot decide for an individual how to please God; the church cannot use force to affect individual civil interests.[6] An individual must not violate his or her own conscience.[7] "If a man does not believe in God, he cannot be forced to swear an oath to God to guarantee his loyalty to the state."[8] Locke was a classical liberal; he "emphasized individual freedom in civic, economic and religious life."[9]

Puritans set the tone of early American politics. They never wanted the separation of church and state. Religiously, they were "right thinkers, not freethinkers."[10] In Puritan theology, the saved were God's "elect." Those who did not obey the command of God were evil messengers. Puritans denounced Roger Williams, who believed in "soul-liberty," the right of everyone to practice religion in his or her own way. Although Rev. Thomas Hooker was a Puritan, some of his co-religionists disagreed with his argument that people should have the God-given right to choose their own leaders and place limits on the powers granted to them. The way a leader thinks, feels, and acts is influenced by the immense power of religion.[11]

In the article "Divine Order vs. Sacred Liberty" in the Winter 2007 edition of *UU World*, Forrest Church connects our religious heritage and political history. James Madison, one of the Founding Fathers of the United States, wanted Americans to protect religion from politicians [because] "religion and Government will both exist in greater purity, the less they are mixed together."[12] George Washington said that America may have been based on a "providential agency," but its principles are based on "private morality." He "disclaimed any interest in whether people were Mohammedans, Jews, Christian, or Atheists, for his sole concern was the right [of citizens] to freedom of worship, expression, and thought."[13] In the case of George Washington, however, his church attendance smoothed his way in Virginia's politics at the time. But throughout volumes of his correspondence, he mentions Christ by name only once. He felt that religion had no business intruding in government affairs. He wanted every individual to conduct himself or herself as a good citizen and be accountable to the dictates of his or her own conscience.

Unitarian-leaning John Adams and Thomas Jefferson said more. Adams claimed that liberty was a gift from God, but democracy was a creation of man.[14] In America's formation, "any persons employed in [government] service had [no] interviews with the gods or...the influence of heaven any more than other laborers of ships, farmers, business persons or homes."[15] Thomas Jefferson "dismissed the Christian clergy as 'the greatest obstacles to the advancement of the real doctrines of Jesus.'"[16] He was attacked by the Federalist Party in 1800 as a "no god" president. He built a wall of separation between church and state that began in 1802. In his drafts of the Declaration of Independence, Jefferson "included no references at all to the divinity,"[17] however he did sue the term "Nature's God.". Several writers of the final draft, however, added the words "Creator," "Supreme Judge of the World," and "Divine Providence."

The only acknowledgment of religion in the original draft of the Constitution was the date: "in the year of our Lord 1787." Even the First Amendment is framed without reference to any particular faith. To speak of God in the Constitution, the framers advised a language of common sense and understanding of every faith so that a system of government would pass the scrutiny of time as an invention of mere human wisdom. The founders were not anti-religious. Many were faithful in their personal life, and they evoked God in their public speeches. But they wanted faith to be only one thread in the country's tapestry, not the whole tapestry. If "truth comes from on high, from God, this is a very authoritarian approach to truth."[18] In a democracy, truth invites evidence.

In the Declaration of Independence, colonists assumed that their community was moving to separate from Britain. But the words enshrined in the Declaration did not match the founders' social deeds. In truth, people were not created equal. White women, the enslaved, and Indigenous people weren't granted equal rights. There was no political equality when many inhabitants did not have the right to vote or serve on juries or run for elected political office. White Americans dominated Americans of color, whether native or non-native, and the country's "patriarchal social structures" were strong.[19]

The Declaration of Independence leads to a discussion of how "religion and politics intertwine."[20] Do equality, liberty, and freedom depend on God?[21] The Declaration directs "a heap of people to come together in a shared fate"[22] for a "refined common life" of peace.[23] Freedom, liberty, and happiness are gifts of peace. Human beings use politics for freedom and happiness and survival. "Politics is the activity that flows from self-consciousness about power."[24] Right or wrong, colonists appealed to God to judge their intentions to separate from the power of Britain.

Many Americans think that we have settled the question of the separation of religion and politics, but we haven't. In her book *The Mighty and the Almighty: Reflections on America, God, and World Affairs,* former Secretary of State Madeleine Albright contends that "most of us do not want our leaders confusing their will with God's."[25] Citizens want leaders to make moral and ethical decisions. Many leaders accept that there should be "no religious tests for public office, no established state religion, and no abridgement of the right of religious liberty."[26] However, the deep roots of religion in America still influence leaders' decisions. Many leaders who attempt to separate "logic from beliefs" find it difficult to keep church and state apart.[27] They see God's purpose creep into the way they think, feel, and act. Self-righteous leaders tend to believe that God has a specific plan for the United States. In 1898, President William McKinley told a group of clergymen that "the expansion of American power [was] part of a divine plan."[28] Former President Reagan declared that "we were a people who believed we were chosen by God to create a greater world."[29]

Furthermore, states Albright, "We will never unite anyone around the proposition that to disagree with the president of the United States is to pick a quarrel with God."[30] In President George W. Bush's inaugural address, he assured us that God would continue to favor the United States as long as its policies were moral and just. He asserted that religion "influences his public discussions."[31] President Bush cited Christ as his favorite "political philosopher." Perhaps former President Bush wasn't following divine principles when he entered an unnecessary war in Iraq. Faith in God does not always "lead to wisdom."[32] Bush's albatross was the influence of religious faith on his leadership. Incalculably, the Bush Administration put its religious "heart" above "intellect" in government affairs.

Albright notes that "religious convictions, if they are convictions, can't be pulled on and off like boots. We walk with these convictions wherever we go."[33] "You can't pretend if you're a person of faith that religion doesn't affect your politics, but if you believe you know all there is to know, then you'll think of others as less holy, less worthy, less deserving of respect."[34] This is a problem when you are dealing with world affairs. Respect for the rights and well-being of each individual is the place where religious faith connects to politics.[35] Albright doesn't think we can keep religion out of foreign policy. Religion motivates people and shapes their views of justice and right behavior. We cannot expect leaders to make decisions in isolation from their religion. Spiritual enlightenment, intellectual reasoning, and emotional conviction cannot be separated from the human condition.

As a practitioner of foreign policy, Albright claims that "to separate religion from world politics [is to] liberate logic from beliefs that transcend logic.... I would not seek to mediate disputes on the basis of religious principles more than I would try to negotiate alone the more intricate details of trade agreements or a pact on arms control.... I would ask people more expert...to begin the process...."[36]

Since 2000, the role of religion has widened political divisions in the United States. For example, we give taxpayer money to faith-based institutions to provide social services. And we don't require religious institutions that promote specific political agendas to pay taxes. "Dogmatic belief is deemed a virtue and open-mindedness a weakness, and sarcasm and slanderous attacks frequently drown out intelligent discussion."[37] "A nation (or group) that believes its success or failure is a direct consequence of the wishes of God is likely either to invite or create trouble."[38] By deferring to God, we relinquish our ability to make a difference, and we ignore our obligation to act on the basis of our own conscience. We hand over our responsibility to fate instead of listening to our honest, inner, moral voice. The test of whether an action is moral is whether it achieves a moral result.[39] For example, nationally, a moral result is when it expands the nation's influence, even wins allies, secures support in a crisis, or protects the life and liberty of the nation's citizens.

Unitarian Universalists believe that each person of whatever faith has inherent worth and dignity. We strive to understand the mystery and wonder of God. We are guided by a spirit of justice, equality, and compassion in human relations. Wisdom from the world's religions inspires us in our spiritual life. The right of conscience and the democratic process affirm our belief in a loving God. We are guided by reason and science; we seek peace, compassion, and spiritual growth. We celebrate the circle of life, and in our theology we stress not only what is, but what should be.

Notes to The Politics of God

1. Pamela J. Annas and Robert C. Rosen, eds., *Literature and Society: An Introduction to Fiction, Poetry, Drama, Nonfiction,* 3rd ed. (Upper Saddle River, NJ: Prentice Hall, 2000), 1303.
2. Annas and Rosen, *Literature and Society,* 1313.
3. Annas and Rosen, *Literature and Society,* 1307.
4. Tom Sorrell, "Thomas Hobbes, English Philosopher," *Encyclopaedia Britannica Online,* accessed March 20, 2021. www.britannica.com/biography/Thomas-Hobbes.
5. Quoted in Garry Wills, *Head and Heart: American Christianities* (New York: Penguin Press, 2007), 178.
6. Wills, *Head and Heart,* 178.
7. Wills, *Head and Heart,* 178.
8. Quoted in Wills, *Head and Heart,* 182.
9. Jon Meacham, *Thomas Jefferson: The Art of Power* (New York: Random House, 2012), 113.
10. Madeline Albright, *The Mighty and the Almighty: Reflections on America, God, and World Affairs* (New York: Penguin Group, 2004), 16.
11. Albright, *The Mighty,* 67.
12. Quoted in Forrest Church, "Divine Order vs. Sacred Liberty: America's Founding Faiths," *UU World,* Winter 2007, 18.
13. Church, "Divine Order vs. Sacred Liberty," 19.
14. Albright, *The Mighty,* 19.
15. Albright, 19.
16. Albright, 19.
17. Danielle Allen, *Our Declaration: A Reading of the Declaration of Independence in Defense of Equality* (New York: Liveright Publishing, 2014), 74.
18. Allen, *Our Declaration,* 137.
19. Allen, 227.
20. Allen, 135.
21. Allen, 135.
22. Allen, 121.

23. Allen, 100.
24. Allen, 163-164.
25. Albright, *The Mighty*, 104.
26. Albright, 27.
27. Albright, 73.
28. Albright, 23
29. Quoted in Albright, *The Mighty*, 28.
30. Albright, *The Mighty*, 161.
31. Albright, 98.
32. Albright, 161.
33. Albright, xi.
34. Albright, 278.
35. Albright, 289.
36. Albright, 74-75.
37. Albright, 89-90.
38. Albright, 149.
39. Albright, 53.

The Three Essentials
by Anne Lamott

According to Jack Mendelsohn in *Why I Am a Unitarian,* "prayer is both a problem and a challenge" for Unitarians.[1] Prayer can be many things: meditation, communication, petition, supplication, intercession, confession, or praise. According to the author Anne Lamott, in reaching for a spiritual horizon or "high," there are three essential prayers we might turn to: asking for *help,* giving *thanks* for the good we witness, and saying *wow* to something amazing.

A bumper sticker plastered on a car in Corinth, Mississippi stated, "Prayer is a Truck Headed for God's Warehouse."[2] Robert Louis Stevenson championed joy and inspiration when he composed this public prayer: "The day returns and brings us the petty round of irritating concerns and duties. Help us to play the man, help us to perform them with laughter and kind faces; let cheerfulness abound with industry. Let us go blithely on our business all this day; bring us to our resting beds weary and content and undishonored; and grant us in the end the gift of sleep."[3] We might utter this prayer each day without feeling craven. Thomas Jefferson believed that prayer was "a subject each was bound to study assiduously for himself, unbiased by the opinions of others—it was a matter solely of conscience."[4] In retirement, Jefferson prayed daily for health and well-being, but he would not want to bring God down to earth to interfere in the affairs of man.[5]

People experience many feelings, including pain, anger, gratitude, and awe. According to Anne Lamott, a novelist and non-fiction writer, a person in a fabulously good mood might say, "Hey! Me again. Thank you for my sobriety, my flowering pear tree, and my grandson."[6] An ailing person might shout, "I hate you God for the real and true pain going on in me for months. Hello? Am I too far gone or can you help me get out of my self-obsession?"[7] Most likely, the best possible idea when a person is bitter or broken is to utter in all honesty, "I'm exhausted emotionally, and I need help."[8] A miserable self might have the courage to show up in prayer and make a contract with some unseen force. But intellect might direct a person to ask for help and give thanks when it comes.

But why do Unitarians find prayer a problem and a challenge when it is simply a matter of asking for help, giving thanks, and saying wow? First, among Unitarian Universalists and other people, there are many different spiritual ideas. Jules Renard, a writer in the eighteenth century, said, "I don't know if God exists, but it would be better for His reputation if He didn't." The philosopher Friedrich Nietzsche asked, "Is man one of God's blunders or is God one of man's?" Contemporary religious thinker Karen Armstrong wonders, "Do I believe God is going to take away my illness when he turned an entire deaf ear to the six million Jews who went into the gas chambers?"[9] And Bertrand Russell stated, "And if there were a God, I think it very unlikely that He would have such an uneasy vanity as to be offended by those who doubt His existence."[10] Therefore, if there is not conformity of ideas for members to even acknowledge God, prayer doesn't satisfy expectations, and thus, for some people praying would be tantamount to communicating with an entity they may not believe in.

When Lamott visited a staunch agnostic friend whose daughter was diagnosed with aggressive lung cancer, Lamott didn't expect a miracle to make things better, but she hoped that doctors could break the grips of cancer and help the daughter live. When I had brain surgery to remove a tumor, I believe it was the skill of the surgeon that saved my life, not God. However, the question I asked myself was: "Where do I find the strength to go through this ordeal?"

A second reason Unitarians might find prayer troublesome is our strong reliance on intellect and reason as the trusted tools to secure human independence, rather than some "higher power" that mesmerizes us. We like to believe we can and must take care of ourselves and be responsible for our lives, even with our human frailty and vulnerability to tragedy. We take pride in our power to solve problems. But self-esteem may blind us to acknowledging our constant dependence on forces beyond ourselves.[11]

Third, Unitarian Universalists desire to conduct ourselves in the most exemplary ways that we can. We affirm and promote the inherent worth and dignity of every person; accept justice, equity, and compassion for each human being; respond to truth; accept the right of conscience; use the democratic process; seek world peace; and respect the interdependent web of all existence. When we personally live up to any of these principles, we heartily thank whatever force brought us to this point of truth.

Finally, the Unitarian Universalist religion is not separate from human activity.[12] Humans need to foster love in physical and spiritual ways. "We cultivate the strength that comes with sharing, with caring, with reaching out, with bestowing [compassion] where we can."[13] Thereupon, when Unitarian Universalists face questions we cannot deal with, we covenant with each other, with family, or with friends. We seek out these sources for consolation. But, if I may testify from personal experience, private prayer for believers is a communication with a mysterious force, undefined, but spiritual in nature.

Anne Lamott contends that "when we cry out for Help, or whisper it inside our chest, we enter the paradox of not going limp and not feeling… hopeless…. We release ourselves from trying to be [on] our own."[14] "Help" can mean we ask "something" to give us courage to stop in our tracks and turn our eyes to the hills or mountains for a breath of fresh air. We can take a moment to express thanks that we dodged a bullet, our child didn't drown, the brakes held when our car had to stop, or the increased level of white blood cells in our body is about allergies, not leukemia. Thanks is also due, says Lamott, when "I found my son; he's in jail, but he's alive."[15] We might express Wow and Thanks for continued health and a good day of work.

Lamott notes that, as human beings, we want leaders to act for the common good. We want help to give aid and comfort to people after catastrophes. We want to repair broken families. We want to show tremendous compassion, mercy, and generosity for other people in the world, including friends, doctors, nurses, and hospice providers. And we want to fix the unfixable.[16]

When things go well, it's easy to thank someone or something. Sometimes, however, humans face exhaustion and defeat. Often we do not get our way, but we gather stamina and try again. We are haunted sometimes by our failures, but the world keeps on spinning and people keep on loving us.[17] "We come to know—or reconnect with—something rich and okay about ourselves, [so] we cast our eyes on the beautiful skies above all the crap we are wallowing in and whisper, 'Thank you.'"[18]

Lamott records an experience she had that was a bridge to understanding. She met two amazing friends, Barbara and Susie, for a "stroll and a roll" because Barbara had Lou Gehrig's disease (ALS) and needed a wheelchair. The disease got full-blown, which meant using a walker, feeding tubes, and a computerized speaking device. So, Susie drove the car to the Pacific Ocean near San Francisco. Barbara was pretty sick, so Lamott moved to the back seat of the car. When the three arrived at the ocean, the view was ruined by fog and the wind was prickly. Hopeless! They stayed in the car and drove through the neighborhood instead. Suddenly, a warm golden sun flooded the car windows and the deep blue of the sky and sea stared at them. They talked for an hour about life, death, families, feeding tubes, and faith. Lamott asked Barbara, "What are you most grateful for these days?" Barbara typed on her iPad, "The beauty of nature, the birds and flowers, the beauty of friends."[19] Lamott thought, "This is called radical gratitude in the face of whatever life throws at you."[20]

Besides help and gratitude, humans also need to express awe. Wonderful! Amazing! Spectacular! It is thinking "with a gasp and a sharp breathless intake of air at the sight of shocking beauty or destruction" or having one's mind blown by an insightful, intuitive, or tragic thought. "Wow! is a child seeing the ocean for the first time."[21] "Wow! is a teenager seeing the second-hand car in the garage he or she received for Christmas."[22] Wow! is appropriate when considering the accomplishments of John Muir, John Grissom, Albert Einstein, and Ruth Bader Ginsberg. Wow! is the magnitude of the solar system with its hundreds of suns and universes. Some movies are Wow: *To Kill a Mockingbird, Spotlight,* and *High Noon.* Or as Robert Macfarlane, author of the book *Landmarks,* states, "Sometimes on the top of a mountain I just say, 'Wow.'"[23] Wow! releases the wonder—even horror—that takes our breath away. In art or in museums we find "framed greatness, genius embracing passion, obsession, discipline, and possibly madness."[24] We stand speechless before the Sphinx, or when viewing works of Monet and Georgia O'Keeffe or listening to the musicians Mozart, Beethoven, and Copland. To watch Fred Astaire dance is to see the "sacred in communal energy."[25]

In 1999 the Unitarian Universalist Association published a pamphlet in which a handful of members expressed their views on prayer. Lynn Ungar wrote, "'Thank you' is the moment of beauty.... It is enough to be grateful and be a witness to wonder."[26] James Ishmael Ford found that in prayer we make compassionate connections "to a moral perspective, a call to justice, and peace."[27] Finally, Dan Harper admitted, "I don't pray. As a Unitarian Universalist child, I learned how to pray. But when I got old enough to take charge of my own spiritual life, I gradually stopped. Every once in a while I try prayer again, just to be sure. The last time was a couple of years ago. My mother spent a long, frightening month in the hospital, so I tried praying once again but it didn't help. I have found my spiritual disciplines—walks in nature, deep conversations, reading ancient and modern scripture, and love—or they have found me. Prayer doesn't happen to be one of them."[28] Inevitably, prayer is an individual matter.

Notes to The Three Essentials by Anne Lamott

1. Jack Mendelsohn, *Why I Am a Unitarian* (New York: Thomas Nelson & Sons, 1960), 193.
2. Tony Horwitz, *Confederates in the Attic: Dispatches from the Unfinished Civil War* (New York: Pantheon Books, 1998), 158.
3. Quoted in Mendelsohn, *Why I Am a Unitarian*, 194.
4. Annette Gordon-Reed and Peter S. Onuf, *"Most Blessed of the Patriarchs": Thomas Jefferson and the Empire of the Imagination* (New York: Liveright Publishing Corporation, 2016), 276.
5. Gordon-Reed and Onuf, *"Most Blessed,"* 281.
6. Anne Lamott, *Help, Thanks, Wow: The Three Essential Prayers* (New York: Riverhead Books, 2012), 4.
7. Lamott, *Help, Thanks, Wow*, 5.
8. Lamott, *Help, Thanks, Wow*, 6.
9. Karen Armstrong, "The God of Imaginative Compassion" in *The Changing Face of God*, ed. Frederick W. Schmidt (Harrisburg, PA: Morehouse Publishing, 2000), 24.
10. Bertrand Russell, "What Is an Agnostic?" in *The Basic Writings of Bertrand Russell*, ed. Robert E. Egner and Lester E. Denonn (New York: Routledge Classics, 2009), 561.

11. Mendelsohn, *Why I Am a Unitarian*, 101.
12. Mendelsohn, 111.
13. Mendelsohn, 174.
14. Lamott, *Help, Thanks, Wow*, 40.
15. Lamott, 46.
16. Lamott, 13-14.
17. Lamott, 51.
18. Lamott, 51.
19. Lamott, 56.
20. Lamott, 56.
21. Lamott, 72.
22. Lamott, 72.
23. Robert Macfarlane, *Landmarks* (New York: Penguin Books, 2016), 10.
24. Lamott, *Help, Thanks, Wow*, 82.
25. Lamott, 83.
26. Catherine Bowers, ed., *UU Views of Prayer* (Boston: Unitarian Universalist Association, 1999).
27. Bowers, *UU Views of Prayer.*
28. Bowers, *UU Views of Prayer.*

PART 8

The Natural World

The Ducks

Friday, May 25, 2018 started out as an ordinary day. A neighbor, Pat, invited me to join a former neighbor, Ellie, from Lincoln Avenue where I live, for lunch at Willow Brook, a retirement community in Delaware, Ohio. In the middle of Willow Brook's dining area there was a courtyard where a mother duck and her ducklings were housed. The courtyard contained a small tree, many shrubs, a small pond where the ducklings could flutter in the water, a green grass cover, and a brush nest where the mother duck could settle. A maintenance crew had appropriately provided for the comfort of the family of ducks. A high, floor-to-ceiling glass window let residents of this village watch the ducks during mealtime. Everyone stopped at the window to observe the progress of little ducklings beginning life. I was captivated by this attraction during my lunch.

But I learned later that a tragedy had occurred after my visit. According to a bulletin published by Willow Brook, a raccoon scaled the barrier wall, alighted in the top of a tree, and climbed down into the courtyard. To satisfy his appetite, he killed every one of the fourteen ducklings. Blood and feathers spattered the glass windows. Luckily, the mother duck had escaped, but when she returned the next day after the cleanup to look for her babies, they were gone. Sadness reigned. Fortunately, the retirement center placed a new mother hen and her ducklings in the courtyard.

In the face of this tragic story, my soul was revived by an amazing report in *The New York Times* on July 24, 2018 about a merganser—a fish-eating, diving duck with a narrow bill that is hooked at the tip and serrated at the edges.[1] A wildlife photographer had spotted a female merganser coasting across Lake Bemidji in Minnesota, followed by seventy-six ducklings in a row. Although it is not unusual to see twenty to thirty ducklings gathered together with a single female duck, it is rare to see a female duck with more than six dozen ducklings in tow.

According to the National Audubon Society, a female merganser can only lay up to a dozen or so eggs, but she often "dumps" some of her eggs in the nests of other ducks in an effort to spread out her offspring and increase the chances of their survival. Of course, it would be impossible for one duck to incubate fifty eggs in a single nest. Some birds, including mergansers and ostriches, raise their babies in a day care system that is called a crèche. "In a crèche, females leave their ducklings in the care of one female—often an older female who is experienced at raising babies," noted Dave Rave, a wildlife manager in the Minnesota Department of Natural Resources.[2] He went on to say, "The females at Lake Bemidji, many of which are related, lay eggs that hatch around the same time.... Afterwards, the adult ducks go off to molt their feathers, leaving their broods in the care of a matriarchal female." While this practice is common, crèches normally only have about thirty-five to fifty ducklings. The photographer has gone back to Lake Bemidji several times to observe the seventy-six ducklings instinctively following the adult female he has named "Mama." This is an amazing phenomenon of nature.

Notes to The Ducks

1. Sarah Mervosh, "1 Hen, 76 Ducklings: What's the Deal with This Picture?" *New York Times*, July 28, 2018. http://www.nytimes.com/2018/07/24/science/merganser-duckilings-photo.html.
2. Mervosh, "1 Hen."

Looking out the Window

Stationed at the computer one day in early March, I was preoccupied with writing a letter. I was composing when I lifted my gaze and saw two little miracles outside the window on the east side of my home. Twenty feet away from me a chipmunk was running down the waterspout on my neighbor's garage. Now, you might wonder why that is unusual. Evidently, chipmunks hibernate during the winter months, and this was the first time I had seen a chipmunk appear out of hibernation. It was a warm welcome sign of spring.

Further, I observed another little miracle in the rosebud tree situated beside our neighbor's garage. Two years earlier, we had moved a globe-sized gourd from a limb in the spruce tree to a higher elevation in the rosebud tree, anticipating that some lucky bird would come and find this gourd a paradise home. For two years no bird had ever made a nest in this beautiful hanging gourd. But on this day I fixated my eyes on a sparrow crawling into an opening in the gourd. Another sparrow flew to the opening with a dried twig in his mouth. They were building a nest! When both sparrows were inside the gourd, it wavered slightly from their busy movement. What other sign of spring do we need except birds nesting, getting ready to support their young? This second miracle of spring that I divined outside the window warmed my soul.

The Squirrel Haven

My grandson Zachary and his wife Sarah had placed a small package in the pile of unwrapped Christmas gifts. The package had no bow or decorative tie; it was just wrapped in cheerful Christmas paper. When I opened it on Christmas Day, a little magic stream of delight hovered in the air. I was touched that Zachary and Sarah—both busy with their medical careers in New Haven, Connecticut—had cared enough to come to Ohio to give this gift to Tom and me. We are both bird lovers.

Significantly, the gift was a small-sized, saucer-shaped, clear-glass birdfeed holder with an opening accessible for birds and squirrels. It had a magnetic base, acceptable for mounting on a window. Zachary tried to figure out the best location on our picture window to place the holder so that it would not interfere with our view of birds and squirrels in the backyard. This didn't get resolved.

The glass holder lingered in limbo for a week after Zachary left. Finally, we examined the birdseed holder more closely and found that it would be difficult to fill the holder with birdseed if it were attached to the window. So where could we securely put this gift? Standing outside on the patio, the answer was apparent; because the holder was magnetized, we could place it on the metal cap in the center of the patio table. After placing the glass holder on the tabletop, we filled it with birdseed. Then the drama began. Squirrels located the birdfeeder first. Approaching this treasure of food, they cautiously walked around it a couple of times, nosed up to the opening, gave it a sniff, and then dove in greedily. The squirrels would sit on their haunches, ferociously nibbling each seed in their paws. It was such an endearing scene to behold. How cute squirrels are, gorging themselves gleefully! Each day we filled the holder with birdseed, and each day the seeds were devoured. Only a few birds came; primarily, it was squirrels that were tempted.

Sadly, one morning we looked out the window and saw no glass birdseed holder on the patio table. Instead, crashed glass pieces were scattered all around on the patio bricks. Some eager, strong, zealous squirrel had pushed the glass holder off its base and slid it over the edge. Nature's playful squirrels had outwitted us. Our fun and delight watching these creatures perform their antics came to an abrupt end. However, the gift still lingers on in our memory.

When Elephants Weep

I once remarked to a friend that I supported wildlife with my dollars to relieve suffering, pain, sorrow, and sadness. She turned to me and asked, "But what about all the human beings who are suffering?"

Animals are endangered almost everywhere on the planet. As the scientist John Lilly states, "We are the ones who are endangering them, it, and ourselves. They are innocent sufferers in a hell of our making."[1] With guns, nets, snares, and poison arrows, hunters and poachers capture and kill wild animals. Consider elephants: "These highly intelligent animals (elephants) who mirror us humans in terms of emotion, who have the sense of family and of death,...should not die for their teeth... [and their tusks that] could be turned into trinkets."[2] These kind and kindred creatures "demand less of the world. They take less from the world. They live in better [harmony] with the rest of the world."[3] Fortunately, committed people in Africa and India are rescuing these animals on our behalf.

Charles Darwin observed that elephants weep tears as a sign of grief. Tears also accompany pain, fear, stress, and loneliness in animals. For example, tears flow "incessantly" from Indian elephants that are tied up and bound motionless on the ground.[4] Also, tears roll down as adult seals watch seal pups clubbed to death by hunters.[5] Humans cannot know the world of sorrow that make the tears of animals appear.

Interestingly, as Jeffrey Masson and Susan McCarthy note in their 1995 book *When Elephants Weep*, scientists hesitate to draw conclusions about the complex and multifaceted emotions of animals. Humans tend to see their own emotions in animals, promoting anthropomorphism. However, in his book *Beyond Words: What Animals Think and Feel*, Carl Safina states, "When someone says you can't attribute human sensations to animals, they forget that human sensations *are* animal sensations."[6] Neurologist Jaak Panksepp confirms that "brain scans show core emotions of sadness, happiness, rage, or fear...appear in direct electrically stimulated parts of the brain of both a cat and a human."[7] Humans and animals produce hormones such as oxytocin, epinephrine, serotonin, and testosterone that influence emotions.[8] The question remains whether emotions in both humans and animals are reflexes, instincts, or conditioned behavior.

David Sheldrick, a warden for thirty years at Kenya's Tsavo National Park in Africa, believes that "every living organism, however humble, [is] an integral and vital cog in the complex wheel of life, each with its own function, important to the wellbeing of the whole."[9] "In order to interpret elephant behavior, you must simply analyze it from a human point of view and that way you will end up close to the truth, something the scientists have yet to learn. They seem to have an arrogant mental block attributing to animals human aspects of behavior, particularly in terms of emotions."[10]

Cynthia Moss, a crusader for elephants, was a writer for *Newsweek* magazine in New York in the 1960s. She went on a safari in Kenya and fell in love with elephants. She stayed in Kenya for the rest of her life. She has observed how much joy elephants experience in their family units, among friends, and with plenty of food and water. Iain Douglas Hamilton notes that "even in times of distress and danger," elephants "behave with exceptional tolerance to their own kind.[11] Elephants face few predators except humans, lions, and hyenas. The oldest female elephant in 2015 was 64 years old. Female elephants are the matriarchs in a family. Aunts, cousins, and grandmothers are babysitters. Babies stay with family members for the first five years. Mothers are essential for baby elephants to survive in the wild. Mothers communicate with their babies by touching them with their tails. When a young elephant dies, a mother acts depressed for many days. In one documented case, a female elephant gave birth to a stillborn and carried the body in her trunk for four days, guarding it from lions.[12] According to Daphne Sheldrick, a long-time animal conservationist, "an elephant can die of grief."[13] "[Elephants] grieve and mourn the loss of loved ones as deeply as [humans] do, and their capacity for love is humbling."[14] They even fondle bones of a dearly departed.[15]

Other incidents demonstrate elephant emotions. "A mother elephant wanted to stay with her baby who fell in a well. No one was helping her. Instead of fighting for attention, she sat on top of the park vehicle and made calls of trumpeting. The two victims were reunited."[16] "Elephants show empathy" when a spear is lodged in another elephant.[17] A friend will remove it and put food in the mouth of the wounded elephant.[18] A female elephant once wondered off her path and at night lay under a tree. A group of elephants covered her up with leaves and branches when they sensed her helplessness.[19] Compassion is also an elephant trait. "Male elephants have been seen carrying young branches [of foliage] to a bull elephant lying injured on the ground, too sick to forage for food."[20]

According to ecologist Carl Safina, elephants communicate by making sounds, trumpeting, flapping their ears, clicking tusks, and stamping the ground with their feet.[21] Other communication comes from snorts, barks, roars, grunts, cries, and squeaks.[22] The intensity of the sounds has value, for the elephants know among themselves what information they need to convey. Some sounds they make cannot be heard by the human ear. They can warn other elephants of danger as much as ninety miles away. They have complex social behavior.

Elephants can feel fear and terror. In a baby elephant orphanage, "a baby elephant who has seen [his family] killed by poachers and witnessed the tusks being cut off the bodies, can wake up screaming at night."[23] Wild animals held in captivity and confined in solitude are sad.[24] Even if well-fed and treated well, they will try to escape time after time.[25] When animals are under stress, they are vulnerable to illness.[26] But animals also express joy. For example, two related elephants had emotional "highs" when meeting each other after a long separation. They communicated as far away as a quarter of a mile, but ran toward each other trumpeting, then rubbed each other and clasped trunks.[27]

In her book *Love, Life, and Elephants,* Daphne Sheldrick lovingly explains elephants. When her ancestors came to British Colony in Kenya in the 1800s, profuse wildlife roamed in the Tsavo National Park area near their settlement. But in World War II, thousands of animals were massacred to provide food for British and Kenyan troops. Also, when the natural balance between animal users and vegetation is considered, some animals need to be culled. An onslaught of poachers and tribesmen wanting land began in the 1950s. By 1955, the largest tusked elephants in the world, magnificent creatures with 100-pound tusks of ivory, were a target for poachers. At least 1,280 elephant carcasses and hundreds of dead rhinos were discovered at this time. The market for elephant ivory for piano keys, billiard balls, carvings, chessmen, and chopsticks was a lucrative business.[28]

Daphne and her husband David devoted their lives to conserving wildlife. They established a reserve that housed animals, especially baby elephants and rhinos. During the colonial era, a field force of David's army unit arrested many poachers. The Game Department of Kenya prosecuted offenders. But when throngs of fifty to three hundred poachers descended on the park with poison arrows and killed many elephants, British and Kenyan officials worked harder to protect the elephants.[29] In fact, Sheldrick had a deep empathy for elephants. "We [humans] should not be so arrogant as to believe that we have all the answers."[30] Animals are not put here only for the benefit of humankind.

Daphne and David Sheldrick witnessed time after time that animals must have emotions like humans. Both elephants and humans have similar brain structure, hormones, and mammary glands. Animals and humans are also psychologically similar. For example, female elephants remain bonded for life to their families. They guide family members to the sources of food and water, walking miles. Bull elephants are also supportive; for example, they share water holes with the tiniest calves. They appear polite with "a rigid code of ethics reinforced in their society down the ages."[31] Elephants always find a custodial home for adopted or dependent young ones who need care.

On the Sheldrick reserve, Huppety, a baby zebra, followed Daphne all around the house. Then, Eleanor, an orphan elephant, was sent to their home. Her mother had been shot on a safari expedition. Eleanor had been sent to a Nairobi Agricultural Show in 1961. She was imprisoned in Nairobi National Park Orphanage as a zoo attraction. Deprived of exercise, proper food, and individual attention, she became obese and lethargic. The Sheldricks rescued her at Tsavo in 1965. Even though Eleanor hesitated to walk down the ramp out of the van, she extended her trunk as a greeting to each adult standing there. Another elephant, Samson, greeted her with the touch of his trunk. Later, she recovered from fear and became a peace-loving, gentle mother to all the other baby elephants on the farm.

Soon the Sheldricks built more stables and enclosures next to their house. They made a large garden area available to the animals. A hoard of orphaned baby animals arrived, including rhinos (Raru and Bukanesi); Wiffle the antelope, who slept on a blanket in the bedroom; Honk the buffalo; and a peacock, too. All the animals took a walk together each day.

In the words of Daphne Sheldrick, Eleanor and a female elephant named Sobo "enabled me to understand the depths of bonds that bind family members together [in the elephant herd and in human families], and these giants were not so different from us.[32] For example, a baby elephant, Gulliver, was never left unattended by Eleanor or Sobo. Three weeks passed and Gulliver died. Eleanor lay down beside his dead body. Sobo grieved. Both touched him lovingly with their trunks as he was lowered into a grave near the garden.[33] They visited the grave every day until Sobo, at four, was reunited with his original family. Daphne found that this joyous family reunion was such a satisfying moment for the elephants that it brought tears to her human eyes.[34]

The Kenyan elephant population declined rapidly in the 1970s. In 1973, the ivory market exported 2.2 million elephant products. In 1972, the elephant population was 500,00; by 1973 the population was 300,000. Mature elephants were readily being slaughtered. Most parts of their body were turned into products: the meat was dried; the feet were turned into wastepaper; the ears were turned into handbags, briefcases, and wallets; the hide was made into luxury leather; the bones were crushed into bone meal; and the ivory was carved into many objects.[35] Daphne Sheldrick describes a magnificent, 5-ton, fifty-five-year-old Bull elephant killed by poison arrow. Ahmed, another elephant with tusks that were 9 feet, 6 inches long, fell to poachers. "The beautiful tusks were worth a small fortune to any trophy hunter, but they were the very mark of his majesty and rank."[36] Avaricious people were violating the precious wilderness and inflicting chaos on elephant families.

Animals kept flooding into the Sheldrick farm, including baby elephants, piglets whose mother had been eaten by a lion, and ostrich chicks. One baby elephant, Deka, was filled with thorns from the underbrush where he had hidden when his mother was killed. For weeks he stood dejectedly beside his tent, tears oozing from his eyes and his trunk hanging limply on the ground.[37] Slowly he took milk, standing alone almost comatose. He improved after befriending another baby elephant, Edo. Daphne saved another baby elephant named Shmetty by feeding her human baby formula. But Daphne went away for a month to her daughter's wedding in England, and when she returned, she found Shmetty dying of illness and loneliness because Daphne had deserted her. Her death was evidence to Daphne that baby elephants require motherly care, just like humans. Of Shmetty, Daphne concluded, "I was contributing something to the wilderness I loved so much."[38]

David Sheldrick spent thirty years working in Tsavo National Park; Daphne spent a lifetime in Kenya. When the Kenyan government took control of all the National Parks from the British, poaching increased in the parks and the orphan farm faced an uncertain future. When David died in 1977 at the age of fifty-seven, Daphne established the David Sheldrick Wildlife Trust Fund which acquired further land. By then, the corrupt Kenyan government was doing little to stop entire herds from being gunned down with automatic weapons. Many more orphans came—elephants, rhinos, and antelopes. Wyeth Laboratories, which developed an infant formula for elephants, funded construction of new elephant stables, and fifty new elephant keepers were hired. In 1989, Daphne was awarded the title "Dame Commander of the Most Excellent Order of the British Empire." She died in Nairobi, Kenya on April 12, 2018.

When parties to the multilateral Convention on International Trade in Endangered Species of Wild Fauna and Flora met in 1989, poachers in Kenya had killed 100,000 elephants in the previous ten years. The population of elephants in 1973 in Kenya was 167,000 but fell to 16,000 in 1989. In Tsavo National Park, the population had fallen from 145,000 to only 6,000. According to Carl Safina, in 2015 an estimated 30,000 to 40,000 elephants were being killed every year around the world.[39] Only 8,000 black rhinos are left in the world. Poaching is fueled by poverty, ethnic rivalry, terrorism, and civil war. But by destroying elephants, it also deprives thousands of Kenyans of potential jobs in the tourism sector.[40] Alfred Russell Wallace in 1869 said that animals must surely show us that all living things are sacred.[41] Biologist Richard Ruggiero concludes that the elephant "is somehow aware that something terrible is happening to it, a very sentient creature who really knows that there's a genocide going on.[42]

Notes to When Elephants Weep

1. Quoted in Jeffrey Moussaieff Masson and Susan McCarthy, *When Elephants Weep: The Emotional Lives of Animals* (New York: Delacorte Press, 1995), 236.
2. Daphne Sheldrick, *Love, Life, and Elephants: An African Love Story* (New York: Farrar, Straus, and Giroux, 2012), 280-281.
3. Carl Safina, *Beyond Words: What Animals Think and Feel* (New York: Henry Holt, 2015), 107.
4. Masson and McCarthy, *When Elephants Weep*, 106.
5. Masson and McCarthy, 108.
6. Safina, *Beyond Words*, 29.
7. Safina, 31.
8. Masson and McCarthy, *When Elephants Weep*, 18.
9. Sheldrick, *Love, Life, and Elephants*, 86.
10. Sheldrick, 88.
11. Quoted in Sheldrick, *Love, Life, and Elephants*, 38.
12. Sheldrick, *Love, Life, and Elephants*, 69.
13. Quoted in Safina, *Beyond Words*, 73.
14. Safina, *Beyond Words*, 73.
15. Safina, 74.
16. Safina, 58.
17. Safina, 61.
18. Safina, 61.
19. Safina, 61.
20. Masson and McCarthy, *When Elephants Weep*, 159.
21. Safina, *Beyond Words*, 78.
22. Safina, 82.
23. Masson and McCarthy, *When Elephants Weep*, 45.
24. Masson and McCarthy, 99.
25. Masson and McCarthy, 120.
26. Masson and McCarthy, 99.
27. Masson and McCarthy, 116.
28. Sheldrick, *Love, Life, and Elephants*, 75.
29. Safina, *Beyond Words*, 104.
30. Sheldrick, *Love, Life, and Elephants*, 138.
31. Sheldrick, 116.
32. Sheldrick, 198.
33. Sheldrick, 199.

34. Sheldrick, 200.
35. Sheldrick, 172.
36. Sheldrick, 226-227.
37. Sheldrick, 276.
38. Sheldrick, 235.
39. Safina, *Beyond Words,* 121.
40. Safina, 118.
41. Safina, ix.
42. Quoted in Safina, *Beyond Words,* 101.

BIBLIOGRAPHY

Albom, Mitch. *Tuesdays with Morrie*. New York: Broadway Books, 1997.

Albright, Madeline. *The Mighty and the Almighty: Reflections on America, God, and World Affairs*. New York: Penguin Group, 2004.

Allen, Danielle. *Our Declaration: A Reading of the Declaration of Independence in Defense of Equality*. New York: Liveright Publishing, 2014.

Annas, Pamela J. and Robert C. Rosen, eds. *Literature and Society: An Introduction to Fiction, Poetry, Drama, Nonfiction*. 3rd ed. Upper Saddle River, NJ: Prentice Hall, 2000.

Appleby, Joyce. *Thomas Jefferson*. New York: Times Books, 2003.

Armstrong, Karen. "The God of Imaginative Compassion." In *The Changing Face of God*. Edited by Frederick W. Schmidt, 15-32. Harrisburg, PA: Morehouse Publishing, 2000.

Arnade, Chris. *Dignity: Seeking Respect in Back Row America*. New York: Sentinel, 2019.

Ashley, Leonard R. N. *What's in a Name?: Everything You Wanted to Know*. Baltimore, MD: Genealogical Publishing Co., 1989.

Barber, Benjamin. "A Failure of Democracy, Not Capitalism." *New York Times*, July 29, 2002.

Basler, Roy P., ed. *The Collected Works of Abraham Lincoln*. Volumes I, II, III, IV. New Brunswick, NJ: Rutgers University Press, 1953.

Benson, Jackson J. *Looking for Steinbeck's Ghosts*. Las Vegas: University of Nevada Press, 2002.

Benson, Jackson J. *The True Adventures of John Steinbeck, Writer*. New York: Penguin, 1984.

Bentley, Rosalind. "Exhibit Juxtaposes Slavery, Jefferson's Ideas of Liberty." *The Columbus Dispatch* (Columbus, OH), March 10, 2013.

Berkow, Ira. "Louis Zamperini, Olympian and 'Unbroken' World War II Survivor, Dies at 97." *New York Times*, July 4, 2014.

Bernstein, R. B. *Thomas Jefferson: The Revolution of Ideas*. Oxford: Oxford University Press, 2003.

Bloom, Harold. *The Ringers in the Tower*. Chicago: University of Chicago Press, 1971.

Blow, Charles M. "Who Loves America?" *New York Times*, February 23, 2015.

Boles, John B. *Jefferson: Architect of American Liberty*. New York: Basic Books, 2017.

Bowers, Catherine, ed. *UU Views of Prayer*. Boston: Unitarian Universalist Association, 1999.

Branch, John. "Pursuing the Impossible, and Coming Out on Top." *New York Times*, January 15, 2015.

Brenowitz, Eliot. Letter to the editor. *New York Times*, October 23, 2013.

Bridges, William. *Transitions: Making Sense of Life's Changes*. Reading, MA: Addison-Wesley Publishing Co., 1980.

Brodie, Fawn. *Thomas Jefferson: An Intimate History*. New York: W. W. Norton, 1974.

Brooks, David. "Integration Now and Forever." *New York Times*, March 30, 2018.

Brooks, David. "The Benedict Option." *New York Times*, March 14, 2017.

Brooks, David. "The Self-Reliant Generation." *New York Times*, January 8, 2016.

Burnstein, Andrew. *Jefferson's Secrets: Death and Desire at Monticello*. New York: Basic Books, 2005.

Caliendo, Stephen M. *Inequality in America: Race, Poverty, and Fulfilling America's Promise*. Boulder, CO: Westview Press, 2015.

Caraher, Lee. *Millennials and Management: The Essential Guide to Making It Work at Work*. Brookline, MA: Bibliomotion, Inc., 2015.

Carlitz, Katherine. "It's O.K. Not to Believe." Letter to the editor. *New York Times*, December 8, 2006.

Children's Defense Fund. *The State of America's Children 2020*. Washington, DC: Children's Defense Fund, 2020. https://www.childrensdefense.org/wp-content/uploads/2020/02/The-State-Of-Americas-Children-2020.pdf.

Church, Forrest. "America's Founding Faiths." *UU World* XXI, no. 4 (Winter 2007): 26-32.

Church, Forrest. "Divine Order vs. Sacred Liberty: America's Founding Faiths." *UU World*, Winter 2007.

Church, Forrest. *The Cathedral of the World: The Universalist Theology*. Boston: Beacon Press, 2009.

Cohen, Patricia. "On Health and Welfare, Moral Arguments Can Outweigh Economics." *New York Times*, May 8, 2017.

Colombo, Gary, Robert Cullen, and Bonnie Lisle, eds. *Rereading America: Cultural Contexts for Critical Thinking and Writing*. 7th ed. Boston: Bedford/St. Martin's, 2007.

Crawford, Alan Pell. *Twilight at Monticello: The Final Years of Thomas Jefferson*. New York: Random House, 2008.

Cunningham, Noble E. *The Pursuit of Reason: The Life of Thomas Jefferson*. Baton Rouge, LA: Louisiana State University Press, 1987.

Dabney, Virginius. *The Jefferson Scandals: A Rebuttal*. New York: Dodd, Mead & Co., 1981.

Dáte, S. V. *Jeb: America's Next Bush*. New York: Tarcher, 2007.

Davis, M. Kathryn. "Edward F. Ricketts: Man of Science and Conscience." *Steinbeck Studies* 15, no. 2 (2004): 15-22.

Dawkins, Richard. *The God Delusion*. Boston: Houghton Mifflin, 2006.

Effron, Daniel A. "Why Trump Supporters Don't Mind His Lies." *New York Times*, April 29, 2018.

Ellis, Joseph J. *American Sphinx: The Character of Thomas Jefferson*. New York: Vintage, 1998.

Ferling, John. *Adams vs. Jefferson: The Tumultuous Election of 1800*. New York: Oxford University Press, 2004.

Ferreira, Stacey, and Jared Kleinert, eds. *2 Billion Under 20: How Millennials Are Breaking Down Age Barriers and Changing the World*. New York: St. Martin's Press, 2015.

Finkelman, Paul. "The Monster of Monticello." *New York Times*, December 1, 2012.

Finkelman, Paul. *Slavery and the Founders: Race and Liberty in the Age of Jefferson*. London: M.E. Sharpe, 1996.

Fisher, David Hackett. *Albion's Seed: Four British Folkways in American History*. New York: Oxford University Press, 1989.

Friedman, Thomas L. "Social Media: Destroyer or Creator." *New York Times*, February 3, 2016.

Friedman, Thomas L. "Who Can Win America's Politics of Humiliation?" *New York Times*, September 9, 2020.

Fromm, Jeff, and Marissa Vidler. *Millennials with Kids: Marketing to This Powerful and Surprisingly Different Generation of Parents*. New York: American Management Association (AMACOM), 2005.

Galbraith, John Kenneth. *The Affluent Society*. Boston: Houghton Mifflin Co., 1998.

Gaustad, Edwin. *Sworn on the Altar of God: The Religious Biography of Thomas Jefferson*. Grand Rapids, MI: William B. Eerdmans Publishing Co., 1996.

Gettleman, Jeffrey. "No Moon Suits, Just Trunks and the Healing Surf." *New York Times*, January 11, 2015.

Gladwell, Malcolm. *Outliers: The Story of Success*. New York: Little, Brown & Co., 2008.

Goldberg, Michelle. "The End of Impunity." *New York Times*, August 8, 2019.

Goldburg, Brad. Letter to the editor. *New York Times,* October 23, 2013.

Goodstein, Laurie. "Study Finds That the Number of Protestant Americans Is in Steep Decline." *New York Times,* October 10, 2012.

Gordon-Reed, Annette. *The Hemingses of Monticello: An American Family.* New York: W. W. Norton, 2008.

Gordon-Reed, Annette. *Thomas Jefferson and Sally Hemings: An American Controversy.* Charlottesville, VA: University Press of Virginia, 1997.

Gordon-Reed, Annette. "Young Elizabeth Hemings's World." *The Root,* June 23, 2008. https://www.theroot.com/young-elizabeth-hemingss-world-1790900190.

Gordon-Reed, Annette, and Peter S. Onuf. *"Most Blessed of the Patriarchs": Thomas Jefferson and the Empire of the Imagination.* New York: Liveright Publishing Corporation, 2016.

Green, Penelope. "Peggy Cooper Cafritz: Everything in a Big Way." *New York Times,* January 15, 2015.

Guasco, Suzanne Cooper. *Confronting Slavery: Edward Coles and the Rise of Antislavery Politics in Nineteenth-Century America.* DeKalb, IL: Northern Illinois University Press, 2013.

Halliday, E. M. *Understanding Thomas Jefferson.* New York: HarperCollins Publishers, 2001.

Hayden, Michael V. "The End of Intelligence." *New York Times,* April 29, 2018.

Hillenbrand, Laura. *Unbroken: A World War II Story of Survival, Resilience, and Redemption.* New York: Random House, 2010.

Hirshman, Linda. *Sisters in Law: How Sandra Day O'Connor and Ruth Bader Ginsburg Went to the Supreme Court and Changed the World.* New York: Harper Perennial, 2015.

Hitchens, Christopher. *God Is Not Great: How Religion Poisons Everything.* New York: Twelve, 2007.

Hitchens, Christopher. *Thomas Jefferson: Author of America.* New York: Harper Perennial, 2005.

Horwitz, Tony. *Confederates in the Attic: Dispatches from the Unfinished Civil War.* New York: Pantheon Books, 1998.

Hyland, William G., Jr. *In Defense of Thomas Jefferson: The Sally Hemings Sex Scandal.* New York: St. Martin's Press, 2009.

Jefferson, Thomas. *The Jefferson Bible.* New York: Penguin, 1940.

Jeffrey, Alex. "Find Your Gift, Give Your Gift!" In *2 Billion Under 20: How Millennials Are Breaking Down Age Barriers and Changing the World*, edited by Stacey Ferreira and Jared Kleinert, 136-189. New York: St. Martin's Press, 2015.

Johnson, Barbara. "My Monster/My Self." In *A World of Difference*, 144-154. Baltimore, MD: Johns Hopkins University Press, 1987.

Johnston, David Cay. *Divided: The Perils of Our Growing Inequality*. New York: The New Press, 2014.

Jordan, Winthrop D. *White over Black: American Attitudes Toward the Negro, 1550-1812*. Chapel Hill, NC: The University of North Carolina Press, 1968.

Joshi, Nirmal. "Doctor, Shut Up and Listen." *New York Times*, January 5, 2015.

Kakutani, Michiko. "How Reading Nourished Obama in Office." *New York Times*, January 16, 2017.

Kempf, Edward J. *Abraham Lincoln's Philosophy of Common Sense: An Analytical Biography of a Great Mind (Part 1)*. New York: The New York Academy of Sciences, 1965.

Kenigsberg, Ben. "On the Way to School." Movie review. *New York Times*, February 6, 2015.

Kimmelman, Michael. "Finding Comfort in the Safety of Names." *New York Times*, August 31, 2003.

Kolbert, Elizabeth. "Skin Deep." *The Race Issue*, special issue of *National Geographic*, April 2018: 28-45.

Kosmin, Barry A., and Ariela Keysar. *American Religious Survey Report (ARIS 2008): Summary Report*. Trinity College, Program on Public Values, March 2009. https://www.washingtonpost.com/wp-srv/metro/documents/aris030609.pdf.

Kowalski, Gary. *Revolutionary Spirits: The Enlightened Faith of American Founding Fathers*. New York: Blueridge, 2008.

Kristof, Nicholas. "Slavery Isn't a Thing of the Past." *New York Times*, November 7, 2013.

Krugman, Paul. "Economics and Elections." *New York Times*, April 6, 2015.

Krugman, Paul. "Knowledge Isn't Power." *New York Times*, February 23, 2015.

Krugman, Paul. "Our Invisible Rich." *New York Times*, September 29, 2014.

Krugman, Paul. "Privilege, Pathology, and Power." *New York Times*, January 1, 2016.

Krugman, Paul. "The Long-Run Cop-Out." *New York Times*, February 2, 2015.

Krugman, Paul. "The Social Contract." *New York Times*, September 23, 2011.

Krugman, Paul. "Weimar in the Aegean." *New York Times*, February 16, 2015.

Kubler-Ross, Elisabeth. *Death: The Final Stage of Growth*. Englewood Cliffs, NJ: Prentice-Hall, 1975.

Lamont, Erika, and Anne Bruce. *The Talent Selection and Onboarding*. New York: McGraw-Hill, 2014.

Lamott, Anne. *Bird by Bird: Some Instructions on Writing and Life*. New York: Anchor Books, 1994.

Lamott, Anne. *Help, Thanks, Wow: The Three Essential Prayers*. New York: Riverhead Books, 2012.

Landis, Michael. "A Proposal to Change the Words We Use When Talking about the Civil War." *Smithsonian Magazine*, September 9, 2015. https://www.smithsonianmag.com/history/proposal-change-vocabulary-we-use-when-talking-about-civil-war-180956547/.

Leichtle, Kurt E. and Bruce G. Carveth. *Crusade against Slavery: Edward Coles, Pioneer of Freedom*. Carbondale, IL: Southern Illinois University Press, 2011.

Macfarlane, Robert. *Landmarks*. New York: Penguin Books, 2016.

Mailer, Norman. *On God: An Uncommon Conversation*. New York: Random House, 2007.

Malone, Dumas. *Jefferson and the Rights of Man*. Boston: Little, Brown & Co., 1951.

Malone, Dumas. *Jefferson the Virginian*. Boston: Little, Brown & Co., 1948.

Mapp, Alf J., Jr. *The Faiths of Our Fathers: What America's Founders Really Believed*. New York: Fall River Press, 2003.

Martin, Douglas. "Pauline Maier, Historian Who Described Jefferson as 'Overrated,' Dies at 75." Obituary. *New York Times*, August 14, 2013.

Martin, Jonathan, and Michael D. Shear. "With 'Virginia Way,' State Thought It Didn't Need Rules." *New York Times*, January 23, 2014.

Masson, Jeffrey Moussaieff, and Susan McCarthy. *When Elephants Weep: The Emotional Lives of Animals*. New York: Delacorte Press, 1995.

Mazel, Ella, ed. *"And Don't Call Me a Racist!" A Treasury of Quotes on the Past, Present and Future of the Color Line in America*. Lexington, MA: Argonaut Press, 1998.

McKibben, Bill. "A Modest Proposal to Destroy Western Civilization as We Know It: The $100 Christmas." *Mother Jones*, November 1, 1997.

McKibben, Bill. "The Christian Paradox: How a Faithful Nation Gets Jesus Wrong." *Harper's Magazine*, August 2005.

McKibben, Bill. "The Planet Doesn't Have Time for This." *New York Times Sunday Review*, April 23, 2017.

McKibben, Bill. "The Social Contract." *New York Times*, September 23, 2011.

McLaughlin, Jack. *Jefferson and Monticello: The Biography of a Builder*. New York: Henry Holt, 1988.

Meacham, Jon. *The Soul of America: The Battle for Our Better Angels*. New York: Random House, 2018.

Meacham, Jon. *Thomas Jefferson: The Art of Power*. New York: Random House, 2012.

Mellor, Anne K. "Possessing Nature: The Female in *Frankenstein*." In *Frankenstein*, by Mary Shelley. Edited by J. Paul Hunter, 274-286. New York: W. W. Norton, 1996.

Mendelsohn, Jack. *Being Liberal in an Illiberal Age*. Boston: Beacon Press, 1964.

Mendelsohn, Jack. *Being Liberal in an Illiberal Age: Why I Am a Unitarian*. 2nd ed. Boston: Skinner House Books, 2006.

Mendelsohn, Jack. *Why I Am a Unitarian*. New York: Thomas Nelson & Sons, 1960.

Mervosh, Sarah. "1 Hen, 76 Ducklings: What's the Deal with This Picture?" *New York Times*, July 28, 2018. https://www.nytimes.com/2018/07/24/science/merganser-ducklings-photo.html.

Mesnik-Greene, Zoe. "What's a Smile Worth to You?" In *2 Billion Under 20: How Millennials Are Breaking Down Age Barriers and Changing the World*, edited by Stacey Ferreira and Jared Kleinert, 105-109. New York: St. Martin's Press, 2015.

Miller, Walter James. "Foreword: The Future of Frankenstein." In *Frankenstein*, by Mary Shelley, v-xviii. New York: Signet Classic, 2000.

Naipaul, V. S. *A Bend in the River*. New York: Alfred A. Knopf, 1979. National Philanthropic Trust. "Charitable Giving Statistics." Accessed April 3, 2021. https://www.nptrust.org/philanthropic-resources/charitable-giving-statistics/.

National Philanthropic Trust. "Charitable Giving Statistics." Accessed April 3, 2021. https://www.nptrust.org/philanthropic-resources/charitable-giving-statistics/.

Noah, Timothy. *The Great Divergence: America's Growing Inequality Crisis and What We Can Do about It*. New York: Bloomsbury Press, 2012.

Nocera, Joe. "The 3 Roles of Michael J. Fox." *New York Times*, October, 22, 2013.

O'Brien, Tim. *The Things They Carried*. New York: Penguin Books, 1990.

Olson, Elizabeth. "Write Grandma a What?" *New York Times*, March 16, 2006.

Ornstein, Allan. *Class Counts: Education, Inequality, and the Shrinking Middle Class*. Lanham, MD: Rowman & Littlefield, 2007.

Painter, Nell Irvin. *Sojourner Truth: A Life, A Symbol*. New York: W. W. Norton & Co., 1996.

Pérez-Peña, Richard. "Gift from a Loving Husband: Part of Himself." *New York Times*, August 2, 2003. https://www.nytimes.com/2003/08/02/nyregion/gift-from-a-loving-husband-part-of-himself.html.

Peterson, Merrill E., ed. *Thomas Jefferson: A Profile*. New York: Hill & Wang, 1967.

Pew Forum on Religion and Public Life. "Faith in Flux: Changes in Religious Affiliation in the U.S." Pew Forum on Religion and Public Life. April 2009. https://www.pewresearch.org/wp-content/uploads/sites/7/2009/04/fullreport.pdf.

Piketty, Thomas. *Capital in the Twenty-First Century*. Translated by Arthur Goldhammer. Cambridge, MA: The Belknap Press of Harvard University Press, 2014.

Quindlen, Anna. "Public & Private; One Vote." *New York Times*, July 1, 1992.

Rainer, Thom S., and Jess W. Rainer. *The Millennials: Connecting to America's Largest Generation*. Nashville, TN: B & H Publishing Group, 2011.

Randall, Willard Sterne. *Thomas Jefferson: A Life*. New York: Henry Holt, 1993.

Russell, Bertrand. "What Is an Agnostic?" In *The Basic Writings of Bertrand Russell*. Edited by Robert E. Egner and Lester E. Denonn. New York: Routledge Classics, 2009.

Safina, Carl. *Beyond Words: What Animals Think and Feel*. New York: Henry Holt, 2015.

Salamon, Julie. *Rambam's Ladder: A Meditation on Generosity and Why It Is Necessary to Give*. New York: Workman Publishing, 2003.

Sandel, Michael J. "The Consequences of the Diploma Divide." *New York Times*, September 5, 2020.

Sanders, Scott Russell. *A Private History of Awe*. New York: North Point Press, 2006.

Sanders, Scott Russell. *Hunting for Hope: A Father's Journeys*. Boston: Beacon Press, 1998.

Sanders, Scott Russell. *The Force of Spirit*. Boston: Beacon Press, 2000.

Sanders, Scott Russell. *Writing from the Center*. Bloomington, IN: Indiana University Press, 1995.

Sandomir, Richard. "Stuart Scott, ESPN's Voice of Exuberance, Dies at 49." *New York Times*, January 5, 2015.

Schwalbe, Will. *The End of Your Life Book Club*. New York: Vintage Books, 2013.

Sheldrick, Daphne. *Love, Life, and Elephants: An African Love Story*. New York: Farrar, Straus, and Giroux, 2012.

Shelley, Mary. *Frankenstein*. Edited by J. Paul Hunter. A Norton Critical Edition. New York: W. W. Norton, 1996.

Singer, Peter. *The President of Good and Evil: The Ethics of George W. Bush*. New York: Penguin Group, 2004.

Skinner, Donald E. "Membership Growth in UUA Slows Down." *UU World*, May 11, 2009. https://www.uuworld.org/articles/membership-growth-in-uua-slows-down.

Sorrell, Tom. "Thomas Hobbes, English Philosopher." *Encyclopaedia Britannica Online*. Accessed March 20, 2021. www.britannica.com/biography/Thomas-Hobbes.

Staples, Brent. "The Legacy of Monticello's Black First Family." *New York Times*, July 5, 2018.

Steinbeck, John. *America and Americans and Selected Nonfiction*. Edited by Jackson J. Benson and Susan Shillinglaw. New York: Viking, 2002.

Steinbeck, John. *The Log from the Sea of Cortez*. New York: Viking, 1951

Steinbeck, John. *Working Days: The Journals of "The Grapes of Wrath" 1938-1941*. Edited by Robert DeMott. New York: Viking Penguin, 1989.

Steinmetz, Katy. "*Help! My Parents Are Millennials.*" *Time*, October 26, 2015.

Stewart, James B. "Tough Times for Disciples of Ayn Rand." *New York Times*, July 14, 2017.

Stiglitz, Joseph E. *The Price of Inequality: How Today's Divided Society Endangers Our Future*. New York: W. W. Norton and Co., 2013.

Strom, Stephanie. "An Organ Donor's Generosity Raises the Question of How Much Is Too Much." *New York Times*, August 17, 2003. https://www.nytimes.com/2003/08/17/us/an-organ-donor-s-generosity-raises-the-question-of-how-much-is-too-much.html.

Strom, Stephanie. "Ideas & Trends: Extreme Philanthropy; Giving of Yourself, Literally, to People You've Never Met." *New York Times*, July 27, 2003. https://www.nytimes.com/2003/07/27/weekinreview/ideas-trends-extreme-philanthropy-giving-yourself-literally-people-you-ve-never.html.

Taylor, Paul. *The Next America: Boomers, Millennials, and the Looming Generational Showdown*. New York: PublicAffairs, 2014.

Thompson, Michael J. *The Politics of Inequality: A Political History of the Idea of Economic Inequality in America*. New York: Columbia University Press, 2007.

Tolan, Sandy. *The Lemon Tree: An Arab, a Jew, and the Heart of the Middle East*. New York: Bloomsbury, 2006.

"UUA Membership Statistics, 1961-2020." Unitarian Universalist Association. Accessed April 15, 2021. https://www.uua.org/data/demographics/uua-statistics.

Warren, Elizabeth. *A Fighting Chance*. New York: Metropolitan Books, 2014.

Wiencek, Henry. "Master of Monticello." *Smithsonian* (October 2012): 40-49, 92-97.

Wiencek, Henry. *Master of the Mountain: Thomas Jefferson and His Slaves.* New York: Farrar, Straus, and Giroux, 2012.

Wilentz, Sean. "Hard Times." Review of *The Soul of America: The Battle for Our Better Angels,* by Jon Meacham. *New York Times Book Review,* June 10, 2018.

Wills, Garry. *Head and Heart: American Christianities.* New York: Penguin Press, 2007.

Wills, Garry. *"Negro President": Jefferson and the Slave Power.* Boston: Houghton Mifflin, 2003.

Winograd, Morley, and Michael D. Hais. *Millennial Momentum: How a New Generation Is Remaking America.* New Brunswick, NJ: Rutgers University Press, 2011.

Wood, Gordon S. *Empire of Liberty: A History of the Early Republic, 1789-1815.* New York: Oxford University Press, 2009.

Woodson, Byron W., Sr. *A President in the Family: Thomas Jefferson, Sally Hemings, and Thomas Woodson.* Westport, CT: Praeger, 2001.

Wright, Robert. *The Evolution of God.* New York: Little, Brown and Company, 2009.

Yardley, William. "Abraham Nemeth, Creator of a Braille Code for Math, Is Dead at 94." *New York Times,* October 7, 2013.

CPSIA information can be obtained
at www.ICGtesting.com
Printed in the USA
LVHW031326181221
706535LV00004B/13/J

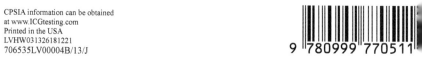

9 780999 770511